Entertaining Is Easy With Surefire Recipes

EVER SINCE we published the first edition of *Taste of Home's Holiday & Celebrations Cookbook* in 2001, folks across the country have been asking us for more…more sure-to-please recipes, more party menus, more easy decorating ideas.

So we're pleased to present *Taste of Home's Holiday & Celebrations Cookbook 2002*. This all-new, photo-filled treasury features 285 mouth-watering recipes to make your Christmas, Thanksgiving, Easter and other celebrations throughout the year easy and enjoyable. Like last year, we've done the planning, offered menu options and provided timetables to minimize last-minute fuss.

'Tis the Season. From formal sit-down dinners to casual cookie exchanges, your Christmas season is likely buzzing with activities. You'll stir up magical memories for every holiday gathering with some of this chapter's 137 delightful dishes, including Bacon-Wrapped Scallops…Candy Cane Coffee Cake…Perfect Prime Rib Roast…Herbed Mashed Potatoes and Chocolate Truffle Dessert. Do some folks on your shopping list have you stumped? You can easily and inexpensively create gift baskets brimming with homemade goodies (turn to page 100 for five unique ideas).

Giving Thanks. Add a twist to your traditional Thanksgiving table with a special supper showcasing succulent Goose with Corn Bread Stuffing. Then round out the meal with a bounty of side dishes and desserts. We also show you how to add life to Thanksgiving leftovers with surefire second-time-around recipes.

Easter Gatherings. With 20 fast-to-fix brunch items, you don't need to get up at the crack of dawn when entertaining early on Easter Day. For hearty dinner fare, go back in time to Grandma's kitchen with Plum-Glazed Gingered Ham.

Special Celebrations. We offer 85 family-favorite recipes for a host of other gatherings throughout the year. Express your love for someone special on Valentine's Day with a magical meal for two, display your patriotism with a true-blue Memorial Day menu or show Pop he's tops with stick-to-your-ribs Father's Day fare.

You'll also find a baby shower buffet, a family reunion picnic, a selection of wintertime soups and breads plus a bounty of birthday cakes.

Can-Do Decorating Ideas. There are dozens of ideas for simple centerpieces (turn to page 170 for a dazzling daisy and carrot display), great-looking garnishes (adorn desserts with the Candied Flowers on page 237) and fun party favors (see the fudge-filled cookie cutters on page 99).

With unforgettable fare, easy decorating ideas and perfect party menus, *Taste of Home's Holiday & Celebrations Cookbook 2002* will help you make magical memories at every gathering with family and friends throughout the year!

WOULD YOU like to see one of your family-favorite recipes featured in a future edition of this timeless treasury? See page 256 for details!

HOLIDAY & Celebrations COOKBOOK 2002

Editor: Julie Schnittka
Art Director: Linda Dzik
Food Editor: Janaan Cunningham
Craft Editor: Jane Craig
Associate Editors: Kristine Krueger, Heidi Reuter Lloyd
Associate Food Editor: Coleen Martin
Senior Recipe Editor: Sue A. Jurack
Recipe Editor: Janet Briggs
Test Kitchen Director: Karen Johnson
Test Kitchen Home Economists: Sue Draheim,
Peggy Fleming, Julie Herzfeldt, Joylyn Jans, Kristin
Koepnick, Mark Morgan, Patricia Schmeling,
Wendy Stenman, Karen Wright
Test Kitchen Assistants: Rita Krajcir, Megan Taylor
Food Photography: Rob Hagen, Dan Roberts
Food Photography Artists: Stephanie Marchese,
Vicky Marie Moseley
Photo Studio Manager: Anne Schimmel
Production: Ellen Lloyd, Catherine Fletcher
Publisher: Roy Reiman

Taste of Home Books
©2002 Reiman Media Group, Inc.
5400 S. 60th St., Greendale WI 53129
International Standard Book Number: 0-89821-351-7
International Standard Serial Number: 1535-2781
All rights reserved.
Printed in U.S.A.

For additional copies of this book, write *Taste of Home* Books, P.O.
Box 908, Greendale WI 53129. Or to order by credit card, call
toll-free 1-800/344-2560 or visit our Web site at
www.reimanpub.com.

PICTURED ON THE COVER: Turkey with Sausage Stuffing
(p. 17), Herbed Mashed Potatoes (p. 16), Dressed-Up Broccoli
(p. 20), Beets in Orange Sauce (p. 18) and Cranberry Ice (p. 19).

'TIS THE Season

The magic of Christmas lies in memorable moments
with family and friends. So plan a neighborhood
round-robin, where you "make the rounds" to
each others' homes to sample a spread of
appetizers, or host a candy and cookie exchange.
Instead of spending a small fortune on gifts,
assemble some inexpensive baskets brimming with
homemade goodies. We also present two complete menus
and a merry array of entrees, breads and desserts.

Christmas Eve Seafood Supper

YOU WON'T have to go fishing for compliments when you serve this distinctive holiday dinner on Christmas Eve.

Shrimp with Lemon Linguine —featuring shrimp, mushrooms and red pepper swimming in a light cream sauce—rivals any fare found in seafood restaurants.

(For a more meaty meal, you'll reel in rave reviews with Beef Burgundy.)

To round out either entree, pour glasses of Brilliant Christmas Sunset, pass around a basket of Homemade Crescent Rolls and toss together Crown Jewel Salad.

Dinner guests will dive into Chocolate Mousse, a "must have" on any holiday menu.

TRUE-BLUE MENU

(Left to right)

Homemade Crescent Rolls (p. 9)

Crown Jewel Salad (p. 12)

Brilliant Christmas Sunset (p. 13)

Shrimp with Lemon Linguine (p. 8)

Shrimp with Lemon Linguine

(Pictured on page 7)

Guests always think I fussed whenever I serve this special dish.
When I tell them how easy it is to prepare, recipe requests come my way!
—Merrilee Chambers, Haines Junction, Yukon Territory

1-1/2 cups sliced fresh mushrooms
   1 small sweet red pepper,
     julienned
   2 tablespoons sliced green
     onion
   1 garlic clove, minced
   3 tablespoons butter *or*
     margarine
   3 tablespoons all-purpose flour
1/4 teaspoon salt
1/4 teaspoon dried tarragon
1/8 teaspoon pepper
1-1/2 cups half-and-half cream
   1 pound uncooked shrimp,
     peeled and deveined
1/2 cup white wine *or* chicken
     broth

LEMON LINGUINE:
  10 cups water
1/2 cup lemon juice
   1 teaspoon salt
   8 ounces linguine *or* other pasta
   1 tablespoon grated lemon peel
   1 tablespoon minced fresh parsley

In a large skillet, saute the mushrooms, red pepper, green onion and garlic in butter until vegetables are crisp-tender. Stir in the flour, salt, tarragon and pepper until blended. Gradually add cream. Bring to a boil; cook and stir for 1 minute or until thickened. Add the shrimp; simmer, uncovered, for 5 minutes or until shrimp turn pink. Stir in wine or broth; heat through.

In a large saucepan, bring water, lemon juice and salt to a boil. Add linguine. Cook for 10-13 minutes or until tender; drain. Sprinkle with lemon peel and parsley. Toss with the shrimp mixture. **Yield:** 4 servings.

PEELING AND DEVEINING SHRIMP

1. Remove the shell from raw or cooked shrimp by opening the shell at the underside or leg area and peeling back.

2. To remove the black vein running down the back of the shrimp, make a slit with a paring knife along the back from the head area to the tail.

3. Rinse shrimp under cold water to remove the vein.

Chocolate Mousse

(Pictured at right)

Our home economists created this rich dessert for chocolate lovers.

12 squares (1 ounce *each*)
   semisweet *or* bittersweet
   chocolate, finely chopped
1-1/3 cups whipping cream, *divided*
1/3 cup water
1/4 cup dark corn syrup
1 teaspoon rum extract
1 package (8 ounces) cream
   cheese, cubed

In a heavy saucepan over medium-low heat, combine the chocolate, 1/3 cup of cream, water and corn syrup.

Cook and stir until chocolate is melted and mixture is smooth. Remove from the heat; cool for 20 minutes. Whisk in extract and cream cheese until blended; set aside.

In a small mixing bowl, beat remaining cream until stiff peaks form. Fold into chocolate mixture. Spoon into individual dessert dishes. Cover and refrigerate for at least 4 hours. **Yield:** 8 servings.

Homemade Crescent Rolls

(Pictured on page 6)

This handy recipe lets me start the preparation the night before. The day of the party, I shape the rolls before guests arrive, let them rise and pop them into the oven for fresh-baked rolls in minutes.
—Lynn McAllister, Mt. Ulla, North Carolina

1 package (1/4 ounce) active
   dry yeast
1 cup warm water (110° to
   115°)
1 cup butter *or* margarine,
   melted
1/2 cup sugar
3 eggs
1/2 teaspoon salt
4 to 4-1/2 cups all-purpose flour

In a small bowl, dissolve yeast in warm water. In a mixing bowl, beat butter and sugar. Add eggs, salt and yeast mixture. Stir in enough flour until dough leaves sides of bowl and is soft (do not knead). Cover and refrigerate overnight.

Punch dough down. Turn onto a floured surface; divide in half. Roll each portion into a 12-in. circle; cut each circle into 12 wedges. Roll up wedges from the wide end and place with pointed end down on greased baking sheets. Curve ends to form crescents. Cover and let rise in a warm place until doubled, about 1-1/2 hours. Bake at 350° for 20-22 minutes or until golden brown. Remove from pans to wire racks. **Yield:** 2 dozen.

SCHEDULE FOR CHRISTMAS EVE DINNER

A Few Weeks Before:

- Prepare two grocery lists—one for non-perishable items to purchase now and one for perishable items to purchase a few days before Christmas Eve.
- Make the Icy Votive Candle Holders (see page 11).

The Day Before:

- Buy shrimp for Shrimp with Lemon Linguine and remaining grocery items.
- Set the table.
- Make the Chocolate Mousse. Cover and refrigerate.
- If you're also serving Beef Burgundy, cube the sirloin tip roast and marinate overnight. Prepare the pearl onions; cover and refrigerate.
- Prepare dough for Homemade Crescent Rolls. Cover and chill overnight.

Christmas Eve Day:

- In the morning, crush ice for the Brilliant Christmas Sunset.
- For Shrimp with Lemon Linguine, peel and devein shrimp, squeeze lemons for juice and grate lemon peel.
- Assemble salad greens and fruit for Crown Jewel Salad; cover and refrigerate. Prepare salad dressing and store at room temperature.
- Bake Homemade Crescent Rolls. Cool and store in an airtight container at room temperature.
- If serving Beef Burgundy, prepare it 2 to 3 hours before dinner is to be served.
- As guests arrive, assemble the Brilliant Christmas Sunset.
- Make Shrimp with Lemon Linguine; serve with Beef Burgundy, Crown Jewel Salad and Homemade Crescent Rolls.
- For dessert, serve Chocolate Mousse.

Beef Burgundy

When I made this recipe for our kids' French club more than 20 years ago, their teacher said it was better than any "authentic" versions of Beef Bourguignonne she'd tried.
—Edna Lanam, Stockton, California

1-1/3 cups red wine
1 small onion, sliced
2 sprigs fresh parsley, stems removed
4-1/2 teaspoons vegetable oil
1 garlic clove, crushed
1 bay leaf
1/8 teaspoon white pepper
Dash dried thyme

1 beef sirloin tip roast (about 2 pounds), cut into 1-inch cubes
2 tablespoons all-purpose flour
3 tablespoons butter *or* margarine, *divided*
1/2 cup beef consomme, undiluted
6 cups water
20 pearl onions
1 cup sliced fresh mushrooms
Hot cooked noodles

In a large resealable plastic bag, combine the first eight ingredients; add the beef. Seal and turn to coat; refrigerate for 4 hours or overnight, turning bag occasionally. Remove meat from marinade; pat dry with paper towel. Strain marinade and set aside; discard onion, parsley and bay leaf.

Coat beef with flour. In a Dutch oven, brown meat on all sides in 2 tablespoons butter over medium-high heat. Stir in the consomme and reserved marinade. Bring to a rolling boil; boil for 1 minute. Reduce heat; cover and simmer for 1-1/2 hours or until meat is tender.

In a large saucepan, bring water to a boil. Add pearl onions; boil for 3 minutes. Drain and rinse in cold water; peel. In a skillet, saute mushrooms and onions in remaining butter until tender. Add to beef mixture. Simmer 10 minutes longer. Thicken if desired. Serve over noodles. **Yield:** 6-8 servings.

Icy Votive Candle Holders

(Pictured at right and on page 7)

Corn syrup is the secret to bringing a bit of Jack Frost to your table! We set the "painted" candle holders on a cobalt blue glass tray and added some clear sparkling stones, but the candle holders can also be used by themselves.

Editor's Note: Handle the candle holders with dry hands. If your hands are wet, some of the syrup may rub off. To remove the corn syrup from the candle holders, simply wash in warm soapy water.

2 tablespoons light corn syrup
Blue gel *or* paste food coloring,
   optional
Three clear glass votive candle
   holders and candles
Pastry brush
Waxed paper

Place corn syrup in a small bowl; tint with food coloring if desired. Immediately apply the corn syrup to the outside of candle holders with pastry brush, using a random pattern of brush strokes. Set candle holders on waxed paper until dry to the touch. These candle holders can be made weeks in advance.

"PAINTING" CANDLE HOLDERS

HOLDING the candle holder on the inside, apply corn syrup with a pastry brush to the outside, using random brush strokes. To achieve the icy look, let the strokes of the brush show…don't try to smooth them out. Set on waxed paper to dry.

Crown Jewel Salad

(Pictured on page 6)

*A raspberry dressing and fruits liven up a package of mixed salad greens
in this recipe from our Test Kitchen home economists.*

1 cup fresh raspberries*
1 package (5 ounces) mixed
   salad greens
2 medium navel oranges, peeled
   and sectioned
1 star fruit, sliced
2 kiwifruit, peeled and chopped
DRESSING:
1/3 cup olive *or* vegetable oil
1/4 cup sugar
1/4 cup raspberry vinegar
1/2 teaspoon salt
1/2 teaspoon onion powder

In a small bowl, mash 2 tablespoons raspberries; strain, reserving juice. Place greens on salad plates. Top with the orange sections, star fruit, kiwi and remaining raspberries.

In another bowl, whisk the oil, sugar, vinegar, salt, onion powder and reserved raspberry juice. Drizzle over salads. Serve immediately. **Yield:** 6-8 servings.

*Editors Note: One medium pomegranate may be substituted for the raspberries. Remove the pomegranate seeds (see box below); mash 2 tablespoons of seeds, reserving juice. Use the juice in the salad dressing, and serve the remaining pomegranate seeds in the salad.

SEEDING A POMEGRANATE

THIS underwater method for seeding a pomegranate helps keep the mess to a minimum and prevents the fruit's crimson juices from staining clothes and fingers.

1. Cut off the crown end of the pomegranate, removing some of the white pith and taking care not to pierce the seeds. Score into quarters.

2. Soak the scored fruit in a large bowl of cool water for 5 minutes. Holding the fruit under water, break the scored sections apart with your fingers. For each section, separate the seed clusters from the skin and membranes. Discard the skin and the membranes; dry the seeds on paper towels.

Brilliant Christmas Sunset

(Pictured at right and on page 7)

This beverage is so beautiful, people
think it takes hours to make.
But busy cooks will be pleased to know
it calls for only three ingredients.
—Rita Farmer, Houston, Texas

Crushed ice
    4 **tablespoons pomegranate juice**
    or **grenadine syrup**
    4 **cups orange juice**

Add ice to four glasses. Pour 1 tablespoon pomegranate juice or grenadine syrup over ice in each glass. Slowly add 1 cup orange juice. Stir if desired. **Yield:** 4 servings.

POMEGRANATE PRIMER

REFER to these pointers when buying, storing and working with pomegranates.
- Pomegranates are available from late Sep-
  tember to November. Select those with fresh
  leather-like skin free from cracks and splits.
  Skin color varies from bright to deep red.
- The crimson juice of this flavorful fruit
  stains skin and clothing easily, so be care-
  ful when cutting it open.
- Whole pomegranates keep well in a cool
  dark place at room temperature for several days. They will last for 3 months in the
  refrigerator.

- You can refrigerate pomegranate seeds for
  up to 3 days. To freeze them, place in a
  single layer in a baking pan. When frozen,
  transfer to an airtight container. Freeze
  for up to 6 months.
- Pomegranate juice can be refrigerated for
  3 days or frozen for 6 months in an airtight container.
- There are two ways to juice a pomegranate.
  One way is to cut the pomegranate in half
  and juice it like an orange. Or remove the
  seeds and mash with a fork or process in a
  blender; strain, reserving juice.

Turkey Dinner for Christmas Day

FAMILY and friends will sing your praises when they see your Christmas Day dinner table decked out in this feast featuring turkey and all the fixings.

It's no surprise that Turkey with Sausage Stuffing is the festive focal point. The outside roasts to a rich golden brown, while the meat and stuffing remain wonderfully moist.

Trim the table with such satisfying side dishes as Herbed Mashed Potatoes, Beets in Orange Sauce, Dressed-Up Broccoli and Salad with Blue Cheese Dressing.

There's no better way to wrap up this mouth-watering meal than with refreshing servings of Cranberry Ice.

A VERY MERRY MEAL
(Clockwise from top right)

Turkey with Sausage Stuffing (p. 17)

Herbed Mashed Potatoes (p. 16)

Dressed-Up Broccoli (p. 20)

Cranberry Ice (p. 19)

Herbed Mashed Potatoes

(Pictured on page 15 and on cover)

A blend of herbs and garlic makes this an extra-special side dish for the holidays.
My family won't let me prepare mashed potatoes any other way.
—Stephanie McKinnon, Salt Lake City, Utah

6-1/2 cups cubed peeled potatoes
2 garlic cloves, peeled and halved
1/2 cup milk
1/2 cup sour cream
2 tablespoons minced fresh parsley
2 tablespoons minced fresh oregano
1 tablespoon minced fresh thyme

1 tablespoon butter *or* margarine
3/4 teaspoon salt
1/4 teaspoon pepper

Place potatoes and garlic in a large saucepan; cover with water. Bring to a boil over medium-high heat. Cook for 15-20 minutes or until tender; drain. Place potatoes and garlic in a large mixing bowl. Add the remaining ingredients; mash. **Yield:** 6 servings.

Turkey-Carving Basics

AFTER removing the roasted turkey from the oven, cover and let stand for 20 minutes. Remove all stuffing to a warm serving bowl; cover with foil to keep warm. Then carve the turkey following these simple steps:

1. Pull the leg away from the body until the thigh bone pops out of its socket. Cut between the thigh joint and the body to remove the entire leg. Repeat with the other leg. Separate the drumstick and thigh by cutting through the ball joint. Hold each part by the bone and cut off 1/4-inch slices.

2. Hold the turkey with a meat fork and make a deep cut into the breast meat just above the wing area. This marks the end of each breast meat slice.

3. Slice down from the breast into the cut made in Step 2. Slice meat 1/4 inch thick.

Turkey with Sausage Stuffing

(Pictured at right, on page 15 and on cover)

All year long, my family looks forward to Christmas when I prepare this pretty and pleasing stuffing. Cream-style corn and sausage make every bite moist and delicious.
—*Janet Danner, Peebles, Ohio*

8 cups cubed day-old bread
1 pound bulk pork sausage, cooked and drained
3 medium onions, chopped
1 can (14-3/4 ounces) cream-style corn
2 tablespoons minced fresh parsley
1-1/2 teaspoons poultry seasoning
1/2 teaspoon salt
1/4 teaspoon pepper
1 turkey (10 to 12 pounds)
Melted butter *or* margarine
2 teaspoons chicken bouillon granules
2 cups boiling water
1/4 to 1/3 cup all-purpose flour

In a large bowl, combine the first eight ingredients. Just before baking, loosely stuff the turkey. Place remaining stuffing in a greased 1-1/2-qt. baking dish; refrigerate. Skewer openings of turkey; tie drumsticks together. Place on a rack in a roasting pan. Brush with butter.

Bake, uncovered, at 325° for 2-3/4 to 3 hours or until a meat thermometer reads 180° for turkey and 165° for stuffing. Bake additional stuffing, covered, for 45-50 minutes or until heated through.

When the turkey begins to brown, baste with drippings; cover loosely with foil if turkey browns too quickly. Cover turkey and let stand for 20 minutes before removing stuffing and carving.

For gravy, dissolve bouillon in water; set aside. Transfer turkey to warm platter. Remove stuffing. Pour 1/4 cup pan drippings into a saucepan; whisk in flour until smooth. Gradually add bouillon mixture. Bring to a boil; cook and stir for 2 minutes or until thickened. Serve with turkey and stuffing. **Yield:** 6-8 servings.

Beets in Orange Sauce

(Pictured on cover)

*To ensure your family eats their veggies, our Test Kitchen home economists
suggest you top beets with an irresistible orange glaze.*

8 medium fresh beets*
1/4 cup sugar
2 teaspoons cornstarch
Dash pepper
1 cup orange juice
1 medium navel orange, sliced
   and halved, optional
1/2 teaspoon grated orange peel

Place beets in a large saucepan; cover with water. Bring to a boil. Reduce heat; cover and cook for 25-30 minutes or until tender. Drain and cool slightly. Peel and slice; place in a serving bowl and keep warm.

In a saucepan, combine the sugar, cornstarch and pepper; stir in orange juice until smooth. Bring to a boil; cook and stir for 2 minutes or until thickened. Remove from the heat; stir in orange slices if desired and peel. Pour over beets. **Yield:** 8 servings.

*Editor's Note: A 15-ounce can of sliced beets may be substituted for the fresh beets. Drain the canned beets and omit the first step of the recipe.

Salad with Blue Cheese Dressing

*This salad is a tradition in my home each Christmas. The chunky blue cheese dressing coats
the lettuce beautifully. Toss in extra vegetables to suit your family's taste.*
—Shirley Bedzis, San Diego, California

DRESSING:
1 cup small-curd cottage cheese
1/2 cup crumbled blue cheese,
   divided
1/4 cup mayonnaise
1/4 cup plain yogurt
1/4 cup white wine vinegar *or*
   cider vinegar
2 garlic cloves, minced
1/4 teaspoon salt
1/4 teaspoon white pepper

SALAD:
12 cups torn Bibb *or* Boston lettuce
2 cups cherry tomatoes
1 small red onion, sliced
1 can (2-1/4 ounces) sliced ripe olives, drained
2 cups seasoned salad croutons

In a blender or food processor, place cottage cheese, 1/4 cup blue cheese, mayonnaise, yogurt, vinegar, garlic, salt and pepper. Cover and process until smooth. Pour into a small bowl; stir in the remaining blue cheese. Cover and refrigerate for 2-3 hours. In a large salad bowl, toss lettuce, tomatoes, onion, olives and croutons. Serve with dressing. **Yield:** 14-16 servings.

Cranberry Ice

*(Pictured at right,
on page 14 and on cover)*

*This traditional Christmas dessert was
first made in our family by my grandma.
She handed the recipe down to my
mother, who then shared it with me
and my two sisters. The cold tart treat
is a wonderful accompaniment to a
traditional turkey dinner.*
—*Carolyn Butterworth*
Spirit Lake, Iowa

3 cups fresh *or* frozen
    cranberries
2 cups water
1-1/2 cups sugar
1 teaspoon unflavored gelatin
1/2 cup cold water
1/2 cup lemon juice

In a large saucepan, bring cranberries
and water to a boil. Cook over medium
heat until the berries pop, about 10 minutes. Remove from the heat; cool slightly. Press mixture through a sieve or food mill, reserving juice and discarding skins and seeds.

In a small bowl, sprinkle gelatin over cold water; set aside. In a saucepan, combine cranberry mixture and sugar; cook and stir until sugar is dissolved and mixture just begins to boil. Remove from the heat. Stir in gelatin mixture until dissolved. Add lemon juice. Transfer to a shallow 1-qt. freezer container. Cover and freeze until ice begins to form around the edges of container, about 1 hour. Freeze until slushy, stirring occasionally. **Yield:** 8 servings.

CRANBERRY BASICS

WITH THEIR ruby color, cranberries are a perfect staple item when cooking around the holidays. Follow these guidelines when storing and using these beautiful berries.

- When stored in a resealable plastic bag and refrigerated, cranberries will remain fresh for 1 month.
- To freeze cranberries, place them in a single layer on a 13-inch x 9-inch baking pan. When frozen, transfer to an airtight container and freeze for up to 1 year. Freezing berries individually allows you to measure only as many as needed.
- Just before using, wash the cranberries and pluck off any stems. There's no need to defrost frozen cranberries first.

CHRISTMAS DINNER COUNTDOWN

A Few Weeks Before:
- Prepare two grocery lists—one for non-perishable items to purchase now and one for perishable items to purchase a few days before Christmas Day.
- Order a fresh 10- to 12-pound turkey or buy and freeze a frozen turkey.

Two to Three Days Before:
- Buy remaining grocery items (including the fresh turkey if you ordered one) and berries and greens for the Cranberries & Boughs Centerpiece (see page 21).
- Thaw frozen turkey in a pan in the refrigerator. (Allow 24 hours of thawing for every 5 pounds.)
- Prepare Cranberry Ice.

Christmas Eve:
- Set the table.
- For the Sausage Stuffing, cube bread and store at room temperature in an airtight container. Cook bulk pork sausage and drain; cover and refrigerate.
- For the Dressed-Up Broccoli, cut broccoli into spears. Store in a large resealable plastic bag; chill.
- Chop onions for the stuffing and broccoli dish; refrigerate in airtight containers.
- Make the Blue Cheese Dressing; cover and chill.

Christmas Day:
- In the morning, assemble the Cranberries & Boughs Centerpiece.
- Peel and cube potatoes for Herbed Mashed Potatoes; cover with cold water and let stand at room temperature.
- Tear lettuce for the tossed salad; place in a resealable plastic bag and chill. Slice the red onion; refrigerate in an airtight container.
- Prepare the stuffing; stuff turkey and bake.
- Make the Beets in Orange Sauce, Dressed-Up Broccoli and Herbed Mashed Potatoes.
- Let cooked turkey stand for 20 minutes. Meanwhile, make the gravy. Remove the stuffing and carve the turkey.
- Assemble the salad ingredients for Salad with Blue Cheese Dressing; serve dressing alongside.
- Serve Cranberry Ice for dessert.

Dressed-Up Broccoli

(Pictured on page 14 and on cover)

To liven up ordinary broccoli, our Test Kitchen tops the tender spears with a special wine sauce.
The light topping coats the broccoli nicely without being overpowering.
Experiment by sampling the sauce on other vegetables.

1-1/2 **pounds fresh broccoli, cut into spears**
   1 **medium onion, chopped**
   3 **garlic cloves, minced**
1/2 **cup butter (no substitutes), *divided***
3/4 **cup white wine *or* chicken broth**
   2 **tablespoons whipping cream**

Place 1 in. of water and broccoli in a large saucepan. Bring to a boil. Reduce heat; cover and simmer for 5-8 minutes or until crisp-tender. Meanwhile, in a small skillet, saute onion and garlic in 1/4 cup butter until golden brown. Add wine or broth; bring to a boil over high heat. Cook until liquid is reduced by half. Remove from the heat. Stir in cream and remaining butter. Drain broccoli and place in a serving bowl; drizzle with sauce. **Yield:** 4-6 servings.

Cranberries & Boughs Centerpiece

(Pictured at right, on page 11 and on cover)

WHEN CREATING a centerpiece for your Christmas buffet table, look no further than the foods and foliage readily available during the season.

For our stunning arrangement shown at right, we relied on fresh cranberries. The crimson color of this tart berry blends beautifully with such dishes as Beets in Orange Sauce and Cranberry Ice (as seen on page 14 and the cover). To carry that hue through, we opted for cranberry-colored napkins instead of the traditional Christmas red.

To fill out the vase, simply snip off some boughs from your Christmas tree or garlands. (We used both juniper and blue spruce branches, but you can use whatever boughs you have available.) Also feel free to tuck in some sprigs of holly or baby's breath and some white roses, lilies or daisies.

For the finishing touch, add a gold cord bow at the top of the vase.

Neighborhood Round-Robin

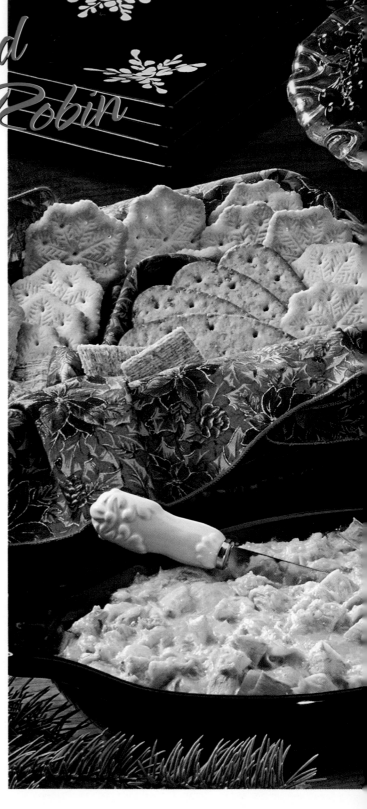

ARE YOU and your neighbors looking for an alternative to the traditional progressive dinner party, where each family hosts a different course in the meal?

This holiday season, consider organizing an appetizer round-robin, where families "make the rounds" to each other's homes to enjoy hearty hors d'oeuvres.

This is a great way to entertain because no family has to cook an elaborate part of the meal.

Oven-fresh fare like Chili Artichoke Dip really warms you up, while Herbed Cheesecake and Antipasto Platter can conveniently be made ahead and refrigerated. (All shown at right.)

This chapter offers a host of innovative appetizers, from hot and cold to fancy and casual.

SEASONAL SNACKING

(Clockwise from top right)

Herbed Cheesecake (p. 27)

Antipasto Platter (p. 25)

Chili Artichoke Dip (p. 24)

Chili Artichoke Dip

(Pictured on page 22)

*It's not tricky to prepare this warm tempting dip. It's cheesy and satisfying with
a bit of zip from the chilies and marinated artichokes.*
—Leanne Mueller, Stockton, California

1 can (14 ounces) water-packed
  artichoke hearts, drained and
  chopped
1 jar (6-1/2 ounces) marinated
  artichoke hearts, drained and
  chopped
1 can (4 ounces) chopped green
  chilies
3 cups (12 ounces) shredded
  cheddar cheese

1/4 cup mayonnaise*
Assorted crackers *or* tortilla chips

In a bowl, combine the artichokes, chilies, cheese and mayonnaise. Transfer to a greased 8-in. square baking dish. Bake, uncovered, at 350° for 20-25 minutes or until cheese is melted. Serve warm with crackers or tortilla chips. **Yield:** about 3-1/2 cups.

*Editor's Note: Reduced-fat or fat-free mayonnaise may not be substituted for regular mayonnaise in this recipe.

PLANNING A NEIGHBORHOOD ROUND-ROBIN

ORGANIZING a holiday gathering is simple when others help with the hosting. Here are some pointers for planning a successful round-robin for you and your neighbors:

- Early in fall, send a note to your neighbors inviting them to participate in an appetizer round-robin, where neighbors go from house to house (staying about 1 hour at each) to enjoy an assortment of appetizers (two to three per house). You may want to list several possible dates or just offer one date and see who can attend.
- Six weeks before the party, send the participating neighbors a schedule for the evening. You may want to ask each family what appetizers they plan on serving to avoid duplicates.
- When selecting recipes, think about the schedule of the evening. If company comes

to your house first, you can prepare a recipe that has a little more last-minute fussing. If not, choose dishes that can either be completely prepared and refrigerated before serving or that can be partially assembled before baking.

- A month before the party, make some outdoor Holiday Luminaries for your walkway (see page 37). You might want to tell your neighbors about this enlightened idea! Or if you're ambitious and there aren't too many families partaking in the event, think about making enough luminaries for each stop along the way.
- The day before the party, do whatever food preparation you can. Set the table with serving trays, plates, napkins and utensils. Although the focus is on the food, you'll want to offer a variety of beverages as well.

Antipasto Platter

(Pictured at right and on page 23)

We entertain often, and this is one of our favorite "party pleasers". It's such a refreshing change from the usual chips and dip.
— Teri Lindquist, Gurnee, Illinois

1 jar (24 ounces) pepperoncinis, drained
1 can (15 ounces) garbanzo beans *or* chickpeas, rinsed and drained
2 cups halved fresh mushrooms
2 cups halved cherry tomatoes
1/2 pound provolone cheese, cubed
1 can (6 ounces) pitted ripe olives, drained
1 package (3-1/2 ounces) sliced pepperoni
1 bottle (8 ounces) Italian vinaigrette dressing
Lettuce leaves

In a large bowl, combine the peppers, beans, mushrooms, tomatoes, cheese, olives and pepperoni. Pour vinaigrette over mixture and gently toss to coat. Refrigerate for at least 30 minutes or overnight. Arrange on a lettuce-lined platter. Serve with toothpicks. **Yield:** 14-16 servings.

Garlic Herb Spread

Garlic and a host of herbs pleasantly season this savory spread. It's a "must" on my holiday menu because I can make it in advance.
— Cheryl Fortier, Athabasca, Alberta

1 package (8 ounces) cream cheese, softened
1/2 cup butter *or* margarine, softened
2 tablespoons minced fresh parsley
1 garlic clove, minced
1/4 teaspoon salt
1/4 teaspoon dill weed
1/4 teaspoon *each* dried basil, thyme and marjoram
Assorted crackers *or* raw vegetables

In a small mixing bowl, combine the cream cheese, butter, parsley, garlic and seasonings. Beat until blended. Refrigerate overnight. Serve with crackers or vegetables. **Yield:** 1-1/2 cups.

Eggplant Dip

This deliciously different appetizer is loved by family and friends...even by those who usually avoid eggplant. The pretty red color makes it great for the holidays.
—*Linda Roberson, Cordova, Tennessee*

3 cups cubed eggplant
1 medium onion, chopped
1/3 cup finely chopped sweet red pepper
1 jar (4-1/2 ounces) sliced mushrooms, drained
4 garlic cloves, minced
1/3 cup olive *or* vegetable oil
1 jar (6 ounces) stuffed olives, drained and chopped
1 can (6 ounces) tomato paste
2 tablespoons red wine vinegar *or* cider vinegar
1-1/2 teaspoons sugar
1 teaspoon salt
1/2 teaspoon dried oregano
Hot pepper sauce to taste
Pita bread wedges *or* tortilla *or* corn chips

In a large skillet, combine the eggplant, onion, red pepper, mushrooms, garlic and oil. Cover and cook over medium heat for 10 minutes or until tender. Stir in the next seven ingredients; bring to a boil. Reduce heat; cover and simmer for 20-30 minutes or until flavors are blended. Serve warm or at room temperature with pita wedges or chips. **Yield:** 3 cups.

ADVICE ABOUT EGGPLANT

SELECT EGGPLANT with smooth skin; avoid those with soft or brown spots. Store eggplant in a cool dry place for 1 to 2 days. To store up to 5 days, place in a plastic bag and refrigerate. A 1-pound eggplant yields 3 to 4 cups cubed. You don't need to peel an eggplant before using.

Meaty Chili Dip

A meaty dish like this is a must for the men in my family.
They scrape the serving bowl clean! For the best dipping, use large corn chips.
—*Karen Kiel, Camdenton, Missouri*

1 pound ground beef
1 medium green pepper, chopped
1 cup water
1 can (6 ounces) tomato paste
1 package (3 ounces) cream cheese, cubed
1 envelope chili seasoning mix
Corn chips

In a large skillet, cook beef and green pepper over medium heat until meat is no longer pink; drain. Add the water, tomato paste, cream cheese and chili seasoning mix. Bring to a boil. Reduce heat; simmer, uncovered, until cheese is melted. Transfer to a small slow cooker or chafing dish to keep warm. Serve with corn chips. **Yield:** 3 cups.

Herbed Cheesecake

(Pictured at right and on page 23)

Cheesecake isn't just for dessert! This savory version is my family's favorite for merry munching around the holidays.
—*Julie Tomlin, Watkinsville, Georgia*

3 packages (8 ounces *each*) cream cheese, softened
2 cups (16 ounces) sour cream, *divided*
1 can (10-3/4 ounces) condensed cream of celery soup, undiluted
3 eggs
1/2 cup grated Romano cheese
3 garlic cloves, minced
1 tablespoon cornstarch
2 tablespoons minced fresh basil *or* 2 teaspoons dried basil
1 tablespoon minced fresh thyme *or* 1 teaspoon dried thyme
1/2 teaspoon Italian seasoning
1/2 teaspoon coarsely ground pepper
Assorted crackers

In a large mixing bowl, beat the cream cheese, 1 cup sour cream and soup until smooth. Add the eggs, Romano cheese, garlic, cornstarch, basil, thyme, Italian seasoning and pepper; beat until smooth.

Pour into a greased 9-in. springform pan. Place pan on a baking sheet. Bake at 350° for 55-60 minutes or until center is almost set. Cool on a wire rack for 10 minutes. Carefully run a knife around edge of pan to loosen; cool 1 hour longer.

Refrigerate for at least 4 hours or overnight. Remove sides of pan. Spread remaining sour cream over top. Serve with crackers. Refrigerate leftovers. **Yield:** 24 servings.

MAKING A POINSETTIA GARNISH

A POINSETTIA GARNISH (shown above and at right) is a great way to add color to a dish during the holidays. Here's how to make it:

Place six fresh basil leaves in a circle with the stems toward the center. Cut five petal-shaped pieces from a sweet red pepper; set between the basil leaves. Chop some sweet yellow pepper; place in the center of the "poinsettia".

Taco Roll-Ups

Our friend made these roll-ups for a Mexican-themed garden party.
A sprinkling of onion soup mix makes them a little different.
— Denice Louk, Garnett, Kansas

2 packages (8 ounces *each*)
   cream cheese, softened
1 cup (8 ounces) sour cream
2 cups (8 ounces) finely
   shredded cheddar cheese
1/2 cup picante sauce
1 can (4-1/2 ounces) chopped
   ripe olives, drained
2 tablespoons taco seasoning
1 tablespoon onion soup mix
8 flour tortillas (10 inches)

In a small mixing bowl, beat cream cheese and sour cream until smooth; stir in the cheddar cheese, picante sauce, olives, taco seasoning and soup mix. Spread over tortillas; roll up jelly-roll style. Wrap in plastic wrap; refrigerate for at least 1 hour. Just before serving, cut into 1-in. pieces. **Yield:** about 3-1/2 dozen.

Marinated Mushrooms

These are a nice addition to an appetizer buffet table. For the best flavor,
allow the mushrooms to marinate a few days before serving.
—JoAnn Stevens, Durham, North Carolina

1 pound fresh whole
   mushrooms
1 large onion, sliced
3/4 cup olive *or* vegetable oil
1/4 cup white vinegar
2 garlic cloves, minced
1/2 teaspoon salt
1/4 teaspoon ground mustard
1/8 teaspoon pepper
Crushed red pepper flakes to taste

In a large bowl, combine all ingredients. Cover and refrigerate for 1 to 2 days. Serve with a slotted spoon. **Yield:** 6-8 servings.

Baked Brie

(Pictured at right)

I always come home with an empty plate when I take this special appetizer to holiday parties. It looks fancy but is actually quite easy to make.
—*Carolyn DeKryger, Fremont, Michigan*

1/4 cup butter (no substitutes), softened
1 package (3 ounces) cream cheese, softened
3/4 cup all-purpose flour
1 round (8 ounces) Brie
1 egg
1 teaspoon water
Assorted crackers and fresh fruit

In a large mixing bowl, beat the butter, cream cheese and flour on low speed until mixture forms a ball. Divide in half and wrap each portion in plastic wrap; refrigerate for 30 minutes.

On a lightly floured surface, roll out each portion into a 7-in. circle about 1/8 in. thick. Place one circle on an ungreased baking sheet. Place Brie on pastry and top with remaining pastry circle; pinch edges to seal. Flute bottom edge if desired.

In a small bowl, beat egg and water; brush over top and sides of pastry. Bake at 400° for 15-20 minutes or until golden brown. Immediately remove from the baking sheet. Let stand for 30 minutes before serving. Serve with crackers and fruit. **Yield:** 8 servings.

Holiday Vegetable Dip

This dip is sure to tickle your taste buds. When I got the recipe, I was warned one batch is never enough. So whenever I make it, I double the recipe and never have any left over.
—*Nancy Hofman, Lethbridge, Alberta*

1 cup mayonnaise
1 tablespoon grated onion
2 teaspoons cider vinegar
2 teaspoons chili sauce
1/4 teaspoon pepper
1/4 teaspoon dried thyme

2 teaspoons minced chives
Assorted raw vegetables *or* potato chips

In a bowl, combine the first six ingredients; cover and refrigerate for at least 1 hour. Sprinkle with chives. Serve with vegetables or chips. **Yield:** 1 cup.

Toasted Almond Party Spread

*This rich spread goes a long way at holiday parties. Almonds and Swiss cheese
are a classic combination that never goes out of style.*
—Kim Sobota, Plymouth, Minnesota

1 package (8 ounces) cream
cheese, softened
1-1/2 cups (6 ounces) shredded
Swiss cheese
1/2 cup sliced almonds, toasted,
divided
1/3 cup mayonnaise
2 tablespoons sliced green
onions
1/8 teaspoon pepper

1/8 teaspoon ground nutmeg
Assorted crackers

In a small mixing bowl, beat the cream cheese until smooth.
Stir in the Swiss cheese, 1/3 cup almonds, mayonnaise,
onions, pepper and nutmeg. Spoon onto a lightly greased pie
plate. Bake at 350° for 14-15 minutes or until heated
through. Sprinkle with remaining almonds. Serve warm
with crackers. **Yield:** 1-1/2 cups.

Luscious Fruit Platter

*I often make this fruit and dip dish in summer, when the finest fruits are at their best.
Paired with angel food cake, this also makes a marvelous dessert.*
—Dixie Terry, Marion, Illinois

1 package (8 ounces) cream
cheese, softened
1/2 cup milk
2 tablespoons lemon juice
4 teaspoons sugar
1/4 teaspoon salt
1 medium honeydew, peeled,
seeded and cut into wedges
1-1/2 cups halved fresh
strawberries

1-1/2 cups cubed seeded watermelon
1 cup fresh blueberries
1 medium firm banana, cut into 1-inch pieces
2 medium ripe peaches, pitted and quartered
Clusters of red and green seedless grapes

In a small mixing bowl, beat cream cheese. Add milk, lemon
juice, sugar and salt; beat until smooth. Transfer to a small
serving bowl. On a large serving platter, arrange honeydew wedges in a spoke pattern. Place strawberries, watermelon, blueberries, banana, peaches and grapes between the
wedges. Place dip in the center. Serve immediately. **Yield:**
8-10 servings (2 cups dip).

Bacon-Wrapped Scallops

(Pictured at right)

When I'm looking for a more special appetizer, this is the recipe I reach for. I've also served these savory scallops for dinner.
—*Pamela MacCumbee*
Berkeley Springs, West Virginia

20 fresh baby spinach leaves
10 uncooked sea scallops, halved
10 bacon strips, halved widthwise
Lemon wedges

Fold a spinach leaf around each scallop half. Wrap bacon over spinach and secure with a toothpick. Place on a baking sheet or broiler pan. Broil 3-4 in. from the heat for 6 minutes on each side or until bacon is crisp. Squeeze lemon over each. Serve immediately. **Yield:** 20 appetizers.

Fiesta Corn Dip

I first came across this recipe at a friend's bridge party. To give it a little more flair, I added the cilantro and olives.
—*Shirley Herring, Conroe, Texas*

2 cups (16 ounces) sour cream
1/2 cup mayonnaise
2 cans (11 ounces *each*) Mexicorn, drained
2-1/2 cups (10 ounces) shredded cheddar cheese
4 green onions, chopped
1/4 cup diced canned jalapeno peppers, drained

2 tablespoons chopped ripe olives
2 tablespoons minced fresh cilantro *or* parsley
Corn chips

In a bowl, combine the first eight ingredients. Cover and refrigerate for at least 2 hours. Serve with corn chips. **Yield:** 5-1/2 cups.

Peppered Meatballs

Plenty of ground pepper gives these saucy meatballs their irresistible zest.
They're so hearty, I sometimes serve them over noodles as a main course.
—Darla Schroeder, Stanley, North Dakota

1/2 cup sour cream
2 teaspoons grated Parmesan *or*
   Romano cheese
2 to 3 teaspoons pepper
1 teaspoon salt
1 teaspoon dry bread crumbs
1/2 teaspoon garlic powder
1-1/2 pounds ground beef
SAUCE:
1 cup (8 ounces) sour cream
1 can (10-3/4 ounces)
   condensed cream of
   mushroom soup, undiluted
2 teaspoons dill weed

1/2 teaspoon sugar
1/2 teaspoon pepper
1/4 teaspoon garlic powder

In a bowl, combine sour cream and Parmesan cheese. Add pepper, salt, bread crumbs and garlic powder. Crumble meat over mixture and mix well. Shape into 1-in. balls. Place in a greased 15-in. x 10-in. x 1-in. baking pan. Bake at 350° for 20-25 minutes or until no longer pink.

Transfer meatballs to a slow cooker. Combine the sauce ingredients; pour over meatballs. Cover and cook on high for 2 hours or until heated through. **Yield:** 1-1/2 dozen (2 cups sauce).

Tomato Spinach Spread

Tomatoes add a tasty twist to a traditional spinach spread.
The red and green colors make this an appropriate appetizer for Christmas.
—Connie Buzzard, Colony, Kansas

1 package (8 ounces) cream
   cheese, softened
1 package (10 ounces) frozen
   chopped spinach, thawed and
   squeezed dry
1 cup (4 ounces) shredded
   Monterey Jack cheese
2 medium tomatoes, seeded and
   chopped
1/3 cup half-and-half cream
1 small onion, chopped
1/2 teaspoon garlic salt
Assorted crackers

In a mixing bowl, beat cream cheese until fluffy. Stir in the spinach, Monterey Jack cheese, tomatoes, cream, onion and garlic salt. Transfer to a greased 1-qt. baking dish. Bake, uncovered, at 350° for 20-25 minutes or until heated through. Serve with crackers. **Yield:** 4 cups.

Macaroon Fruit Dip

(Pictured at right)

*I rely on make-ahead dishes like this
when entertaining. Serving the dip
in a pineapple shell makes for
a pretty presentation.*
—*Jean Forster, Elmhurst, Illinois*

2 cups (16 ounces) sour cream
1/4 cup packed brown sugar
1-1/2 cups crumbled macaroons
Assorted fresh fruit
Small macaroon cookies

In a bowl, combine the sour cream,
brown sugar and crumbled cookies.
Cover and refrigerate for 12 hours or
overnight. Serve with fruit and macaroons. **Yield:** 3 cups.

PINEAPPLE SERVING BOWL

TO MAKE a Pineapple Serving Bowl (pictured
above with Macaroon Fruit Dip), stand a medium
fresh pineapple upright; cut in half lengthwise,
leaving top attached. Cut pineapple from one section
and discard shell. Cut pineapple from the other
half, leaving a 1/2-in. shell. Spoon fruit dip into shell.
Serve pineapple with dip or save for another use.

BLT Dip

*Fans of bacon, lettuce and tomato sandwiches will fall for this creamy dip.
It's easy to transport to different functions and always draws recipe requests.*
—*Emalee Payne, Eau Claire, Wisconsin*

2 cups (16 ounces) sour cream
2 cups mayonnaise *or* salad
  dressing
2 pounds sliced bacon, cooked
  and crumbled
6 plum tomatoes, chopped

3 green onions, chopped
Assorted crackers *or* chips

In a bowl, combine the sour cream, mayonnaise, bacon,
tomatoes and onions. Refrigerate until serving. Serve with
crackers or chips. **Yield:** 6 cups.

Southwestern Seafood Egg Rolls

Scallops, shrimp, spicy seasonings and phyllo dough combine to make these unique egg rolls.
Assemble them in the morning, refrigerate, then bake as guests arrive.
—*Lori Coeling, Hudsonville, Michigan*

1/4 pound uncooked bay scallops
1/4 pound uncooked medium
    shrimp, peeled and deveined
1 teaspoon minced garlic,
    divided
2 tablespoons olive *or* vegetable
    oil, *divided*
1 large tomato, peeled, seeded
    and chopped
1/4 cup finely chopped onion
3 tablespoons minced fresh
    parsley
3 tablespoons minced fresh
    cilantro *or* additional parsley
3/4 teaspoon ground cumin
1/2 teaspoon paprika
1/4 teaspoon salt
1/8 teaspoon pepper
Dash cayenne pepper
Dash ground turmeric
1/4 cup soft bread crumbs

1/2 pound frozen phyllo dough, thawed
1/2 cup butter *or* margarine, melted

In a large skillet, saute scallops, shrimp and 1/2 teaspoon garlic in 1 tablespoon oil for 2 minutes or until seafood is opaque. With a slotted spoon, remove from the pan and coarsely chop; set aside. In the same skillet, combine the tomato, onion and remaining garlic and oil; simmer for 5 minutes. Stir in parsley, cilantro, cumin, paprika, salt, pepper, cayenne and turmeric. Simmer, uncovered, until liquid is evaporated, about 5 minutes. Stir in seafood mixture and bread crumbs.

Cut the phyllo dough into 14-in. x 4-1/2-in. strips. Cover with a damp towel until ready to use. Lightly brush one strip with butter. Top with another strip; brush with butter. Place a tablespoonful of seafood mixture near one short side; fold in the long sides and roll up. Brush lightly with butter. Place on a greased baking sheet. Repeat with remaining phyllo and filling. Bake at 375° for 12-15 minutes or until golden brown. **Yield:** 2 dozen.

Baked Cheddar Bacon Spread

Potlucks at work just aren't the same without this deliciously rich spread.
—*Kathy Fehr, Fairbury, Illinois*

2 packages (8 ounces *each*)
    cream cheese, softened
2 cups (16 ounces) sour cream
1 medium onion, chopped
2 tablespoons mayonnaise
1 pound sliced bacon, cooked
    and crumbled

4 cups (16 ounces) shredded cheddar cheese, *divided*
Assorted crackers

In a mixing bowl, beat the cream cheese, sour cream, onion and mayonnaise until smooth. Fold in bacon and 3 cups of cheddar cheese. Transfer to a 2-qt. baking dish. Sprinkle with the remaining cheese. Bake, uncovered, at 375° for 30 minutes or until lightly browned. Serve with crackers. **Yield:** 7 cups.

Cheesy Pizza Fondue

(Pictured at right)

I keep these dip ingredients on hand for spur-of-the-moment gatherings. Folks can't resist chewy bread cubes coated with a savory sauce.
—Nel Carver, Moscow, Idaho

1 jar (29 ounces) meatless spaghetti sauce
2 cups (8 ounces) shredded mozzarella cheese
1/4 cup shredded Parmesan cheese
2 teaspoons dried oregano
1 teaspoon dried minced onion
1/4 teaspoon garlic powder
1 unsliced loaf (1 pound) Italian bread, cut into cubes

In a 1-1/2-qt. slow cooker, combine the spaghetti sauce, cheeses, oregano, onion and garlic powder. Cook for 4-6 hours or until cheese is melted and sauce is hot. Serve with bread cubes. **Yield:** 12 servings (4 cups).

Spicy Hummus

Hummus is a Middle Eastern spread made from seasoned mashed chickpeas. Served with pita wedges, this version from our Test Kitchen home economists is a simple satisfying snack.

1/4 cup packed fresh parsley sprigs
2 tablespoons chopped onion
1 garlic clove
1 can (15 ounces) chickpeas *or* garbanzo beans, rinsed and drained
2 tablespoons sesame seeds, ground
2 tablespoons cider vinegar
2 teaspoons soy sauce
2 teaspoons lime juice
1 teaspoon honey
1 teaspoon Dijon mustard
1/4 teaspoon salt
1/4 teaspoon *each* ground cumin, ginger, coriander and paprika
Pita bread, cut into wedges

In a food processor or blender, combine the parsley, onion and garlic; cover and process until smooth. Add the chickpeas, sesame seeds, vinegar, soy sauce, lime juice, honey, mustard and seasonings; cover and process until smooth. Serve with pita bread. **Yield:** 1-1/2 cups.

Calico Clams Casino

A few years ago, I came across this recipe in the back of my files when I was looking for a special appetizer. Everyone raved about it. Now it's an often-requested dish.
—Paula Sullivan, Barker, New York

3 cans (6-1/2 ounces *each*) chopped clams
1 cup (4 ounces) shredded mozzarella cheese
1 cup (4 ounces) shredded cheddar cheese
4 bacon strips, cooked and crumbled
3 tablespoons seasoned bread crumbs
3 tablespoons butter *or* margarine, melted
2 tablespoons *each* finely chopped onion, celery and sweet red, yellow and green peppers
1 garlic clove, minced
Dash dried parsley flakes

Drain clams, reserving 2 tablespoons of juice. In a large bowl, combine the clams and remaining ingredients; stir in the reserved clam juice. Spoon into greased 6-oz. custard cups or clamshell dishes; place on baking sheets. Bake at 350° for 10-15 minutes or until heated through and lightly browned. **Yield:** 8 servings.

Egg Salad Wonton Cups

Crispy wonton wrappers are a nice contrast to the creamy egg salad in this appetizer from our Test Kitchen. It's a mouth-watering alternative to traditional deviled eggs.

36 wonton wrappers
3 cups prepared egg salad
1/3 cup chopped green onions
1/3 cup shredded carrot
10 bacon strips, cooked and crumbled
9 cherry tomatoes, quartered
Parsley sprigs

Coat one side of each wonton wrapper with nonstick cooking spray; gently press into miniature muffin cups, greased side down. Bake at 350° for 10-12 minutes or until golden brown. Remove to wire racks to cool.

In a bowl, combine the egg salad, onions and carrot; mix well. Stir in the bacon. Spoon about 1 tablespoon into each wonton cup. Garnish with tomatoes and parsley. **Yield:** 3 dozen.

Holiday Luminaries

As you and your neighbors make the rounds from house to house, light the way with these festive luminaries. They can be made well in advance. Simply light them just before your guests arrive.

Sand
Clear glass quart jars
Tea light candles
Red faceted plastic beads
Artificial wired pine garlands
(13-inch lengths)

Place 1 cup sand in the bottom of each jar. Use a long-handled pastry brush to level. Place tea light candle in center of sand. Sprinkle about 1/4 cup of beads around each candle, using pastry brush to distribute them evenly. Wrap garland around outside bottom of jar and twist ends together to hold; arrange garland as desired.

Festive Oven-Fresh Breads

"KNEAD" a homemade gift from the kitchen or looking for a fresh-baked goody to round out a holiday meal? Turn to the bounty of breads in this chapter.

You'll find selections loaded with chocolate, fruits and nuts that will sweeten everyone's day. Hazelnut Swirl Bread, Fruit 'n' Nut Turnovers and Lemon Cranberry Muffins (shown at right) are just three examples.

Plus, you'll uncover a host of savory choices featuring cheese, herbs, spices and seasonings.

With so many mouth-watering recipes to choose from, you'll easily find an appealing assortment of breads, muffins and more that rise to any occasion!

FILLED FAVORITES
(Clockwise from top right)

Hazelnut Swirl Bread (p. 42)

Fruit 'n' Nut Turnovers (p. 43)

Lemon Cranberry Muffins (p. 41)

Sour Cream Herb Bread

My aunt gave me this recipe more than 20 years ago. It's a great bread to serve when entertaining. I also use slices to make sandwiches.
—Sammy Daken, Kelliher, Minnesota

     3 to 3-1/4 cups all-purpose flour
 1/4 cup sugar
   1 package (1/4 ounce) active
     dry yeast
   1 teaspoon salt
 1/2 teaspoon celery seed
 1/2 teaspoon dill seed
 1/2 teaspoon dried minced onion
   1 cup (8 ounces) sour cream
 1/2 cup water
   3 tablespoons plus 2 teaspoons
     butter *or* margarine, *divided*
   1 egg
   1 teaspoon sesame seeds

In a large mixing bowl, combine 2 cups flour, sugar, yeast, salt, celery seed, dill seed and onion. In a small saucepan, heat the sour cream, water and 3 tablespoons butter to 120°-130°. Add to dry ingredients; beat just until moistened. Add egg; beat until smooth. Stir in enough remaining flour to form a firm dough. Turn onto a floured surface; knead until smooth and elastic, about 6-8 minutes. Place in a greased bowl, turning once to grease top. Cover and let rise in a warm place until doubled, about 70 minutes.

Punch dough down. Turn onto a lightly floured surface. Shape into a round loaf. Place in a greased 2-qt. round baking dish. Cover and let rise until doubled, about 40 minutes. Bake at 350° for 35-40 minutes or until golden brown. Melt remaining butter; brush over bread. Sprinkle with sesame seeds. Remove from pan to a wire rack to cool. **Yield:** 1 loaf.

Christmas Bubble Ring

Family and friends will think you fussed when they catch sight of this impressive bread. But frozen dough gives this round loaf a quick and easy start.
—Carolyn Stafford, Stratton, Ontario

 1/2 cup butter *or* margarine
 1/2 cup packed brown sugar
   2 teaspoons ground cinnamon
   1 loaf (1 pound) frozen bread
     dough, thawed
 1/2 cup chopped pecans
 1/4 cup maraschino cherries,
     halved

In a saucepan, combine butter, brown sugar and cinnamon; cook and stir over low heat until sugar is dissolved. Cool. Cut dough into 1-in. pieces. Spread a fourth of the syrup mixture over the bottom of a greased 10-in. tube pan. Sprinkle with half of the pecans and cherries and a third of the dough. Repeat layers once. Top with half of the remaining syrup and remaining dough; drizzle with remaining syrup. Cover with greased plastic wrap. Refrigerate overnight.

Remove from the refrigerator 30 minutes before baking. Remove plastic wrap. Bake at 375° for 35-40 minutes. Immediately invert bread onto a serving platter. Serve warm. **Yield:** 8-10 servings.

Lemon Cranberry Muffins

(Pictured at right and on page 38)

These mouth-watering muffins can be baked in less than half an hour. So I often rely on this recipe when time is tight.
—Noelle Miles Griggs, Columbia, Illinois

   2 cups all-purpose flour
   1 cup sugar
   3 teaspoons baking powder
1/2 teaspoon salt
   2 eggs
   1 cup milk
1/2 cup vegetable oil
   1 teaspoon lemon extract
   1 cup fresh *or* frozen
       cranberries, halved
1/3 cup slivered almonds, toasted

In a large bowl, combine the dry ingredients. In another bowl, beat the eggs, milk, oil and extract. Stir into dry ingredients just until moistened. Fold in cranberries.

Fill paper-lined muffin cups two-thirds full; sprinkle with almonds. Bake at 400° for 18-20 minutes or until a toothpick comes out clean. Cool for 5 minutes before removing from pan to a wire rack. **Yield:** 1 dozen.

Apple Walnut Bread

I first made this bread when I was in high school in 1929. The recipe has stood the test of time!
—Helen Rebic, McAllen, Texas

1/2 cup shortening
   1 cup sugar
   2 eggs
4-1/2 teaspoons buttermilk
   1 teaspoon vanilla extract
   2 cups all-purpose flour
   1 teaspoon baking powder
   1 teaspoon baking soda
1/2 teaspoon salt

   1 cup finely chopped unpeeled tart apple
1/2 cup chopped walnuts

In a mixing bowl, cream shortening and sugar. Add eggs, one at a time, beating well after each addition. Beat in buttermilk and vanilla. Combine the flour, baking powder, baking soda and salt; add to creamed mixtures. Fold in apple and walnuts. Pour into a greased 8-in. x 4-in. x 2-in. loaf pan. Bake at 350° for 55-65 minutes or until a toothpick comes out clean. Cool for 10 minutes before removing from pan to a wire rack. **Yield:** 1 loaf.

Hazelnut Swirl Bread

(Pictured on page 39)

I invented this recipe a few years ago after eating hazelnut whole wheat bread at a restaurant. Each savory slice has a tender crumb that appeals to all palates.
—Loraine Meyer, Bend, Oregon

2 packages (1/4 ounce *each*) active dry yeast
1/2 cup warm water (110° to 115°)
2 cups warm milk (110° to 115°)
1 cup mashed potato flakes
2/3 cup shortening
1/2 cup sugar
2 eggs, lightly beaten
1 teaspoon salt
3 cups whole wheat flour
3 to 4 cups all-purpose flour
FILLING:
3 tablespoons butter *or* margarine, softened
2/3 cup packed brown sugar
2 egg yolks
2 tablespoons milk
1/4 teaspoon vanilla extract
2 cups finely chopped hazelnuts

In a large mixing bowl, dissolve yeast in warm water. Add the milk, potato flakes, shortening, sugar, eggs, salt, whole wheat flour and 1 cup all-purpose flour; beat until smooth. Stir in enough remaining all-purpose flour to form a stiff dough. Turn onto a floured surface; knead until smooth and elastic, about 6-8 minutes. Place in a greased bowl, turning once to grease top. Cover and let rise in a warm place until doubled, about 1 hour. Punch dough down. Turn onto a lightly floured surface; divide in half. Roll each portion into a 14-in. x 9-in. rectangle.

For filling, in a small mixing bowl, beat butter, brown sugar and egg yolks until creamy. Add milk and vanilla; mix well. Stir in hazelnuts. Spread over dough to within 1/2 in. of edges. Roll up jelly-roll style, starting with a short side; pinch seams to seal. Place seam side down in two greased 9-in. x 5-in. x 3-in. loaf pans. Cover and let rise in a warm place until doubled, about 30 minutes. Bake at 375° for 15 minutes. Cover with foil. Bake 20-25 minutes longer or until golden brown. Remove from pans to wire racks to cool. **Yield:** 2 loaves.

Pull-Apart Cinnamon Sticks

I cook for our hired help and appreciate easy recipes. These cinnamon breadsticks disappear fast.
—Elvera Dallman, Franklin, Nebraska

1 tube (11 ounces) refrigerated breadsticks*
3 tablespoons butter *or* margarine, melted
1/3 cup sugar
1/2 teaspoon ground cinnamon

Unroll breadsticks and cut in half widthwise. Place butter in a shallow bowl. In another shallow bowl, combine sugar and cinnamon. Dip one side of each breadstick in butter, then in cinnamon-sugar. Place sugared side up in a greased 9-in. pie plate, overlapping layers. Bake at 375° for 20-25 minutes or until golden brown. Serve warm. **Yield:** 6 servings.

***Editor's Note:** This recipe was tested with Pillsbury refrigerated breadsticks.*

Fruit 'n' Nut Turnovers

(Pictured at right and on page 38)

*These flaky Danish nicely round out
a holiday brunch.*
—Aneta Kish, La Crosse, Wisconsin

1-1/2 cups cold butter (no
    substitutes), cut into
    1/2-inch slices
   5 cups all-purpose flour, *divided*
   1 package (1/4 ounce) active
    dry yeast
1-1/4 cups half-and-half cream
   1/4 cup sugar
   1/4 teaspoon salt
   1 egg
FILLING:
   1 cup chopped dried apricots *or*
    cherries
1-1/2 cups water
   1 cup chopped walnuts
   1/2 cup packed brown sugar
   2 tablespoons all-purpose flour
   1/8 teaspoon ground cinnamon
ICING:
   1 cup confectioners' sugar
   1/4 teaspoon vanilla extract
   2 to 3 tablespoons apricot
    nectar *or* maraschino cherry
    juice

In a bowl, toss butter with 3 cups flour until well coated; refrigerate for 1 hour or until well chilled. In a mixing bowl, combine yeast and 1-1/2 cups flour. In a saucepan, heat the cream, sugar and salt to 120°-130°. Add to yeast mixture with the egg; beat on low speed for 30 seconds. Beat on high for 3 minutes. Stir in the chilled butter mixture just until combined (butter will remain in large pieces).

Turn onto a well-floured surface; gently knead 8 times. Coat rolling pin with the remaining flour. Roll dough into a 21-in. x 12-in. rectangle. Starting with a short side, fold dough in thirds, forming a 12-in. x 7-in. rectangle. Cover and refrigerate for 1 to 1-1/2 hours or until firm but not stiff.

Turn dough onto a well-floured surface; roll into a 21-in. x 12-in. rectangle. Starting with a short side, fold dough in thirds, forming a 12-in. x 7-in. rectangle. Give dough a quarter turn; roll into a 21-in. x 12-in. rectangle. Fold into thirds, starting with a short side. Repeat, flouring surface as needed. (Do not chill dough between each rolling and folding.) Cover and refrigerate for 4 to 24 hours or until firm.

For filling, in a saucepan, bring fruit and water to a boil. Remove from the heat. Cover and let stand for 5 minutes; drain. Stir in the walnuts, brown sugar, flour and cinnamon; set aside.

Cut dough in half lengthwise. Roll each portion into a 12-in. square; cut each square into nine 4-in. squares. Spoon about a rounded tablespoonful of filling onto the center of each square. Brush edges of dough with water; fold dough diagonally in half, forming a triangle. Press edges to seal. Place 4 in. apart on greased baking sheets. Cover and let rise in a warm place until doubled, about 1 hour.

Bake at 375° for 16-18 minutes or until golden brown. Remove to wire racks to cool. Combine icing ingredients; drizzle over turnovers. **Yield:** 1-1/2 dozen.

Orange Sour Cream Muffins

Sour cream makes every bite of these muffins moist, while orange juice concentrate provides pleasant flavor. I keep some in the freezer for a fast breakfast or snack.
—*Nellie Gobeli, Ava, Missouri*

1-1/4 cups all-purpose flour
    1 cup sugar
  1/2 cup chopped pecans
  1/2 teaspoon baking soda
  1/4 teaspoon salt
    1 egg
  1/2 cup sour cream
    6 tablespoons butter *or* margarine, melted
    3 tablespoons orange juice concentrate

In a bowl, combine the flour, sugar, pecans, baking soda and salt. In another bowl, whisk the egg, sour cream, butter and orange juice concentrate. Stir into the dry ingredients just until moistened.

Fill paper-lined muffin cups three-fourths full. Bake at 375° for 18-20 minutes or until a toothpick comes out clean. Cool for 5 minutes before removing from pans to a wire rack. Serve warm. **Yield:** 1 dozen.

Focaccia for a Crowd

I've been making this bread for quite a few years…even my Italian friends tell me it's delicious. When it's in season, I like to substitute 1 tablespoon minced fresh basil for the dried basil.
—*Betty Peyret, Pine Grove, California*

    1 package (1/4 ounce) active dry yeast
    1 cup warm water (110° to 115°)
    2 teaspoons sugar
  1/4 cup plus 3 tablespoons olive *or* vegetable oil, *divided*
  3/4 teaspoon salt
2-2/3 to 3 cups all-purpose flour
    3 tablespoons grated Parmesan cheese
    1 teaspoon dried basil
  1/4 teaspoon garlic salt
  1/4 teaspoon garlic powder

In a large mixing bowl, dissolve yeast in warm water. Add sugar; let stand for 5 minutes. Add 1/4 cup oil, salt and 2 cups flour; beat until smooth. Stir in enough remaining flour to form a soft dough. Turn onto a floured surface; knead until smooth and elastic, about 6-8 minutes. Place in a greased bowl, turning once to grease top. Cover and let rise in a warm place until doubled, about 40 minutes.

Punch dough down. Turn onto a lightly floured surface. Pat dough flat; let rest for 5 minutes. Press dough into a greased 15-in. x 10-in. x 1-in. baking pan. Cover and let rise in a warm place for 20-30 minutes or until dough begins to rise.

With a wooden spoon handle, make indentations in the dough at 1-in. intervals. Brush with 2 tablespoons of the remaining oil. Combine Parmesan cheese, basil, garlic salt and garlic powder; sprinkle over top. Drizzle with remaining oil. Bake at 450° for 12-15 minutes or until golden brown. Cut into squares; serve warm. **Yield:** 2 dozen.

Blue Cheese Garlic Bread

(Pictured at right)

This is a great way to dress up an ordinary loaf of bread. Serve slices as an appetizer or with a meal.
—Kevalyn Henderson
Hayward, Wisconsin

1/2 cup butter *or* margarine, softened
4 ounces crumbled blue cheese
2 tablespoons grated Parmesan cheese
1 tablespoon snipped chives
1 teaspoon garlic powder
1 loaf (1 pound) unsliced French bread

In a small bowl, combine the first five ingredients. Cut bread into 1-in.-thick slices, but not all the way through, leaving slices attached at the bottom. Spread cheese mixture between slices. Wrap loaf in a large piece of heavy-duty foil (about 28 in. x 18 in.). Fold foil around bread and seal tightly. Bake at 350° for 20 minutes or until heated through. Serve warm. **Yield:** 10 servings.

Ginger Yeast Muffins

These feather-light muffins are loaded with the old-fashioned flavor of ginger.
They're best enjoyed the same day they're made.
—Geneva Wood, Granada, Minnesota

1 package (1/4 ounce) active dry yeast
1 cup warm water (110° to 115°)
3 cups all-purpose flour, *divided*
1 cup shortening
1-1/2 cups sugar
3 eggs
1/2 cup molasses
2 teaspoons ground cinnamon
1 teaspoon salt
1/2 teaspoon baking soda

1/2 teaspoon ground ginger
1/2 cup chopped walnuts

In a small mixing bowl, dissolve yeast in warm water. Add 1-1/2 cups flour; beat until smooth. Cover and let rise in a warm place for 30 minutes. In another mixing bowl, cream shortening and sugar. Add eggs, one at a time, beating well after each addition. Beat in molasses until smooth. Add the yeast mixture. Combine cinnamon, salt, baking soda, ginger and remaining flour; gradually add to egg mixture. Stir in nuts.

Fill greased or paper-lined muffin cups two-thirds full. Bake at 350° for 20-25 minutes or until a toothpick comes out clean. Cool for 5 minutes before removing from pans to wire racks. **Yield:** 2 dozen.

Bishop's Bread

This bread is packed with cherries, chocolate and nuts. I give away many loaves at Christmas.
— Yvonne Wheeler, Minneapolis, Minnesota

1 cup sugar
3 eggs
1/2 teaspoon almond extract
1/2 teaspoon vanilla extract
1-1/2 cups flour
1-1/2 teaspoons baking powder
1 teaspoon salt
1 cup whole almonds
1 cup chopped walnuts
1 cup chopped dates
1/2 cup *each* red and green
   maraschino cherries, drained
   and halved

1 milk chocolate candy bar with almonds
   (7 ounces), broken into bite-size pieces

In a large mixing bowl, beat sugar, eggs and extracts. In another bowl, combine the flour, baking powder and salt; stir in almonds, walnuts, dates, cherries and candy bar. Stir into egg mixture until blended.

Pour into a greased and floured 9-in. x 5-in. x 3-in. loaf pan. Press down firmly to eliminate air spaces. Bake at 300° for 2 hours. Cool for 10 minutes before removing from pan to a wire rack. **Yield:** 1 loaf.

Cappuccino Muffins

These airy muffins capture the wonderful flavor of coffee. Folks are pleasantly surprised to find a creamy chocolate center.
— Susan Wagers, Minot, North Dakota

2-1/2 cups all-purpose flour
2/3 cup sugar
2-1/2 teaspoons baking powder
1-1/2 teaspoons ground cinnamon
3/4 teaspoon salt
1/2 teaspoon baking soda
1 egg
1-1/3 cups buttermilk
3 tablespoons vegetable oil
4-1/2 teaspoons instant coffee
   granules
2 teaspoons vanilla extract
12 chocolate kisses
TOPPING:
2 tablespoons sugar
1/2 teaspoon ground cinnamon

In a large bowl, combine the flour, sugar, baking powder, cinnamon, salt and baking soda. In another bowl, beat the egg, buttermilk, oil, coffee granules and vanilla until coffee granules are dissolved. Stir into dry ingredients just until moistened.

Spoon 2 tablespoons batter into greased muffin cups. Place a chocolate kiss in the center of each; top with remaining batter. Combine sugar and cinnamon; sprinkle over batter. Bake at 425° for 16-20 minutes or until a toothpick inserted into muffin comes out clean. Cool for 5 minutes before removing from pan to a wire rack. Serve warm. **Yield:** 1 dozen.

Maple-Nut Cinnamon Rolls

(Pictured at right)

Adding oats to the dough makes these sweet rolls a little more hearty. The gooey topping is finger-licking good!
—Barbara Simonds
Wellsboro, Pennsylvania

3-1/2 cups all-purpose flour, *divided*
1 cup old-fashioned oats
1/3 cup packed brown sugar
1-1/2 teaspoons salt
1 package (1/4 ounce) active dry yeast
1 cup milk
1/2 cup shortening
2 eggs
FILLING:
2/3 cup packed brown sugar
1 tablespoon grated orange peel
1 teaspoon ground cinnamon
TOPPING:
2/3 cup chopped walnuts
1/2 cup maple syrup
1/4 cup butter *or* margarine, melted
1/4 cup packed brown sugar
1/4 teaspoon maple flavoring

In a large mixing bowl, combine 1-1/2 cups flour, oats, brown sugar, salt and yeast. In a saucepan, heat milk and shortening to 120°-130°. Add to the oat mixture; mix well. Add eggs, one at a time, beating well after each. Add enough remaining flour to form a stiff dough. Turn onto a floured surface; knead until smooth and elastic, about 6-8 minutes. Place in a greased bowl, turning once to grease top. Cover and let rise until doubled, about 1 hour.

Punch dough down. Roll into a 16-in. x 12-in. rectangle. Combine filling ingredients; sprinkle over dough to within 1/2 in. of edges. Roll up jelly-roll style, starting with a long side. Cut into 12 slices.

Sprinkle nuts into a greased 13-in. x 9-in. x 2-in. baking pan. Combine the remaining topping ingredients; pour over nuts. Place rolls over topping. Cover and let rise for 30 minutes. Bake at 350° for 30-35 minutes or until golden brown. Cool for 5 minutes before inverting rolls onto a wire rack. **Yield:** 1 dozen.

SLICING CINNAMON ROLLS

IF YOU find it difficult to slice cinnamon roll dough with a knife, try this trick. Place a piece of dental floss under the rolled dough, 1 inch from the end. Bring the floss up around the dough and cross it over the top, cutting through the dough and filling. Repeat at 1-inch intervals.

Chocolate Pinwheel Bread

This swirled yeast bread is chock-full of chocolate chips. The sweet slices don't need any butter.
Keep one loaf for your family and share the other with a neighbor.
—*Dawn Onuffer, Freeport, Florida*

1 package (1/4 ounce) active
   dry yeast
1 cup warm milk (110° to 115°)
1/4 cup sugar
1 teaspoon salt
2 eggs
4 ounces cream cheese, softened
4 to 4-1/2 cups bread flour
FILLING:
   4 ounces cream cheese, softened
1/2 cup confectioners' sugar
2 tablespoons baking cocoa
1 cup (6 ounces) semisweet
   chocolate chips
1 egg, beaten

In a large mixing bowl, dissolve yeast in milk. Add sugar, salt, eggs, cream cheese and 2 cups flour; beat until smooth. Stir in enough remaining flour to form a soft dough. Turn onto a floured surface; knead until smooth and elastic, about 6-8 minutes. Place in a greased bowl, turning once to grease top. Cover and let rise in a warm place until doubled, about 1 hour.

Punch dough down. Turn onto a floured surface; divide in half. Roll each portion into a 12-in. x 8-in. rectangle. In a mixing bowl, beat cream cheese, confectioners' sugar and cocoa until smooth. Spread over each rectangle to within 1/2 in. of edges. Sprinkle with chocolate chips. Roll up jelly-roll style, starting with a short side; pinch seam to seal. Place seam side down in two greased 9-in. x 5-in. x 3-in. loaf pans. Cover and let rise until doubled, about 45 minutes.

Brush tops of loaves with egg. Bake at 350° for 25 minutes. Cover loosely with foil. Bake 15-20 minutes longer or until loaves sound hollow when tapped. Remove from pans to wire racks to cool. **Yield:** 2 loaves.

Orange Bubble Bread

This sweet version of bubble bread is dotted with raisins and topped with
an orange glaze. My great-aunt shared the recipe with me.
—*Cyndie Wowchuk, Saskatoon, Saskatchewan*

1 package (1/4 ounce) active
   dry yeast
1 teaspoon plus 1/4 cup sugar,
   divided
1 cup warm milk (110° to 115°)
3-1/2 to 4 cups all-purpose flour
1 teaspoon salt
1/2 cup cold butter *or* margarine
2 eggs, lightly beaten

ORANGE SYRUP:
3/4 cup orange juice
3/4 cup orange marmalade
   4 to 5 tablespoons sugar
   2 tablespoons plus 1 teaspoon butter *or* margarine
3/4 teaspoon grated orange peel
   1 cup flaked coconut, toasted, *divided*
1/2 cup golden raisins

In a small bowl, dissolve yeast and 1 teaspoon sugar in warm milk; set aside. In a large bowl, combine 3-1/2 cups flour, salt and remaining sugar. Cut in butter until crumbly. Stir in eggs. Stir in yeast mixture and enough remaining flour until mixture forms a firm ball (mixture will be slightly sticky). Turn onto a floured surface; knead until smooth and elastic, about 6-8 minutes. Place in a greased bowl, turning once to grease top. Cover and let rise in a warm place until doubled, about 1-1/4 hours.

Meanwhile, for syrup, combine orange juice, marmalade, sugar, butter and orange peel in a saucepan. Cook and stir until mixture comes to a boil. Reduce heat; simmer, uncovered, for 5 minutes. Cool to room temperature. Place 1/2 cup syrup and 1/2 cup coconut on the bottom of a greased 10-in. tube pan.

Punch dough down; turn onto a lightly floured surface. Divide into 32 pieces; roll each into a 1-in. ball. Dip each into remaining orange syrup. Place 16 balls in prepared pan. Sprinkle with half of the raisins and remaining coconut. Top with remaining balls, raisins and coconut. Cover and let rise until doubled, about 45 minutes.

Bake at 350° for 40-50 minutes or until golden brown. Cool for 5 minutes before inverting bread onto a serving plate. **Yield:** 1 loaf.

Baked Herb Puffs

(Pictured at right)

Ground mustard, parsley and green onions make these savory puffs a nice addition to any meal. I often freeze them, then reheat for a few minutes in the oven.
—Dorothy Smith, El Dorado, Arkansas

   1 cup water
1/2 cup butter (no substitutes)
   1 teaspoon ground mustard
1/4 teaspoon salt
1/8 teaspoon pepper
   1 cup all-purpose flour
   4 eggs
1/3 cup minced fresh parsley
1/4 cup chopped green onions

In a large saucepan, bring water, butter, mustard, salt and pepper to a boil. Add flour all at once and stir until a smooth ball forms. Remove from the heat; let stand for 5 minutes. Add eggs, one at a time, beating well after each addition. Continue beating until smooth and shiny. Add parsley and green onions; mix well.

Drop by rounded 2 tablespoonfuls 2 in. apart onto greased baking sheets. Bake at 400° for 18-20 minutes or until golden brown. Cut a slit in each to allow steam to escape; bake 5 minutes longer. Remove from pans to wire racks to cool. **Yield:** 1-1/2 dozen.

Cracked Wheat Buttermilk Bread

Slices of this crusty bread are great alongside meals or for sandwiches.
It's one of the lightest wheat breads I've ever tried.
— Ruth Stoops, Cincinnati, Ohio

1-1/2 cups water
    6 tablespoons cracked wheat
  3/4 cup warm buttermilk
     (70° to 80°)
    3 tablespoons honey
    3 tablespoons butter *or*
    margarine, softened
1-1/2 teaspoons salt
  1/4 teaspoon baking soda
1-1/2 cups bread flour
1-1/2 cups whole wheat flour
    1 tablespoon active dry yeast

In a saucepan, bring the water and cracked wheat to a boil; boil for 6 minutes. Drain; cool for 15 minutes. Place all ingredients, including cracked wheat, in bread machine pan in order suggested by manufacturer. Select basic bread setting. Choose crust color and loaf size if available. Bake according to bread machine directions (check dough after 5 minutes of mixing; add 1-2 tablespoons of warm buttermilk or flour if needed). **Yield:** 1 loaf (1-1/2 pounds).

Editor's Note: If your bread machine has a time-delay feature, we recommend you do not use it for this recipe.

Toasted Oat Raisin Loaves

Toasting the oats before preparing the dough gives these lovely loaves wonderful flavor and color.
— Penny Kessler, Festus, Missouri

    2 cups quick-cooking oats
    6 to 6-1/2 cups all-purpose flour
  1/4 cup packed brown sugar
    3 packages (1/4 ounce *each*)
    active dry yeast
    2 teaspoons salt
1-3/4 cups warm milk
     (120° to 130°)
  1/4 cup butter *or* margarine,
    softened
  1/4 cup honey
    2 eggs, beaten
    1 cup raisins
    1 cup chopped walnuts
    1 egg yolk
    1 teaspoon cold water

In a large skillet, cook and stir oats over medium-low heat for 10 minutes or until lightly toasted. In a large mixing bowl, combine oats, 3 cups flour, brown sugar, yeast and salt. Beat in the milk, butter, honey and eggs until smooth. Stir in raisins, nuts and enough remaining flour to form a stiff dough. Turn onto a floured surface; knead until smooth and elastic, about 8-10 minutes. Place in a greased bowl, turning once to grease top. Cover and let rise in a warm place until doubled, about 1-1/4 hours.

Punch dough down and divide in half. Shape into two loaves. Place in two greased 9-in. x 5-in. x 3-in. loaf pans. Cover and let rise until doubled, about 45 minutes.

In a small bowl, whisk the egg yolk and cold water; brush over loaves. With a very sharp knife, make three shallow cuts across the top of each loaf. Bake at 350° for 40-45 minutes or until golden brown. Remove from pans to wire racks to cool. **Yield:** 2 loaves.

Editor's Note: Bread may also be shaped into two round loaves and baked on two greased baking sheets.

Sugarplum Spice Bread

(Pictured at right)

I make Christmas Eve magical with hot cocoa and toasted slices of this fragrant, fruit-studded bread. My son and I combined several recipes to come up with this winner.
—Jackie Brown, Tully, New York

3/4 cup butter *or* margarine,
    softened
3/4 cup sugar
  4 eggs
5-1/2 to 6 cups all-purpose flour
  2 packages (1/4 ounce *each*)
    quick-rise yeast
1-1/2 teaspoons ground cardamom
  1 teaspoon salt
3/4 teaspoon ground cinnamon
1/4 teaspoon ground nutmeg
1-1/2 cups milk
  1 cup diced dried fruit
1/2 cup raisins
1/2 cup golden raisins
FROSTING:
  2 tablespoons butter *or*
    margarine, softened
  2 tablespoons shortening
  2 cups confectioners' sugar
1/2 teaspoon vanilla extract
  2 to 3 tablespoons milk

In a large mixing bowl, cream butter and sugar. Add eggs, one at a time, beating well after each addition. Add 4 cups flour, yeast, cardamom, salt, cinnamon and nutmeg. Heat milk to 120°-130°; add to creamed mixture and beat until moistened. Stir in enough remaining flour to form a firm dough. Turn onto a heavily floured surface. Sprinkle with fruit and raisins; knead until smooth and elastic, about 6-8 minutes. Cover and let rise in a warm place until doubled, about 40 minutes.

Punch dough down. Turn onto a lightly floured surface; divide into eight portions. Shape into loaves. Place in eight greased 5-3/4-in. x 3-in. x 2-in. loaf pans. Cover and let rise until doubled, about 30 minutes. Bake at 350° for 30-35 minutes or until golden brown. Remove from pans to wire racks to cool.

For frosting, in a small mixing bowl, cream butter and shortening. Gradually beat in confectioners' sugar, vanilla and enough milk to achieve spreading consistency. Frost loaves. **Yield:** 8 mini loaves.

Blackberry Muffins

No one can resist these buttery muffins bursting with juicy blackberries.
They make a nice addition to any breakfast table.
—Julee Wallberg, Carson City, Nevada

1/2 cup butter *or* margarine,
    softened
1-1/4 cups plus 1 tablespoon sugar,
    divided
    2 eggs
    2 cups all-purpose flour
    2 teaspoons baking powder
1/2 teaspoon salt
1/2 cup milk
    2 cups fresh *or* frozen
    blackberries*

In a mixing bowl, cream butter and 1-1/4 cups sugar. Add eggs, one at a time, beating well after each addition. Combine the flour, baking powder and salt; stir into creamed mixture alternately with milk. Fold in blackberries.

Fill greased or paper-lined muffin cups two-thirds full. Sprinkle with remaining sugar. Bake at 375° for 20-25 minutes or until a toothpick comes out clean. Cool for 5 minutes before removing from pans to wire racks. Serve warm. **Yield:** 1-1/2 dozen.

*Editor's Note: If using frozen blackberries, do not thaw before adding to batter.

Raisin Pumpkin Bread

My family loves pumpkin bread, so I'm always looking for new ways to make it.
My husband and daughter think this variation is the best.
—Naomi Henderson, Ashburn, Virginia

    6 tablespoons butter *or*
    margarine, softened
3/4 cup packed brown sugar
    2 eggs
    1 cup cooked *or* canned
    pumpkin
1/3 cup maple syrup
1/3 cup orange juice
1/2 to 1 teaspoon grated orange
    peel
    2 cups all-purpose flour
    2 teaspoons baking powder
1/2 teaspoon salt
1/2 teaspoon ground cinnamon
1/2 teaspoon ground nutmeg

1/4 teaspoon baking soda
1/4 teaspoon ground cloves
1/2 cup raisins
1/2 cup chopped pecans

In a mixing bowl, cream butter and brown sugar. Beat in the eggs, pumpkin, syrup, orange juice and peel; mix well. Combine the flour, baking powder, salt, cinnamon, nutmeg, baking soda and cloves; add to creamed mixture just until blended. Fold in raisins and pecans.

Transfer to a greased 9-in. x 5-in. x 3-in. loaf pan. Bake at 350° for 55-60 minutes or until a toothpick inserted near the center comes out clean and top is golden brown. Cool for 10 minutes before removing from pan to a wire rack to cool completely. **Yield:** 1 loaf.

Candy Cane Coffee Cake

(Pictured at right)

Our family of seven is thrilled when I serve this cherry-cheese Danish.
—Doris Hostetler
Clarkrange, Tennessee

  1 tablespoon active dry yeast
1/4 cup warm water
    (110° to 115°)
1/2 cup butter *or* margarine,
    softened
1/2 cup sour cream
  2 eggs
  3 tablespoons sugar
1/4 teaspoon salt
  3 cups all-purpose flour
FILLING:
  2 packages (8 ounces *each*)
    cream cheese, softened
1/2 cup sugar
  2 egg yolks
  2 teaspoons vanilla extract
TOPPINGS:
  1 tablespoon confectioners'
    sugar
  1 jar (12 ounces) cherry jam

In a small bowl, dissolve yeast in warm water. In a mixing bowl, combine the butter, sour cream, eggs, sugar and salt. Add yeast mixture and flour; beat until smooth (do not knead). Place in a greased bowl, turning once to grease top. Cover and refrigerate overnight.

For filling, in a mixing bowl, beat cream cheese, sugar, egg yolks and vanilla until blended. Punch dough down. Turn onto a lightly floured surface; divide in half. Roll out each portion into a 16-in. x 10-in. rectangle on a greased baking sheet. Spread filling down center of each rectangle. On each long side, cut 1-1/2-in.-wide strips about 3 in. into center. Starting at one end, fold alternating strips at an angle across filling. Pinch ends to seal. Curve one end, forming a candy cane. Cover and let rise until doubled, about 1 hour.

Bake at 350° for 20-25 minutes or until golden brown. Carefully remove from pans to wire racks to cool. Sprinkle with confectioners' sugar. Stir jam, then spoon over top of loaves, creating candy cane stripes. Refrigerate leftovers. **Yield:** 2 coffee cakes.

SHAPING CANDY CANE COFFEE CAKE

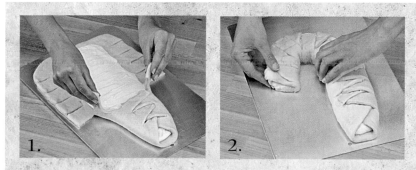

1. Starting at one end, fold strips alternately at an angle across the filling. Seal ends.

2. Curve one end to form a candy cane.

'TIS THE *Season*

Merry Main Dishes

WHEN PLANNING any menu, most cooks first decide on the star attraction—the entree—then round out the meal with side dishes.

And for the holidays, choosing just the right main course is even more important.

To guarantee that every meal with family and friends during the Christmas season is merry, turn to this recipe-packed chapter.

It features an appetizing array of main courses such as Rosemary Chicken Dinner, Halibut with Tomato-Basil Sauce and Parsley-Stuffed Flank Steak (all shown at right).

From beef and seafood to pork and poultry, you'll find an inviting entree to suit any occasion.

APPETIZING ENTREES
(Clockwise from top right)

Rosemary Chicken Dinner (p. 56)

Halibut with Tomato-Basil Sauce (p. 59)

Parsley-Stuffed Flank Steak (p. 57)

Rosemary Chicken Dinner

(Pictured on page 55)

The fragrant rosemary in this hearty meat-and-potatoes dish makes the whole house smell wonderful! All you need to round out the meal is a green salad or vegetable.
—*Christine Yost, Newark, New York*

3 large potatoes, peeled
1 broiler/fryer chicken (3 to 4 pounds), cut into quarters
2 tablespoons olive *or* vegetable oil
1 teaspoon salt
1/4 teaspoon garlic powder
1/4 teaspoon pepper
2 to 3 teaspoons minced fresh rosemary *or* 1 teaspoon dried rosemary, crushed

Cut each potato into four wedges. Place chicken and potatoes in a greased 13-in. x 9-in. x 2-in. baking dish or shallow roasting pan. Drizzle with oil. Combine salt, garlic powder and pepper; sprinkle over chicken and potatoes. Sprinkle rosemary over chicken. Bake, uncovered, at 375° for 45 minutes; drain. Bake 15-20 longer or until potatoes are tender and chicken juices run clear. **Yield:** 4 servings.

Pineapple-Glazed Ham Loaf

This holiday ham loaf was served by a good friend several years ago.
Now it's become a tradition in my family as well.
—*Sherry Golightly, Paducah, Kentucky*

2 eggs, lightly beaten
1 cup milk
1 teaspoon ground mustard
1 cup crushed saltines (about 30 crackers)
2 tablespoons orange juice
1 pound ground fully cooked ham
1 pound ground pork
1 cup packed brown sugar
1 tablespoon white vinegar
1 can (8 ounces) crushed pineapple, undrained

In a bowl, combine the first five ingredients. Crumble ham and pork over mixture; mix well. Press into a 9-in. x 5-in. x 3-in. loaf pan coated with nonstick cooking spray. Combine brown sugar, vinegar and pineapple; spoon over loaf. Bake, uncovered, at 350° for 2 hours or until a meat thermometer reads 160°. Cool for 10 minutes before removing from pan. **Yield:** 6-8 servings.

Parsley-Stuffed Flank Steak

(Pictured at right and on page 54)

*A simple cheese and parsley stuffing
adds flair to ordinary flank steak.
I make this entree often .*
— *Tami Dristiliaris*
Dracut, Massachusetts

  1 beef flank steak (2 pounds)
1/2 cup minced fresh parsley
  4 teaspoons chopped garlic
1/2 cup grated Romano cheese

Butterfly the flank steak, cutting horizontally from a long side to within 1/2
in. of opposite side. Open and place on
a large piece of heavy-duty aluminum foil (about 18 in.
square). Sprinkle parsley, garlic and cheese over meat to
within 1/2 in. of edges. Roll up tightly jelly-roll style, starting with a long side. Wrap tightly in foil.

Place in a 13-in. x 9-in. x 2-in. baking dish. Bake at 325° for
1-1/2 hours or until meat reaches desired doneness (for rare,
a meat thermometer should read 140°; medium, 160°; well-
done, 170°). Unwrap and slice steak. **Yield:** 8 servings.

Brisket with Gingersnap Gravy

*This is the first and only recipe I've ever used to prepare a fresh beef brisket.
Serve it thinly sliced on a platter as an entree or use it for sandwiches.*
— *Teri Lindquist, Gurnee, Illinois*

  1 beef brisket* (about 5 pounds)
  1 cup water
3/4 cup chili sauce
  1 envelope onion soup mix
  5 to 6 gingersnaps, crushed

Place brisket in a roasting pan. In a bowl, combine the water, chili sauce and soup mix; pour over meat. Cover and
bake at 325° for 2-1/2 to 3 hours or until tender. Cool; cover and refrigerate overnight.

Remove meat and cut into 1/4-in.-thick slices; return to
the pan. Sprinkle with gingersnap crumbs. Cover and
bake at 350° for 30-45 minutes or until heated through.
Yield: 16-18 servings.

*Editor's Note: This is a fresh beef brisket, not corned
beef.

Perfect Prime Rib Roast

If you've never made prime rib before, you can't go wrong with this recipe.
It comes from a chef at a favorite local restaurant.
—Pauline Waasdorp, Fergus Falls, Minnesota

1/4 **cup Worcestershire sauce**
1-1/2 **teaspoons garlic salt**
1-1/2 **teaspoons seasoned salt**
1-1/2 **teaspoons coarsely ground**
 pepper
 1 **bone-in beef rib roast (5 to 6**
 pounds)

In a small bowl, combine the first four ingredients; rub over the roast. Place in a large resealable plastic bag; seal and refrigerate overnight, turning often.

Place roast fat side up in a large roasting pan; pour marinade over roast. Tent with foil. Bake at 350° for 1 hour. Uncover and bake 1-1/2 hours longer or until meat reaches desired doneness (for rare, a meat thermometer should read 140°; medium, 160°; well-done, 170°). Let stand for 10-15 minutes before slicing. **Yield:** 8-10 servings.

MAKING SIT-DOWN DINNERS SPECIAL

THE HOLIDAYS are a perfect time to add a little elegance to the table. Instead of a casual family-style supper, where food is passed from one person to another, host a formal sit-down dinner, where individual plates of food are served to guests. Here's how:

- Keep the guest list small.
- Bring out your china, crystal, silver and best linen cloths. Use place cards so guests don't have to guess where to sit.
- When selecting a centerpiece for the table, make sure it isn't too tall (10 to 12 inches is an acceptable maximum height), otherwise guests won't be able to see each other across the table.
- Serve appetizers and beverages in the living room before sitting down. You'll have one less course to bring to the table.
- Before calling guests to the table, fill water goblets and put out the bread and butter for guests to pass.

 If you're serving a salad, fill individual salad plates and set them at each place setting. Consider chilling the salad plates in the refrigerator for several hours to keep greens crisp.

 If your dinner plates are oven-safe, set the oven to the lowest possible temperature and place the stacked plates in the oven to warm while enjoying salad and bread. If your dishes are not oven-safe, rinse them under hot water and dry just before filling.

- When guests have finished with the salad, clear the plates and utensils used. Then prepare and garnish individual dinner plates in the kitchen.
- Before serving dessert, clear the table of all dishes, including extra glasses, salt and pepper shakers and condiment dishes.
- Serve dessert and coffee cups. Place the sugar and creamer on the table.
- Avoid the temptation to clear the table and start washing dishes…that can wait until after your guests leave.

Halibut with Tomato-Basil Sauce

(Pictured at right and on page 54)

Roasted tomatoes and garlic create a succulent sauce in this recipe from our Test Kitchen. Topping the fish with a seasoned mayonnaise mixture before baking keeps it moist.

6 plum tomatoes, cut into 1-1/4-inch slices
1 tablespoon olive *or* vegetable oil
4 to 6 garlic cloves, peeled
1/2 teaspoon balsamic vinegar
2 tablespoons minced fresh basil
Water
4 halibut steaks (1 inch thick)
TOPPING:
1/2 cup mayonnaise
1/2 teaspoon Dijon mustard
1 cup soft bread crumbs
2 tablespoons minced fresh basil
2 tablespoons chopped ripe olives

Place tomatoes on a baking sheet; drizzle with oil. Wrap garlic in aluminum foil and place on the baking sheet. Bake at 450° for 20 minutes or until edges of tomatoes are lightly browned and garlic pierces easily with a fork. Place tomatoes and garlic in a food processor or blender; cover and process until smooth. Add vinegar, basil and water to achieve desired thickness; set aside.

Place halibut in a greased 13-in. x 9-in. x 2-in. baking dish. Combine mayonnaise and mustard; spread over fish. Combine bread crumbs, basil and olives; sprinkle over mayonnaise mixture and press down gently. Bake, uncovered, at 400° for 20 minutes or until topping is golden brown and fish flakes easily with a fork. Spoon tomato sauce onto four dinner plates, top with fish. **Yield:** 4 servings.

Hawaiian Chicken

You can bring a taste of the tropics to your Christmas table with this flavorful entree.
It's been the star of many special meals in our family.
—Lois Miller, Watertown, South Dakota

1 broiler/fryer chicken
   (3 to 4 pounds), cut up
1/4 cup butter *or* margarine,
   melted
1 can (20 ounces) pineapple
   chunks
1/4 cup packed brown sugar
2 tablespoons cornstarch
1 teaspoon salt
1/3 cup ketchup
1/4 cup cider vinegar
1 teaspoon chili powder
1 teaspoon Worcestershire
   sauce

1 teaspoon soy sauce
Pinch ground ginger

Place chicken in a greased 13-in. x 9-in. x 2-in. baking dish; drizzle with butter. Drain pineapple, reserving juice; set pineapple aside. In a saucepan, combine brown sugar, cornstarch and salt; stir in reserved pineapple juice until smooth. Add the ketchup, vinegar, chili powder, Worcestershire sauce, soy sauce and ginger. Bring to a boil; cook and stir for 2 minutes or until thickened. Pour over chicken.

Cover and bake at 350° for 1 hour. Uncover and bake for 30 minutes. Top with reserved pineapple; bake 15 minutes longer or until chicken juices run clear and pineapple is heated through. **Yield:** 6 servings.

Slow-Cooked Round Steak

Quick-and-easy slow cooker recipes like this are a real plus, especially around the holidays.
Serve these saucy beef slices over mashed potatoes, rice or noodles.
—Dona McPherson, Spring, Texas

1/4 cup all-purpose flour
1/2 teaspoon salt
1/8 teaspoon pepper
2 pounds boneless beef round
   steak (3/4 inch thick), cut into
   serving-size pieces
6 teaspoons vegetable oil,
   divided
1 medium onion, thinly sliced
1 can (10-3/4 ounces) condensed
   cream of mushroom soup,
   undiluted
1/2 teaspoon dried oregano
1/4 teaspoon dried thyme

In a large resealable plastic bag, combine the flour, salt and pepper. Add beef, a few pieces at a time, and shake to coat. In a large skillet, brown meat on both sides in 4 teaspoons oil. Place in a 5-qt. slow cooker.

In the same skillet, saute onion in remaining oil until lightly browned; place over beef. Combine the soup, oregano and thyme; pour over onion. Cover and cook on low for 7-8 hours or until meat is tender. **Yield:** 6-8 servings.

Cornish Hens with Cranberry Stuffing

(Pictured at right)

*Serving Cornish hens to our young sons
makes them feel like kings! I often
have to make extra stuffing
to have on hand for leftovers.*
—*Marjorie O'Dell, Bow, Washington*

2 slices whole wheat bread
2 slices white bread
1 cup chopped fresh *or* frozen
  cranberries thawed
3 tablespoons sugar
1 teaspoon grated orange peel
1/2 teaspoon salt
1/8 teaspoon ground cinnamon
2 tablespoons raisins
3 tablespoons butter *or*
  margarine, melted, *divided*
1 to 2 tablespoons orange juice
4 Cornish game hens (22 ounces
  each)

Cut bread into 1/2-in. cubes; place on a baking sheet. Bake at 300° for 15 minutes or until toasted and dry. In a bowl, combine the cranberries, sugar, orange peel, salt and cinnamon; mix well. Stir in bread cubes and raisins. Add 1 tablespoon butter and enough orange juice until stuffing reaches desired moistness.

Loosely stuff hens; rub skin with remaining butter. Place in a shallow roasting pan. Bake, uncovered, at 375° for 1 hour and 15 minutes or until juices run clear and a meat thermometer inserted into stuffing reads 165°. **Yield:** 4 servings.

CORNISH GAME HEN FACTS

CORNISH GAME HENS are a cross between Cornish and White Rock chickens and typically weigh 1-1/2 pounds or less. They look elegant, have tender meat and take less time to cook than a whole chicken, but they are more expensive.

Shrimp Crepes

Several years ago, I came up with this recipe when I was experimenting with my new crepe maker. It was a hit with the whole family and now appears on many special-occasion menus.
—Donna Bartlett, Reno, Nevada

       4 eggs
1-1/2 cups milk
1-1/2 teaspoons sugar
    1/8 teaspoon salt
       1 cup all-purpose flour
Butter *or* **margarine**
FILLING:
       3 tablespoons butter *or*
          margarine
4-1/2 cups chopped fresh broccoli
       6 green onions, chopped
       2 teaspoons minced garlic,
          divided
    1/4 teaspoon Worcestershire
          sauce, *divided*
    1/2 teaspoon salt
    1/4 teaspoon pepper
       1 pound uncooked shrimp,
          peeled and deveined
    1/4 cup white wine *or* chicken
          broth
       1 envelope bearnaise sauce

In a bowl, whisk eggs, milk, sugar and salt. Add flour; beat until smooth. Melt 1 teaspoon butter in an 8-in. nonstick skillet. Pour 2 tablespoons batter into center of skillet; lift and turn pan to cover the bottom. Cook until lightly browned; turn and brown the other side. Remove to a wire rack. Repeat with remaining batter, adding butter to skillet as needed. When cool, stack crepes with waxed paper or paper towels in between.

For filling, in a large skillet, melt butter over medium heat. Add broccoli, onions, 1 teaspoon garlic, 1/8 teaspoon Worcestershire sauce, salt and pepper. Cook and stir for 7-9 minutes or until broccoli is crisp-tender. Remove mixture from the pan and set aside. Add the shrimp, wine or broth, and remaining garlic and Worcestershire sauce to the pan. Saute until shrimp turn pink, about 4 minutes. Return broccoli mixture to skillet.

Spoon filling down center of crepes; roll up. Place in an ungreased 15-in. x 10-in. x 1-in. baking pan. Bake, uncovered, at 350° for 15-20 minutes or until heated through. Meanwhile, prepare bearnaise sauce according to package directions. Serve over crepes. **Yield:** 8 servings (16 crepes).

Raspberry Pork Chops

(Pictured at right)

*These fruity chops look a little fancy,
yet they're quite simple to prepare.
My family can't eat just one,
so I often double the recipe.*
—Barbara Workman, What Cheer, Iowa

4 bone-in pork loin chops
   (1/2 inch thick)
1/4 cup all-purpose flour
1 tablespoon vegetable oil
2 tablespoons lemon juice
1/3 cup seedless raspberry jam
1/4 teaspoon salt
1/8 to 1/4 teaspoon ground ginger
1/8 teaspoon pepper

Coat pork chops with flour and shake off excess. In a large skillet, brown chops in oil for 2-3 minutes on each side. Pour lemon juice over chops. Combine the jam, salt, ginger and pepper; spread over chops. Reduce heat; cover and cook for 5-10 minutes or until chops are tender and meat juices run clear. **Yield:** 4 servings.

Pesto Mushroom Chicken

*My husband is an avid hunter, so we enjoy lots of game. But when I cook chicken,
this is the recipe I turn to. Pesto, cheese and mushrooms make it special.*
—Jennifer Tomlinson, Hamilton, Montana

4 boneless skinless chicken
   breast halves
Salt and pepper to taste
5 tablespoons olive *or* vegetable
   oil, *divided*
1 cup loosely packed fresh basil
   leaves
1/2 cup chopped walnuts
2 garlic cloves, minced
1/2 teaspoon salt
1/3 cup grated Parmesan cheese
4 slices mozzarella cheese
1 cup sliced fresh mushrooms

Flatten chicken to 1/4-in. thickness; sprinkle with salt and pepper. In a large skillet, cook chicken in 1 tablespoon oil for 5-10 minutes on each side or until juices run clear.

Meanwhile, for pesto, combine the basil, nuts, garlic, salt and Parmesan cheese in a blender or food processor; cover and process until well blended. While processing, gradually add remaining oil in a stream. Spoon over chicken. Top each with a slice of mozzarella. Sprinkle mushrooms around chicken. Cover and cook for 5 minutes or until cheese is melted and mushrooms are tender. **Yield:** 4 servings.

Chicken Supreme

Strips of Monterey Jack cheese tucked inside chicken make this entree extra special.
Crushed Caesar croutons are a unique addition to the coating.
—Marlene Nutter, Thedford, Nebraska

    4 ounces Monterey Jack
      cheese
  1/2 cup butter *or* margarine,
      softened
    1 teaspoon minced fresh
      parsley
    1 teaspoon dried oregano
  1/2 to 1 teaspoon dried marjoram
    8 boneless skinless chicken
      breast halves (about 3
      pounds)
  1/2 teaspoon seasoned salt
  1/2 cup all-purpose flour
    2 eggs, beaten
1-3/4 cups crushed Caesar salad
      croutons
  1/2 cup white wine *or* chicken
      broth

Cut Monterey Jack cheese into eight 2-1/4-in. x 1-in. x 3/8-in. strips. In a bowl, combine the butter, parsley, oregano and marjoram; spread 1-1/2 teaspoons over each cheese strip. Cover and refrigerate cheese and remaining butter mixture for at least 2 hours.

Flatten chicken to 1/8-in. thickness; sprinkle with seasoned salt. Place a cheese strip on each piece of chicken. Roll up and tuck in ends; secure with a toothpick. Coat chicken on all sides with flour. Dip in eggs, then coat with croutons.

Place seam side down in a greased 13-in. x 9-in. x 2-in. baking dish. Bake, uncovered, at 350° for 30 minutes. In a saucepan, combine wine or broth and reserved butter mixture; heat until butter is melted. Pour over chicken. Bake 20-25 minutes longer or until chicken juices run clear. Discard toothpicks before serving. **Yield:** 8 servings.

Marinated Pork Tenderloin

Nothing could be more convenient when you're entertaining than this recipe.
Marinate the pork for a few hours, bake, then pull together the side dishes.
—Alyce Wyman, Pembina, North Dakota

  1 can (5-1/2 ounces) apricot
    nectar
1/2 cup soy sauce
  3 tablespoons vegetable oil
  2 garlic cloves, minced
  2 teaspoons minced fresh
    parsley
  2 pork tenderloins (about 1
    pound *each*)

In a large resealable bag, combine the first five ingredients. Add the pork; seal bag and turn to coat. Refrigerate for at least 2 hours. Drain and discard marinade. Line a shallow baking pan with foil and coat with nonstick cooking spray. Place tenderloins in pan. Bake, uncovered, at 425° for 25-30 minutes or until a meat thermometer reads 160°. Let stand for 10 minutes before slicing. **Yield:** 6 servings.

Salmon Steaks with Dill Sauce

(Pictured at right)

I first made this recipe when we lived in Alaska and my husband did a lot of fishing. Dill is a wonderful complement to salmon.
—Joan Peterson
Colorado Springs, Colorado

1-1/2 cups water
 1 medium onion, sliced
 1 tablespoon lemon juice
 1 teaspoon chicken bouillon
 granules
 1 teaspoon salt
 4 salmon steaks (1 inch thick)
DILL SAUCE:
 1 tablespoon finely chopped
 onion
 2 tablespoons butter *or*
 margarine
 2 tablespoons all-purpose flour
 1 teaspoon dill weed
 1/2 teaspoon salt
 1/8 teaspoon pepper
1-1/2 cups milk

In a large skillet, combine the first five ingredients; bring to a boil. Add salmon. Reduce heat; cover and simmer for 15-20 minutes or until fish flakes easily with a fork. Meanwhile, in a saucepan, saute onion in butter until tender. Stir in flour, dill, salt and pepper until blended; gradually add milk. Bring to a boil; cook and stir for 2 minutes or until thickened. Serve with the salmon. **Yield:** 4 servings.

Family Traditions

ON CHRISTMAS DAY, my siblings and I and our families gather at our parents' house and take part in the Polish custom of sharing "oplatki", a thin bread wafer much like the unleavened host at Mass.
We're each given a large piece and go from person to person, breaking off small pieces of each other's wafer and exchanging good wishes. It's a heart-warming way to reflect on the importance of family.
—*Carol Fischer, Pewaukee, Wisconsin*

'Tis the Season

Decked Out in Desserts

THERE IS no better way to wrap up a holiday dinner than by presenting a selection of sweets to relatives and friends.

Chocolate Truffle Dessert, Almond Puff Pastries and Peppermint Ice Cream (all shown at right) are just a small taste of the tempting treats this chapter has to offer.

From tender cakes and pleasing pies to creamy ice cream and elegant desserts, you'll find a fitting finale for casual family suppers and special sit-down dinners for Christmas and throughout the year.

We also offer some thirst-quenching drinks and easy-to-make beverage stirrers to serve alongside all of your delectable desserts.

LAST BUT NOT LEAST
(Clockwise from top right)

Chocolate Truffle Dessert (p. 69)

Almond Puff Pastries (p. 68)

Peppermint Ice Cream (p. 70)

Almond Puff Pastries

(Pictured on page 66)

My husband comes from a family of almond growers, so I use almonds often in my baking.
These puff pastries have a crisp topping and creamy filling.
— Barbara Harrison, Monte Sereno, California

1 package (17.3 ounces) frozen
  puff pastry, thawed
1 egg, *separated*
1 tablespoon water
1 cup sliced almonds
1 cup sugar
2 cups whipping cream,
  whipped
Confectioners' sugar

Unfold pastry sheets onto a lightly floured surface. Cut each sheet into nine 3-in. squares. Place 1 in. apart on greased baking sheets. In a small bowl, beat egg yolk and water; brush over pastry squares. In another bowl, beat egg white; add almonds and sugar. Spread over each square. Bake at 375° for 20-25 minutes or until well puffed and browned. Cool completely on wire racks.

Split pastries in half horizontally. Fill with whipped cream; replace tops. Sprinkle with confectioners' sugar. Serve immediately. **Yield:** 18 servings.

Macaroon Cheesecake

No one can resist a slice of creamy cheesecake, especially around the holidays.
This version features coconut in the crust and topping.
— Tracy Powers, Cedar Springs, Michigan

1 cup flaked coconut, toasted
1/2 cup ground pecans
2 tablespoons butter *or*
  margarine, melted
FILLING:
3 packages (8 ounces *each*)
  cream cheese, softened
1/2 cup sugar
3 eggs
1/2 teaspoon vanilla extract
1/4 teaspoon almond extract
TOPPING:
1 egg white
1/2 teaspoon vanilla extract
1/3 cup sugar
2/3 cup flaked coconut, toasted

In a bowl, combine the coconut and pecans; stir in butter. Press onto the bottom of a greased 9-in. springform pan; set aside. In a mixing bowl, beat cream cheese and sugar until smooth. Add eggs, beating on low speed just until combined. Beat in extracts just until blended. Pour over crust. Place pan on a baking sheet. Bake at 350° for 35 minutes.

In a small mixing bowl, beat egg white and vanilla until soft peaks form. Gradually add sugar, beating until stiff peaks form. Fold in coconut. Carefully spread over top of cheesecake. Bake 20-25 minutes longer or until center is almost set. Cool on a wire rack for 10 minutes. Carefully run a knife around edge of pan to loosen; cool 1 hour longer. Refrigerate overnight. Remove sides of pan. **Yield:** 12-14 servings.

Chocolate Truffle Dessert

(Pictured at right and on page 67)

*Chocolate lovers will savor
this impressive dessert, featuring
a brownie base and
chocolate mousse filling.*
—Lisa Otis, New Paltz, New York

1/4 cup butter (no substitutes),
    softened
1 cup sugar
2 squares (1 ounce *each*)
    unsweetened chocolate,
    melted and cooled
2 eggs, *separated*
1/4 cup milk
1 teaspoon vanilla extract
3/4 cup all-purpose flour
1/2 teaspoon baking powder
1/4 teaspoon salt

TRUFFLE MOUSSE:
2 cups (12 ounces) semisweet
    chocolate chips
1-1/4 cups butter
3/4 cup sugar
1 tablespoon instant coffee
    granules
5 egg yolks, lightly beaten
3 tablespoons vanilla extract
1 envelope unflavored gelatin
1/3 cup cold water
1 cup whipping cream, whipped
14 to 16 creme-filled Pirouette
    cookies, cut into 1-1/2-inch
    pieces

In a mixing bowl, cream butter and sugar. Add chocolate; mix well. Add egg yolks, one at a time, beating well after each addition. Add milk and vanilla; mix well. Combine the flour, baking powder and salt; stir into chocolate mixture just until blended. In a small mixing bowl, beat egg whites until soft peaks form. Fold into chocolate mixture. Pour into a greased and floured 9 in. springform pan. Place pan on a baking sheet. Bake at 350° for 25-30 minutes or until a toothpick inserted near the center comes out clean. Cool completely on a wire rack.

For mousse, combine chocolate chips, butter, sugar and coffee granules in a saucepan. Cook and stir over low heat until sugar is dissolved and chips are melted. Stir a small amount of hot liquid into egg yolks; return all to pan. Cook and stir for 2 minutes or until mixture is slightly thickened. Remove from the heat; stir in vanilla. Sprinkle gelatin over cold water; let stand for 2 minutes. Add a small amount of hot liquid to gelatin; stir until gelatin is dissolved. Stir into chocolate mixture. Pour into a bowl. Set the bowl in a larger bowl of ice water; stir occasionally until thickened, about 30 minutes.

Remove sides of springform pan. Set aside 1/4 cup of mousse for garnish. Spoon half of the remaining mousse over brownie layer, spreading evenly over top and around sides.

In a mixing bowl, beat the remaining mousse and about a third of the whipped cream on low. Fold in remaining whipped cream. Spread over mousse layer. Place cookies around sides of dessert, gently pushing into mousse. Place reserved mousse in a resealable plastic bag or pastry bag; decorate top of dessert as desired. Cover and refrigerate for at least 4 hours or until firm. **Yield:** 12-16 servings.

Peppermint Ice Cream

(Pictured on page 66)

With flecks of peppermint candy, this ice cream is perfect for the holidays.
—Berneice Metcalf, Leavenworth, Washington

4 egg yolks
1-1/2 cups half-and-half cream
3/4 cup sugar
1/4 teaspoon salt
2 cups whipping cream
4-1/2 to 6 teaspoons vanilla extract
1 to 1-1/4 cups crushed
peppermint candy

In a heavy saucepan, whisk egg yolks, half-and-half, sugar and salt. Cook and stir over low heat until mixture reaches 160° and coats the back of a metal spoon. Remove from the heat. Place pan in a bowl of ice water; stir for 2 minutes. Stir in whipping cream and vanilla. Press plastic wrap onto surface of custard. Refrigerate for several hours or overnight.

Fill cylinder of ice cream freezer two-thirds full. (Refrigerate any remaining mixture until ready to freeze.) Freeze according to the manufacturer's directions. Stir in peppermint candy. Allow to ripen in ice cream freezer or firm up in the refrigerator freezer for 2-4 hours before serving. **Yield:** 1 quart.

Pineapple Dream Dessert

I often serve this creamy dessert because it's a light and refreshing end to any meal.
My mother made it when I was young, and now my daughters ask for it.
—Darlene Markel, Sublimity, Oregon

1-1/2 cups graham cracker crumbs
(about 24 squares)
1/4 cup sugar
1/3 cup butter *or* margarine,
melted
FILLING:
1/3 cup sugar
3 tablespoons cornstarch
2 cups milk
1 egg, beaten
1-1/2 teaspoons vanilla extract
1 can (20 ounces) crushed
pineapple, drained
1 cup whipping cream, whipped
1/2 cup pastel miniature
marshmallows

In a bowl, combine the cracker crumbs, sugar and butter. Set aside 1/4 cup for topping. Press the remaining crumb mixture onto the bottom of a greased 11-in. x 7-in. x 2-in. baking dish. Bake at 350° for 10-14 minutes or until lightly browned and set. Cool on a wire rack.

For filling, combine sugar and cornstarch in a saucepan. Gradually whisk in milk until smooth. Bring to a boil; cook and stir for 2 minutes or until thickened. Remove from the heat. Stir a small amount of hot filling into egg; return all to the pan, stirring constantly. Bring to a gentle boil; cook and stir for 1 minute. Remove from the heat; stir in vanilla. Cool for 30 minutes, stirring several times.

Stir in pineapple. Pour over crust. Top with whipped cream (pan will be full). Sprinkle with marshmallows and reserved crumb mixture. Cover and refrigerate for at least 3 hours. **Yield:** 12-16 servings.

Chiffon Fruitcake

(Pictured at right)

Unlike typical fruitcakes, this tall cake is nice and light. The cinnamon whipped cream adds a bit of festive flair.
— *Tonya Farmer, Iowa City, Iowa*

2 cups plus 2 tablespoons all-purpose flour, *divided*
1-1/2 cups sugar
3 teaspoons baking powder
1 teaspoon salt
1 teaspoon ground cinnamon
7 eggs, *separated*
3/4 cup water
1/2 cup vegetable oil
2 teaspoons grated lemon peel
2 teaspoons vanilla extract
1/2 teaspoon cream of tartar
3/4 cup finely chopped candied cherries
1/2 cup finely chopped pecans
1/4 cup finely chopped mixed candied fruit

CINNAMON WHIPPED CREAM:
1 cup whipping cream
2 tablespoons sugar
1 teaspoon vanilla extract
1/2 teaspoon ground cinnamon

In a large mixing bowl, combine 2 cups flour, sugar, baking powder, salt and cinnamon. In another bowl, whisk the egg yolks, water, oil, lemon peel and vanilla; add to dry ingredients and beat until well blended.

In another mixing bowl, beat egg whites and cream of tartar until soft peaks form; fold into batter. Toss cherries, pecans and candied fruit with remaining flour; fold into batter. Pour into an ungreased 10-in. tube pan.

Bake at 325° for 55-60 minutes or until top springs back when lightly touched. Immediately invert cake pan; cool completely. Carefully run a knife around edge of pan to loosen. Remove cake from pan and place on a serving plate.

In a small mixing bowl, beat the cream, sugar, vanilla and cinnamon until soft peaks form. Serve with cake. **Yield:** 12 servings (2 cups whipped cream).

Caramel-Chocolate Pecan Pie

This pleasing pie satisfies my family of chocoholics!
It's quick and easy to prepare, yet special enough for company.
—*Betty Thompson, Zionsville, Indiana*

1/2 cup crushed cream-filled
    chocolate sandwich cookies
    (5 cookies)
  4 teaspoons butter *or*
    margarine, melted
20 caramels*
1/2 cup whipping cream, *divided*
  2 cups chopped pecans
3/4 cup semisweet chocolate chips

Combine cookie crumbs and butter. Press onto the bottom of a 9-in. pie plate. Bake at 375° for 8-10 minutes or until set. Cool completely on a wire rack.

    In a saucepan, melt caramels with 1/4 cup cream over low heat; stir until blended. Remove from the heat; stir in pecans. Spread evenly over crust. Refrigerate for 10 minutes or until set. In a small saucepan, melt chocolate chips with remaining cream. Drizzle over the caramel layer. Refrigerate for at least 1 hour before serving. **Yield:** 10-12 servings.

    *Editor's Note: This recipe was tested with Hershey caramels.

Lime Tart

For a change of pace from rich holiday desserts, try this light and cool pie.
When I'm short on time, I use a prepared graham cracker crust with equally good results.
—*Jane Dyrhaug, Andover, Minnesota*

1-1/2 cups graham cracker crumbs
    (about 24 squares)
  1/2 cup sugar
    6 tablespoons butter *or*
    margarine, melted
FILLING:
    1 cup sugar
    3 tablespoons cornstarch
    1 cup whipping cream
  1/3 cup lime juice
  1/4 cup butter *or* margarine, cubed
    1 tablespoon grated lime peel
    1 cup (8 ounces) sour cream
TOPPING:
  1/2 cup whipping cream
    2 tablespoons confectioners'
    sugar
  3/4 teaspoon vanilla extract

Combine cracker crumbs, sugar and butter; press onto the bottom and up the sides of a 9-in. pie plate. Bake at 350° for 12-15 minutes or until lightly browned. Cool completely on a wire rack.

    In a saucepan, combine sugar and cornstarch. Gradually whisk in cream and lime juice until smooth. Add butter. Cook and stir over medium heat; gradually bring to a boil. Boil for 1 minute. Remove from the heat; stir in lime peel. Cool to room temperature; fold in sour cream. Pour into crust.

    In a small mixing bowl, beat cream, confectioners' sugar and vanilla until stiff peaks form. Spread over filling. Chill for 4 hours or until ready to serve. **Yield:** 6-8 servings.

Minted Chocolate Torte

(Pictured at right)

Our family has enjoyed this pretty layered cake for years. It's a favorite for many occasions.
— Barbara Humiston, Tampa, Florida

1/2 cup shortening
1-1/3 cups sugar, *divided*
2-1/4 cups cake flour
3 teaspoons baking powder
1/2 teaspoon salt
1 cup milk
1-1/2 teaspoons vanilla extract
2 squares (1 ounce *each*)
   semisweet chocolate,
   finely chopped
3 egg whites
FILLING/TOPPING:
6 squares (1 ounce *each*)
   semisweet chocolate
1/4 cup butter (no substitutes)
1-1/4 cups confectioners' sugar
3 tablespoons hot water
1 teaspoon vanilla extract
Dash salt
FROSTING:
2 cups whipped topping
1/2 teaspoon vanilla extract
1/8 teaspoon peppermint extract
1 to 2 drops green food
   coloring

In a large mixing bowl, cream shortening and 1 cup sugar. Combine the flour, baking powder and salt; add to the creamed mixture alternately with milk. Stir in vanilla and chocolate. In a small mixing bowl, beat egg whites on medium speed until soft peaks form. Gradually beat in the remaining sugar, 1 tablespoon at a time, on high until stiff peaks form. Fold into batter.

Pour into two greased and floured 9-in. round baking pans. Bake at 350° for 30-35 minutes or until a toothpick inserted near the center comes out clean. Cool for 10 minutes before removing from pans to wire racks.

In a small saucepan, melt the chocolate and butter over low heat until smooth. Remove from the heat; transfer to a mixing bowl. Beat in the confectioners' sugar, hot water, vanilla and salt.

To assemble, split each cake into two horizontal layers. Place bottom layer on a serving plate; top with 1/3 cup of filling. Repeat layers three times. In a bowl, gently combine the whipped topping, extracts and food coloring. Frost the sides of the cake. Store in the refrigerator. **Yield:** 12-16 servings.

Boston Cream Sponge Cake

I'm not a big fan of rich desserts, so I frequently make this light and fluffy cake.
—*Jan Badovinac, Harrison, Arkansas*

   5 eggs
   1 cup sugar
   1/2 teaspoon salt
   1 teaspoon vanilla extract
1-1/4 cups all-purpose flour
CUSTARD:
   3/4 cup sugar
   2 tablespoons cornstarch
1-1/2 cups milk
   6 egg yolks, beaten
   1 teaspoon vanilla extract
   1/2 cup butter (no substitutes),
      softened
CHOCOLATE FROSTING:
   2 tablespoons butter, softened
   1 square (1 ounce)
      unsweetened chocolate,
      melted and cooled
   1 cup confectioners' sugar
   3 tablespoons whipping cream
   1 teaspoon vanilla extract

In a mixing bowl, beat eggs until light and fluffy. Gradually add sugar and salt, beating until thick and lemon-colored. Add vanilla; mix well. Fold in flour, 2 tablespoons at a time. Pour into two greased and floured 9-in. round baking pans. Bake at 350° for 17-20 minutes or until cake springs back when lightly touched. Cool for 10 minutes before removing from pans to wire racks to cool completely.

For custard, combine sugar and cornstarch in a saucepan. Gradually stir in milk until smooth. Bring to a boil; cook and stir for 2 minutes. Remove from the heat. Stir a small amount of hot mixture into egg yolks; return all to the pan. Bring to a gentle boil, stirring constantly. Remove from the heat; stir in vanilla. Cool completely. In a mixing bowl, cream butter. Gradually beat in custard.

To assemble, split each cake into two horizontal layers. Place bottom layer on a serving plate; top with a third of the filling. Repeat layers twice. Top with remaining cake layer. In a small mixing bowl, combine frosting ingredients. Spread over top of cake. Refrigerate. **Yield:** 12-16 servings.

Toasted Almond Ice Cream Balls

You can keep these almond-coated ice cream balls on hand in the freezer for last-minute entertaining. Just whip up the sauce in minutes for a simply satisfying sweet treat.
—*Anita Curtis, Camarillo, California*

   1 cup chopped almonds, toasted
   1 quart French vanilla ice
      cream
HOT FUDGE SAUCE:
   1 can (12 ounces) evaporated
      milk
   2/3 cup semisweet chocolate chips
   1/4 cup butter *or* margarine
   2 cups confectioners' sugar

Place almonds in a shallow dish. Using an ice cream scoop, shape ice cream into balls. Roll each in almonds until well coated. Place on a waxed paper-lined baking sheet; cover and freeze.

For sauce, combine the milk, chocolate chips and butter in a saucepan. Cook and stir over low heat until melted and smooth. Add sugar; bring to a boil. Reduce heat. Simmer, stirring frequently, for 8-10 minutes or until thickened. Serve hot or cold over ice cream balls. **Yield:** 5 servings.

Candied Holly Cupcakes

(Pictured at right)

My mother often made these fruity spice cupcakes. Decorated with cherries and citron, they're so festive for Christmas.
—Pam Goodlet
Washington Island, Wisconsin

1/2 cup shortening
 1 cup sugar
 2 eggs
1-1/2 cups all-purpose flour
1/2 teaspoon baking soda
1/2 teaspoon *each* ground
   cinnamon, allspice, nutmeg
   and cloves
1/2 cup buttermilk
1/2 cup cherry jam *or* flavor of
   your choice
1/2 cup chopped pecans
1/4 cup finely chopped candied
   cherries
1/4 cup finely chopped candied
   orange peel
 2 cups prepared vanilla frosting
 9 candied cherries, halved
18 green citron pieces *or* green
   candied pineapple pieces,
   cut into strips

In a mixing bowl, cream shortening and sugar. Beat in eggs. Combine the flour, baking soda and spices; add to creamed mixture alternately with buttermilk. Stir in jam, pecans, cherries and orange peel. Fill paper-lined muffin cups three-fourths full. Bake at 350° for 20-25 minutes or until a toothpick comes out clean. Cool for 5 minutes before removing from pans to wire racks.

Frost cooled cupcakes. Decorate with cherries for holly berries and citron for leaves. **Yield:** 1-1/2 dozen.

Cranberry Fruit Punch

This not-too-sweet punch is always a part of my Christmas buffet.
It can easily be doubled if you're having a large group.
—Ruth Andrewson, Peck, Idaho

5 cups cranberry juice, chilled
5 cups white grape juice, chilled
5 cups pineapple juice, chilled
3 cups ginger ale, chilled
1 pint orange sherbet

Just before serving, combine the juices and ginger ale in a punch bowl. Add scoops of sherbet. **Yield:** 24 servings (about 4 quarts).

Iced Coffee Slush

We have a tradition of hosting a game night during the holidays with nine other couples.
Our guests come for the camaraderie, but they sure love washing down delicious buffet
items with this sweet slush. Even non-coffee drinkers enjoy it.
—Iola Egle, McCook, Nebraska

3 cups hot strong brewed coffee
1-1/2 to 2 cups sugar
4 cups milk
2 cups half-and-half cream
1-1/2 teaspoons vanilla extract

In a freezer-safe bowl, stir coffee and sugar; until sugar is dissolved. Refrigerate until thoroughly chilled. Add the milk, cream and vanilla; freeze. Remove from the freezer several hours before serving. Chop mixture until slushy; serve immediately. **Yield:** 12 servings (2-1/4 quarts).

Sweet Citrus Punch

The wonderful rosy color of this beverage makes it a natural choice to serve at Christmas.
I keep the ingredients on hand to prepare at a moment's notice.
—Mary Ann Kosmas, Minneapolis, Minnesota

1 can (12 ounces) frozen orange juice concentrate, thawed
1 can (12 ounces) frozen lemonade concentrate, thawed
1 cup grenadine syrup
2 quarts ginger ale, chilled

Ice ring *or* shaved ice, optional

In a punch bowl, combine the first four ingredients. Add an ice ring or shaved ice to the bowl if desired. **Yield:** 10-12 servings (about 2-1/2 quarts).

Chocolate Coffee

(Pictured at right)

*A rich whipped chocolate mixture
from our Test Kitchen is used to flavor
coffee and to make hot chocolate.
Set out a small serving bowl,
spoon some of the mixture into mugs
and add hot coffee or milk.*

 1 **cup sugar**
 1 **cup baking cocoa**
 1 **cup boiling water**
 1 **teaspoon vanilla extract**
1/4 **teaspoon salt**
 4 **cups whipping cream,**
  whipped
 8 **cups hot strong brewed coffee**
  ***or* whole milk**

In a large heavy saucepan, whisk the sugar, cocoa and water until smooth. Cook and whisk over medium-low heat until mixture forms soft peaks when whisk is lifted and resembles thick hot fudge sauce, about 35 minutes. Remove from the heat; stir in vanilla and salt. Transfer to a mixing bowl; refrigerate for at least 2 hours.

Beat the chocolate mixture. Add 2 cups whipped cream; mix well. Fold in remaining whipped cream. For each serving, place about 1/2 cup chocolate cream in 2/3 cup coffee or milk; stir to blend. **Yield:** 12 servings.

TIPS FOR CHOCOLATE COFFEE

THE CHOCOLATE BASE for Chocolate Coffee can be made weeks in advance and refrigerated. The morning of your party, add the whipped cream and spoon into small serving bowls. Cover with plastic wrap and refrigerate.

As a fancy garnish, place some of the chocolate cream in a pastry bag fitted with a star tip and decorate the bowls just before serving.

Set out one serving bowl at a time and replace with another after 2 hours or as needed.

Mulled Holiday Drink

(Pictured at right)

The beverage's burgundy color and tart taste are terrific for winter.
—Richell Welch, Buffalo, Texas

1 bottle (46 ounces) cranberry
   juice
1 bottle (46 ounces) white
   grape juice
6 whole cloves
2 cinnamon sticks (3 inches),
   broken
Citrus-Cinnamon Stir Sticks
   (recipe on page 79), optional

Pour juices into a Dutch oven. Place cloves and cinnamon on a double thickness of cheesecloth; bring up corners of cloth and tie with kitchen string to form a bag. Add to juice mixture. Bring to a boil. Reduce heat; cover and simmer for 30 minutes or until flavors are blended. Discard spice bag. Serve warm with stir sticks if desired. **Yield:** 10 servings (2-1/2 quarts).

Celebration Spoons

(Pictured at right)

You can easily make chocolate-covered spoons with this recipe from
our Test Kitchen. Serve them with coffee or hot chocolate.

1 cup (6 ounces) semisweet
   chocolate chips
24 metal *or* plastic spoons
Peppermints *and/or* Andes candies,
   chopped

In a microwave-safe bowl, melt chocolate chips; stir until smooth. Dip spoons into chocolate. Tap the handle of spoon on the edge of the bowl to remove excess chocolate. Place on waxed paper. Sprinkle with chopped candies. Let stand until set. **Yield:** 2 dozen.

Sparkling Candy Swizzle Sticks

(Pictured above right)

Serve these sweet sticks from our Test Kitchen with tea, cider and hot chocolate.

Assorted candy sticks (sour apple,
   cinnamon, orange *or* flavor of
   your choice)
Warm water

White *or* colored decorating sugar

Dip candy sticks halfway into warm water; sprinkle with sugar. Place on a wire rack until dry.

Citrus-Cinnamon Stir Sticks

(Pictured above)

*To add a little zest to hot cider, our home economists came up with these simple stirrers.
Once the stirrer is added to the beverage, the orange strip will eventually fall off the
cinnamon stick...but that's all right. It will continue to add flavor.*

3 medium navel oranges
1 cup sugar
1 cup water
12 cinnamon sticks (5 inches)
Additional sugar, optional

Using a citrus stripper or vegetable peeler, cut 12 strips of peel from or-

anges, about 4-6 in. long. In a small saucepan, bring sugar and water to a boil over medium heat. Reduce heat; simmer, uncovered, for 12 minutes.

Place one orange strip at a time in hot syrup; cook for 3 minutes. Remove orange strip to waxed paper; when cool enough to handle, wrap strip around a cinnamon stick. Dip into hot syrup; place on a wire rack. Sprinkle with sugar if desired. Let stand until dry. **Yield:** 1 dozen.

Cookie & Candy Exchange

PRETTY PLATTERS piled high with holiday cookies and candies help make Christmas special.

But making a variety of merry morsels often takes more time than you have.

One way to get heaps of homemade goodies with little work is by hosting a holiday cookie and candy exchange.

Each person makes a big batch of their favorite treat for all at the party to share and take home.

If you're crazy about cookies, why not give Cherry Chocolate Cookies, Gingerbread Cookies, Chinese Almond Cookies and Striped Icebox Cookies a try?

Or, if candy making is more to your liking, sample slightly sweet White Chocolate Peppermint Fudge. (All shown at right.)

Cherry Chocolate Cookies

Chinese Almond Cookies

es

FESTIVE CONFECTIONS
(Clockwise from top right)

Cherry Chocolate Cookies (p. 83)

Chinese Almond Cookies (p. 84)

Striped Icebox Cookies (p. 85)

White Chocolate
Peppermint Fudge (p. 87)

Gingerbread Cookies (p. 84)

Toffee Bars

These shortbread bars have the taste of toffee without the hassle of making candy.
They're an attractive addition to a cookie tray.
—Ruth Burrus, Zionsville, Indiana

1 cup butter (no substitutes),
  softened
1 cup packed brown sugar
1 egg yolk
1 teaspoon vanilla extract
2 cups all-purpose flour
1/4 teaspoon salt
6 milk chocolate candy bars
  (1.55 ounces *each*)
1/2 cup finely chopped pecans

In a mixing bowl, cream butter and brown sugar. Beat in egg yolk and vanilla. Gradually add flour and salt, beating until smooth. Press into a greased 15-in. x 10-in. x 1-in. baking pan. Bake at 350° for 17-19 minutes or until light golden brown. Immediately place chocolate bars on top; return to the oven for 1 minute. Spread melted chocolate over bars; sprinkle with pecans. **Yield:** about 4 dozen.

HOSTING A COOKIE AND CANDY EXCHANGE

A NEIGHBORLY cookie and candy exchange saves you lots of time in the kitchen while giving you a chance to gather with family and friends. Hosting such an event is easier than you think with these timely tips:

- Select a date and send out the invitations about 6 weeks in advance. Weekday evenings or weekend afternoons work well because people may be less busy. Schedule the party to be about 2 hours long so guests aren't required to set aside a lot of time.
- Invite 8 to 12 people, keeping in mind that having more guests results in more variety of treats. Make the same kind of cookie or candy, allowing 1 dozen for each person participating. You might also encourage them to bring an extra dozen for sampling at the party.
- Ask what each person is making to avoid duplicates. There's no point to the exchange if everyone arrives with sugar cookies.
- Have participants bring empty containers or resealable plastic bags to collect their goodies. If the gathering is small, they may want to bring the batches already individually wrapped. Also have guests bring a copy of their recipe for each person.
- You can keep your menu to a minimum by focusing on the sweet treats. Simply serve a selection of beverages and the extra cookies and candies. Or if you prefer, offer a few hot and cold appetizers.
- As people arrive, set out the cookies and candies on a long table, leaving enough room for folks to walk around. Label the containers with the recipe name.
- Near the end of the party, have guests fill their containers with a dozen of each kind of cookie and candy.
- For party favors, gather all the different recipe cards into bundles, tie with festive ribbons and hand them out as guests leave. For another party favor idea, see the fudge-filled cookie cutters on page 99.

Cherry Chocolate Cookies

(Pictured at right and on page 81)

*No one can resist the chewy texture
of these fudgy cookies. I always double
the recipe because they disappear
quickly around our house.*
—*Kim Williams, Fort Wayne, Indiana*

2-1/2 cups butter (no substitutes),
    softened
  4 cups sugar
  4 eggs
  4 teaspoons vanilla extract
  4 cups all-purpose flour
1-1/2 cups baking cocoa
  2 teaspoons baking soda
  1 teaspoon salt
  1 package (12 ounces)
    miniature semisweet
    chocolate chips
  1 jar (16 ounces) maraschino
    cherries, drained and halved

In a large mixing bowl, cream butter and sugar. Add eggs, one at a time, beating well after each addition. Beat in vanilla. Combine the flour, cocoa, baking soda and salt; gradually add to creamed mixture. Stir in chocolate chips.

Drop by heaping tablespoonfuls 3 in. apart onto ungreased baking sheets. Top each with a cherry half. Bake at 350° for 10-12 minutes or until edges are firm. Remove to wire racks to cool. **Yield:** about 6-1/2 dozen.

Apricot Coconut Balls

*I appreciate that these fruity candies are easy to prepare and can be made ahead of time.
They're a nice alternative to chocolate sweets.*
—*Barbara Strohbehn, Gladbrook, Iowa*

1-1/2 cups dried apricots
  2 cups flaked coconut
  2/3 cup sweetened condensed
    milk
Confectioners' sugar

Chop apricots in a food processor. Transfer to a bowl; add coconut and milk. Shape into 1-in. balls; roll in sugar. Place on a baking sheet. Refrigerate until firm. Store in an airtight container in the freezer or refrigerator. **Yield:** 3 dozen.

Chinese Almond Cookies

(Pictured on page 81)

Each Christmas, my mother made lots of these tender butter cookies and stored them in clean coffee cans. When she passed away, I started giving our kids a can of these sentimental sweets.
—Jane Garing, Talladega, Alabama

1 cup butter (no substitutes),
  softened
1 cup sugar
1 egg
1 teaspoon almond extract
3 cups all-purpose flour
1 teaspoon baking soda
1/2 teaspoon salt
1/4 cup sliced almonds
1 egg white
1/2 teaspoon water

In a mixing bowl, cream butter and sugar. Beat in egg and extract. Combine the flour, baking soda and salt; gradually add to creamed mixture. Roll into 1-in. balls. Place 2 in. apart on ungreased baking sheets. Flatten with a fork. Sprinkle with almonds.

In a small bowl, beat egg white and water. Brush over cookies. Bake at 325° for 14-16 minutes or until edges and bottoms are lightly browned. Cool for 2 minutes before removing to wire racks. **Yield:** about 5 dozen.

Gingerbread Cookies

(Pictured on page 80)

Our two boys linger around the kitchen when these aromatic cookies are baking. I make them throughout the year using a variety of cookie cutters.
—Christy Thelan, Kellogg, Iowa

3/4 cup butter (no substitutes),
  softened
1 cup packed brown sugar
1 egg
3/4 cup molasses
4 cups all-purpose flour
2 teaspoons ground ginger
1-1/2 teaspoons baking soda
1-1/2 teaspoons ground cinnamon
3/4 teaspoon ground cloves
1/4 teaspoon salt
Vanilla frosting of your choice,
  optional

In a mixing bowl, cream butter and brown sugar. Add egg and molasses. Combine the flour, ginger, baking soda, cinnamon, cloves and salt; gradually add to creamed mixture. Cover and refrigerate for 4 hours or overnight or until easy to handle.

On a lightly floured surface, roll out dough to 1/8-in. thickness. Cut with floured 2-1/2-in. cookie cutters. Place 1 in. apart on ungreased baking sheets. Bake at 350° for 8-10 minutes or until edges are firm. Remove to wire racks to cool. Decorate with frosting if desired. **Yield:** 5 dozen.

Striped Icebox Cookies

(Pictured at right and on page 81)

I've been using this recipe ever since I was a little girl. I like it because it's easier than making cutout cookies. You can easily mix-and-match your favorite ingredients to create different looks.
—Patricia Reese, Pewaukee, Wisconsin

1 cup butter (no substitutes), softened
1-1/2 cups sugar
1 egg
2-1/2 cups all-purpose flour
1-1/2 teaspoons baking powder
1/4 teaspoon salt
1/4 cup chopped maraschino cherries, drained
2 drops red food coloring
1 square (1 ounce) semisweet chocolate, melted
1 tablespoon nonpareils

In a mixing bowl, cream butter and sugar. Beat in egg. Combine the flour, baking powder and salt; gradually add to creamed mixture. Divide into thirds; place in three bowls. Add cherries and food coloring to one portion, chocolate to another portion and nonpareils to remaining portion.

Line a 9-in. x 5-in. x 3-in. loaf pan with waxed paper. Spread cherry dough over bottom. Cover with chocolate dough, then remaining dough. Cover with plastic wrap and refrigerate for 2 hours or until firm.

Remove dough from pan; cut in half lengthwise. Cut each portion into 1/4-in. slices. Place 1 in. apart on lightly greased baking sheets. Bake at 375° for 10-12 minutes or until edges begin to brown. Remove to wire racks to cool. **Yield:** 5 dozen.

Lemon Pecan Slices

These attractive morsels are my daughter's favorite.
The lemon glaze pairs well with the delicate nut-topped cookie.
—Melissa Branning, Fontana, Wisconsin

1 cup butter (no substitutes),
  softened
3/4 cup packed brown sugar
1/2 cup sugar
2 eggs
1-1/2 teaspoons vanilla extract
1 tablespoon grated lemon peel
3 cups all-purpose flour
1-1/2 teaspoons baking powder
3/4 teaspoon salt
TOPPING:
3/4 cup finely chopped pecans
1/4 cup sugar
LEMON GLAZE:
1-1/4 cups confectioners' sugar
5 teaspoons lemon juice
1 drop yellow food coloring,
  optional

In a mixing bowl, cream the butter and sugars. Separate one egg; refrigerate egg white. Add the egg yolk, second egg, vanilla and lemon peel to creamed mixture; mix well. Combine the flour, baking powder and salt; gradually beat in to creamed mixture. Shape into three 7-in. rolls; wrap each in plastic wrap. Refrigerate for 2 hours or until firm.

Unwrap logs. Lightly beat reserved egg white. Combine pecans and sugar. Brush each log with egg white, then roll in pecan mixture, pressing firmly into dough.

Cut into 1/4-in. slices. Place 2 in. apart on ungreased baking sheets. Bake at 400° for 6-7 minutes or until very lightly browned. Remove to wire racks to cool. Combine glaze ingredients; drizzle over cookies. **Yield:** about 7 dozen.

Cinnamon Oatmeal Cookies

A hint of cinnamon makes these chewy oatmeal cookies stand out from all others.
The recipe makes a big batch, so it's perfect when you need a snack for a crowd.
—Terri Crum, Fort Scott, Kansas

2-1/2 cups shortening
5 cups sugar
4 eggs
1/3 cup molasses
1 tablespoon vanilla extract
4-3/4 cups quick-cooking oats
4-1/3 cups all-purpose flour
4 teaspoons baking powder
4 teaspoons ground cinnamon
1 teaspoon baking soda
1 teaspoon salt

In a large mixing bowl, cream shortening and sugar. Add eggs, one at a time, beating well after each addition. Beat in molasses and vanilla. Combine the remaining ingredients; gradually add to creamed mixture. Drop by tablespoonfuls 2 in. apart onto greased baking sheets. Bake at 350° for 10-12 minutes or until edges are firm. Remove to wire racks to cool. **Yield:** about 13 dozen.

White Chocolate Peppermint Fudge

(Pictured at right and on page 80)

I make many batches of this minty fudge to give as Christmas gifts. It's not too sweet, so it appeals to lots of palates.
—Sue Schindler, Barnesville, Minnesota

1-1/2 teaspoons plus 1/4 cup butter (no substitutes), softened, *divided*
2 cups sugar
1/2 cup sour cream
12 squares (1 ounce *each*) white baking chocolate, chopped
1 jar (7 ounces) marshmallow creme
1/2 cup crushed peppermint candy
1/2 teaspoon peppermint extract

Line a 9-in. square pan with foil. Grease the foil with 1-1/2 teaspoons butter; set aside. In a heavy saucepan, combine the sugar, sour cream and remaining butter. Cook and stir over medium heat until sugar is dissolved. Bring to a rapid boil; cook and stir until a candy thermometer reads 234° (soft-ball stage), about 5 minutes.

Remove from the heat; stir in white chocolate and marshmallow creme until melted. Fold in peppermint candy and extract. Pour into prepared pan. Chill until firm. Using foil, lift fudge out of pan. Gently peel off foil; cut fudge into 1-in. squares. Store in the refrigerator. **Yield:** 2 pounds.

Editor's Note: We recommend that you test your candy thermometer before each use by bringing water to a boil; the thermometer should read 212°. Adjust your recipe temperature up or down based on your test.

QUICK CHOCOLATE-COVERED CANDY

MAKING CANDY doesn't need to be a time-consuming task. Here's a simple recipe for making chocolate-covered treats.

Chop eight 1-ounce squares of semisweet chocolate. Melt chocolate and 1 teaspoon shortening in a microwave or heavy saucepan; stir until smooth.

Dip fresh or dried fruit, nuts, pretzels or cookies in chocolate; let excess chocolate drip off. Place on waxed paper until set.

Or stir chopped nuts, flaked coconut, raisins or chow mein noodles into the melted chocolate. Drop by spoonfuls onto waxed paper and let stand until set.

Store the chocolate candies in an airtight container.

Fudge-Topped Orange Cookies

Cookies and fudge are two classic sweets around the holidays, so one day I decided to combine them. The chocolate marshmallow topping works well on a variety of cookies.
—Lisa Evans, Rileyville, Virginia

3/4 cup butter (no substitutes),
    softened
1 cup sugar
1 egg
2 egg yolks
2 teaspoons grated orange peel
1-1/2 teaspoons orange extract
2 cups all-purpose flour
1 teaspoon ground ginger
1/2 teaspoon baking soda
TOPPING:
1 jar (7 ounces) marshmallow
    creme
3/4 cup sugar
1/3 cup evaporated milk
2 tablespoons butter
1/8 teaspoon salt
1 cup (6 ounces) semisweet chocolate chips
1/2 teaspoon vanilla extract

In a mixing bowl, cream butter and sugar. Beat in the egg, egg yolks, orange peel and extract. Combine the flour, ginger and baking soda; gradually add to creamed mixture. Drop by rounded tablespoonfuls 2 in. apart onto ungreased baking sheets. Bake at 300° for 21-23 minutes or until golden brown. Remove to wire racks to cool.

In a saucepan, combine the marshmallow creme, sugar, milk, butter and salt. Bring to a rolling boil over medium heat; boil for 5 minutes, stirring constantly. Remove from the heat. Add chocolate chips and vanilla; stir until chips are melted. Spread over tops of cookies. **Yield:** 2 dozen.

Candied Cherry Nut Bars

Every year at Christmas, my mother and I would make dozens of cookies, including this favorite. Now all the women in my family get together for a baking bonanza, rotating houses each year.
—Barbara Wilson, Thamesville, Ontario

1-1/4 cups all-purpose flour
2/3 cup packed brown sugar,
    divided
3/4 cup cold butter (no
    substitutes)
1 egg
1/2 teaspoon salt
1-1/2 cups salted mixed nuts
1-1/2 cups halved green and red
    candied cherries
1 cup (6 ounces) semisweet
    chocolate chips

In a bowl, combine flour and 1/3 cup brown sugar; cut in butter until mixture resembles coarse crumbs. Press into a lightly greased 13-in. x 9-in. x 2-in. baking pan. Bake at 350° for 15-17 minutes or until set.

In a mixing bowl, beat egg, salt and remaining brown sugar. Stir in nuts, cherries and chocolate chips. Spoon evenly over crust. Bake 20-25 minutes longer or until topping is set. Cool on a wire rack before cutting. **Yield:** 3 dozen.

Frosted Butter Cutouts

(Pictured at right)

I have fond memories of baking and frosting these cutout cookies with my mom. Now I carry on the tradition with my kids. It's a messy but fun day!
—Sandy Nace, Greensburg, Kansas

1 cup butter (no substitutes),
  softened
2 cups sugar
2 eggs
1 cup buttermilk
1 teaspoon vanilla extract
1/2 teaspoon almond extract
5 cups all-purpose flour
2 teaspoons baking powder
1 teaspoon baking soda
1/4 teaspoon salt
FROSTING:
1/4 cup butter, softened
2 cups confectioners' sugar
1/2 teaspoon almond extract
2 to 3 tablespoons whipping
  cream
Green and red food coloring,
  optional

In a mixing bowl, cream butter and sugar. Add eggs, one at a time, beating well after each addition. Beat in the buttermilk and extracts. Combine the flour, baking powder, baking soda and salt; gradually add to creamed mixture. Cover and refrigerate overnight or until easy to handle.

On a lightly floured surface, roll out dough to 1/4-in. thickness. Cut with floured 2-1/2-in. cookie cutters. Place 1 in. apart on greased baking sheets. Bake at 350° for 6-7 minutes or until lightly browned. Remove to wire racks to cool.

For frosting, in a small mixing bowl, combine butter, confectioners' sugar, extract and enough cream to achieve spreading consistency. Add food coloring if desired. Frost cookies. **Yield:** about 8-1/2 dozen.

Chocolate Mint Surprises

I came up with this recipe a few years ago and have shared it with many people.
I would often snack on these treats after my baby's middle-of-the-night feeding.
—Sheila Kerr, Revelstoke, British Columbia

3/4 cup butter (no substitutes),
   softened
1 cup sugar
1 egg
1 teaspoon vanilla extract
3 squares (1 ounce *each*)
   unsweetened chocolate,
   melted
2-1/2 cups all-purpose flour
1-1/2 teaspoons baking powder
1/2 teaspoon salt
MINT FILLING:
4 cups confectioners' sugar
3 tablespoons butter, softened
1/4 cup evaporated milk
2 to 3 teaspoons peppermint
   extract

1/2 teaspoon vanilla extract
2 pounds dark chocolate candy coating, melted

In a mixing bowl, cream butter and sugar. Beat in egg and vanilla. Add melted chocolate. Combine flour, baking powder and salt; gradually add to chocolate mixture. Shape into two 10-in. rolls; wrap each in plastic wrap. Refrigerate for 4 hours or until firm.

Unwrap dough and cut into 1/4-in. slices. Place 2 in. apart on ungreased baking sheets. Bake at 375° for 5-7 minutes or until edges are firm. Remove to wire racks to cool.

For filling, in a bowl, combine the confectioners' sugar, butter, milk and extracts until smooth. Shape into 1/2-in. balls. Place a ball in the center of each cookie; flatten. Freeze for 30 minutes. Dip cookies in melted candy coating to completely cover. Place on waxed paper until set. **Yield:** about 6 dozen.

Swiss Treat Bars

Preferred at our house come Christmas, these scrumptious squares get gobbled up quickly!
With the mix of chocolate, nuts, cherries and coconut, there's plenty of flavor in each tempting bite.
—Fern Vacca, Ventura, California

1 cup butter (no substitutes),
   softened
1-1/4 cups sugar
1 egg
1 teaspoon vanilla extract
2-1/2 cups all-purpose flour
1-1/2 teaspoons baking powder
1/2 teaspoon salt
1 cup (6 ounces) semisweet
   chocolate chips
1/2 cup finely chopped nuts

1/2 cup maraschino cherries, drained and chopped
1/2 cup flaked coconut

In a mixing bowl, cream butter and sugar. Beat in egg and vanilla. Combine flour, baking powder and salt; gradually add to creamed mixture. Fold in chocolate chips, nuts, cherries and coconut (mixture will be thick). Press into a greased 15-in. x 10-in. x 1-in. baking pan. Bake at 375° for 18-22 minutes or until lightly browned. Cool on a wire rack before cutting. **Yield:** 5 dozen.

Jeweled Coconut Crisps

(Pictured at right)

*When I anticipate a busy day during
the holiday season, I make this
cookie dough the night before.
The next day, I just slice and bake.*
—Eileen Milacek
Waukomis, Oklahoma

1 cup butter (no substitutes),
  softened
1 cup sugar
2 tablespoons milk
1-1/2 teaspoons vanilla extract
2-1/2 cups all-purpose flour
3/4 cup finely chopped red and
  green candied cherries
3/4 cup finely chopped pecans
1 cup flaked coconut

In a mixing bowl, cream butter and sugar. Beat in milk and
vanilla. Stir in flour, cherries and pecans. Shape into two
8-in. logs. Sprinkle the coconut over waxed paper; place
each log on waxed paper and roll in coconut. Wrap in plastic wrap. Refrigerate for 4 hours or until firm.

  Unwrap dough and cut into 1/4-in. slices. Place 2 in. apart
on ungreased baking sheets. Bake at 375° for 10-12 minutes
or until edges are lightly browned. Remove to wire racks
to cool. **Yield:** about 5 dozen.

Mocha Nut Fudge

*I was lucky enough to inherit my grandmother's cookbook collection along with all
of her recipe notations. This fudgy candy earned high marks.*
—Brandy LaFountain, Marion, Michigan

1 cup packed brown sugar
1/3 cup evaporated milk
2 tablespoons light corn syrup
1 cup (6 ounces) semisweet
  chocolate chips
2 teaspoons vanilla extract
1 teaspoon instant coffee
  granules
1 cup chopped walnuts

In a heavy saucepan, combine the brown sugar, milk and
corn syrup. Cook and stir over medium heat until sugar is
dissolved and mixture comes to a boil; boil for 2 minutes.
Remove from the heat; stir in chocolate chips, vanilla and
coffee granules with a wooden spoon. Continue stirring
until mixture is smooth and thick, about 5 minutes. Stir in
walnuts. Shape into two 9-in. logs; wrap each in plastic
wrap. Refrigerate for 2 hours or overnight. Unwrap and cut
into slices. **Yield:** 1 pound.

Jelly-Topped Sugar Cookies

On busy days, I appreciate this fast-to-fix drop sugar cookie.
Top each cookie with your favorite flavor of jam or jelly.
—June Quinn, Kalamazoo, Michigan

2 eggs
3/4 cup vegetable oil
2 teaspoons vanilla extract
1 teaspoon lemon extract
1 teaspoon grated lemon peel
3/4 cup sugar
2 cups all-purpose flour
2 teaspoons baking powder
1/2 teaspoon salt
1/2 cup jam *or* jelly

In a mixing bowl, combine eggs, oil, extracts and lemon peel until well blended. Beat in sugar (mixture will become thick). Combine the flour, baking powder and salt; gradually add to egg mixture. Drop by rounded tablespoonfuls 2 in. apart onto ungreased baking sheets.

Spray the bottom of a glass with nonstick cooking spray, then dip in sugar. Flatten cookies with glass, redipping in sugar as needed. Place 1/4 teaspoon jelly in the center of each cookie. Bake at 400° for 8-10 minutes or until set. Remove to wire racks to cool. **Yield:** about 3-1/2 dozen.

Coconut Marshmallow Squares

One of my favorite childhood memories includes eating these coconut-covered candies.
You can make them throughout the year using a variety of food coloring.
—Heather Warner, Salt Lake City, Utah

2 envelopes unflavored gelatin
1-1/4 cups cold water, *divided*
2 cups sugar
2 egg whites, lightly beaten
1 teaspoon vanilla extract
2-1/2 cups flaked coconut, chopped
2 to 3 drops red *or* yellow food coloring, optional

In a large mixing bowl, sprinkle gelatin over 1/2 cup cold water; set aside. In a heavy saucepan, combine sugar and remaining water. Cook and stir over low heat until sugar is dissolved. Cook over medium heat until a candy thermometer reads 234° (soft-ball stage),

stirring occasionally. Remove from the heat; slowly pour over gelatin, beating constantly. Immediately add egg whites. Use the candy thermometer to make sure mixture is at least 160°. Continue to beat 15-20 minutes longer. Beat in vanilla. Pour into a greased 9-in. square pan. Cool for 3 hours or until firm enough to cut into squares.

In a shallow bowl, combine coconut and food coloring if desired. Roll marshmallow squares in coconut. Store in an airtight container in the refrigerator. **Yield:** 3 dozen (about 1-1/2 pounds).

Editor's Note: A stand mixer is recommended for beating the marshmallow mixture after it reaches 160°. We recommend that you test your candy thermometer before each use by bringing water to a boil; the thermometer should read 212°. Adjust your recipe temperature up or down based on your test.

Nutty Caramel Clusters

(Pictured at right)

Don't be fooled by the impressive presentation of these sweet candies. They're so easy to make, even our two young sons can help.
—Charlyn Koistinen
Hayti, South Dakota

25 caramels
1 tablespoon butter (no substitutes)
1 tablespoon milk
1 cup sliced almonds
1/2 cup salted dry roasted peanuts
1/2 cup pecan halves
1/2 cup semisweet chocolate chips
2 teaspoons shortening

In a 1-qt. microwave-safe dish, combine the caramels, butter and milk. Microwave, uncovered, on high for 2 minutes, stirring once. Stir in peanuts and pecans. Drop by tablespoonfuls onto waxed paper-lined baking sheets.

In a microwave-safe bowl, melt chocolate chips and shortening; stir until blended. Drizzle over clusters. Chill until firm. Store in the refrigerator. **Yield:** 1-1/2 dozen.

Editor's Note: This recipe was tested in an 850-watt microwave with Hershey caramels.

Peanut Butter Cups

The classic combination of peanut and chocolate is one my children, grandchildren and great-grandchildren can't resist. They gobble up this candy all year long!
—Doris Price, St. John, New Brunswick

1-1/2 cups confectioners' sugar
1 cup creamy peanut butter*
1/2 cup packed brown sugar
2 tablespoons butter (no substitutes), softened
1 teaspoon vanilla extract
2 cups (12 ounces) semisweet chocolate chips
1/4 cup shortening

In a bowl, combine the confectioners' sugar, peanut butter, brown sugar, butter and vanilla; cover and set aside.

In a microwave-safe bowl, melt chocolate chips and shortening. Pour teaspoonfuls into paper-lined mini muffin cups. Drop a rounded teaspoonful of peanut butter mixture into each cup; top with another teaspoonful of chocolate mixture. Chill until set. **Yield:** about 4 dozen.

*Editor's Note: Reduced-fat or generic brands of peanut butter are not recommended for this recipe.

Chocolate Peppermint Cookies

If anything can get you in the Christmas spirit, these minty chocolate chip cookies can.
A sprinkle of peppermint candy adds an extra-festive touch. They're excellent for dunking.
—Delia True, Forest Ranch, California

1 cup butter (no substitutes),
  softened
3/4 cup sugar
3/4 cup packed brown sugar
2 eggs
2 teaspoons vanilla extract
2-1/2 cups whole wheat flour
1 teaspoon baking soda
1/2 teaspoon salt
1 cup (6 ounces) semisweet
  chocolate chips

1/2 cup crushed peppermint candy
Additional crushed peppermint candy, optional

In a mixing bowl, cream butter and sugars. Beat in eggs and vanilla. Combine flour, baking soda and salt; gradually add to creamed mixture. Stir in chocolate chips and crushed candy. Drop by rounded teaspoonfuls 2 in. apart onto ungreased baking sheets. Sprinkle with additional candy if desired. Bake at 350° for 9-10 minutes or until cookies spring back when lightly touched. Remove to wire racks to cool. **Yield:** about 7-1/2 dozen.

Soft Rum Caramels

I adapted a family recipe to come up with these melt-in-your-mouth caramels.
My husband and daughter eagerly volunteer to eat any scraps from the pan!
—Kelly-Ann Gibbons, Prince George, British Columbia

1 teaspoon plus 1/4 cup butter
  (no substitutes), softened,
  divided
1 cup whipping cream
1 cup packed brown sugar
1 cup light corn syrup
1/4 cup sugar
1/4 teaspoon salt
1 to 2 teaspoons rum extract

Line an 8-in. square pan with foil and grease the foil with 1 teaspoon butter; set aside. In a mixing bowl, cream remaining butter. Beat in cream until smooth; set aside.

In a heavy saucepan, combine the brown sugar, corn syrup, sugar and salt. Bring to a boil over medium heat, stirring constantly. Reduce heat to medium-low; cook until a candy thermometer reads 244° (firm-ball stage). Gradually add cream mixture. Continue cooking until a candy thermometer reads 242°. Remove from the heat; stir in extract.

Pour into prepared pan (do not scrape sides of saucepan). Cool completely. Invert pan onto a cutting board; remove foil. Cut candy into squares. Wrap individually in waxed paper or foil; twist ends. **Yield**: 1-1/2 pounds.

Editor's Note: We recommend that you test your candy thermometer before each use by bringing water to a boil; the thermometer should read 212°. Adjust your recipe temperature up or down based on your test.

Festive Shortbread Logs

(Pictured at right)

I first made these rich and tender cookies as a teenager and now make them for my husband and our two sons. The smiles on their faces are well worth the time and effort.
—Michele Fenner, Girard, Pennsylvania

1 cup butter (no substitutes), softened
1/2 cup confectioners' sugar
1 teaspoon vanilla extract
2 cups all-purpose flour
1-1/2 cups semisweet chocolate chips
4 teaspoons shortening
3/4 cup ground walnuts

In a mixing bowl, cream butter and confectioners' sugar. Add vanilla. Gradually add flour; mix well. With lightly floured hands, shape tablespoonfuls into 2-in. logs. Place 2 in. apart on ungreased baking sheets. Bake at 350° for 9-11 minutes or until edges and bottom are lightly browned. Cool for 2-3 minutes before removing to wire racks.

In a microwave-safe bowl, melt chocolate chips and shortening; stir until smooth. Drizzle chocolate over half of the cookies. Dip one end of remaining cookies into chocolate, then sprinkle with walnuts. **Yield:** 4 dozen.

Sesame Coconut Cookies

Even folks who normally pass on coconut treats can't resist these crisp butter cookies. They make a nice accompaniment to a hot cup of coffee or tea.
—Roberta Myers, Elwood, Indiana

2 cups butter (no substitutes), softened
1-1/2 cups sugar
1 teaspoon vanilla extract
3 cups all-purpose flour
1/2 teaspoon salt
2 cups flaked coconut
1 cup sesame seeds
1/2 cup finely chopped almonds

In a mixing bowl, cream butter and sugar. Beat in vanilla. Combine flour and salt; gradually add to creamed mixture. Stir in the coconut, sesame seeds and almonds. Shape into three 10-in. rolls; wrap each in plastic wrap. Refrigerate for 1-2 hours or until firm.

Unwrap dough and cut into 1/4-in. slices. Place 1 in. apart on ungreased baking sheets. Bake at 300° for 25-30 minutes or until lightly browned. Cool for 2 minutes before removing to wire racks. **Yield:** 10 dozen.

Almond Toffee

I love this recipe because it makes me look like an expert candy maker...it's so easy!
This candy graces our table from Thanksgiving through the New Year.
—Janice Sage, Garretson, South Dakota

1-1/2 teaspoons plus 2 cups butter
  (no substitutes), softened,
  divided
  2 cups sugar
1/3 cup water
  2 tablespoons light corn syrup
  1 package (11-1/2 ounces) milk
  chocolate chips
  1 cup finely chopped almonds,
  toasted

Line the bottom and sides of a 15-in. x 10-in. x 1-in. baking pan with foil. Grease the foil with 1-1/2 teaspoons butter; set aside. In a large heavy saucepan, melt remaining butter. Add sugar, water and corn syrup. Cook and stir over medium heat until a candy thermometer reads 290° (soft-crack stage).

Pour into prepared pan. Cool for 4 minutes. Sprinkle with chocolate chips; let stand for 3 minutes. Spread melted chocolate evenly over candy. Sprinkle with almonds; press down lightly. Cool until chocolate is firm. Break into bite-size pieces. Store in an airtight container. **Yield:** about 1 pound.

Editor's Note: We recommend that you test your candy thermometer before each use by bringing water to a boil; the thermometer should read 212°. Adjust your recipe temperature up or down based on your test.

Hard Maple Candy

During the war, the women at my grandmother's church would donate sugar rations
throughout the year so they'd have enough to make candy as a fund-raiser each Christmas.
I'm lucky enough to have inherited this tried-and-true recipe.
—Dorothea Bohrer, Silver Spring, Maryland

1-1/2 teaspoons butter (no
  substitutes), softened
3-1/2 cups sugar
  1 cup light corn syrup
  1 cup water
  3 tablespoons maple flavoring

Grease a 15-in. x 10-in. x 1-in. baking pan with butter; set aside. In a large heavy saucepan, combine the sugar, corn syrup and water. Cook over medium-high heat until a candy thermometer reads 300° (hard-crack stage), stirring occasionally. Remove from the heat; stir in maple flavoring. Immediately pour into prepared pan; cool. Break into pieces. Store in airtight containers. **Yield:** 1-3/4 pounds.

Editor's Note: We recommend that you test your candy thermometer before each use by bringing water to a boil; the thermometer should read 212°. Adjust your recipe temperature up or down based on your test.

Coconut Chocolate Slices

(Pictured at right)

These crispy cookies with a chewy coconut center travel really well. I send a box to our son in the Army, and they always arrive unbroken.
—Cheri Booth, Gering, Nebraska

1 package (3 ounces) cream cheese, softened
1/3 cup sugar
1 teaspoon vanilla extract
1 cup flaked coconut
1/2 cup finely chopped nuts
COCONUT FILLING:
6 tablespoons butter (no substitutes), softened
1 cup confectioners' sugar
1 egg
2 squares (1 ounce *each*) semisweet chocolate, melted and cooled
1 teaspoon vanilla extract
1-1/2 cups all-purpose flour
1/2 teaspoon baking soda
1/2 teaspoon salt

In a mixing bowl, beat cream cheese, sugar and vanilla until smooth. Stir in coconut and nuts. Refrigerate until easy to handle. For filling, in a small mixing bowl, cream butter and confectioners' sugar. Beat in egg, chocolate and vanilla. Combine the flour, baking soda and salt; gradually add to creamed mixture. Refrigerate for 30 minutes or until easy to handle.

Roll dough between waxed paper into a 14-in. x 4-1/2-in. rectangle. Remove top piece of waxed paper. Shape coconut filling into a 14-in. roll; place on dough, 1 in. from a long side. Roll dough around filling and seal edges. Wrap in plastic wrap. Refrigerate for 2-3 hours or overnight.

Unwrap and cut into 1/4-in. slices. Place 2 in. apart on greased baking sheets. Bake at 350° for 8-10 minutes or until set. Cool for 1 minute before removing to wire racks. **Yield:** about 4 dozen.

Chocolate Peanut Butter Grahams

(Pictured at right)

Because so many people seem to love the combination of chocolate and peanut butter, I came up with this no-bake cookie recipe.
—*Geraldine Sliwa, Elgin, Illinois*

1 jar (18 ounces) peanut butter
1 package (16 ounces) graham crackers, broken into rectangles
1-1/2 pounds milk chocolate candy coating

Spread a rounded teaspoonful of peanut butter on one side of half of the graham crackers. Top with remaining crackers. In a heavy saucepan over low heat, melt candy coating; stir until smooth. Dip cookies in coating to completely cover; allow excess to drip off. Place on waxed paper-lined baking sheets; let stand until firm. Store in an airtight container in a cool dry place. **Yield:** 5 dozen.

Macadamia Nut Fudge

(Pictured at right)

Family and friends look forward to this creamy fudge every holiday season. The macadamia nuts make it extra special.
— Kristine Stokowski, Tremont, Illinois

1 tablespoon plus 1 cup butter
  (no substitutes), *divided*
4-1/2 cups sugar
1 cup milk
36 large marshmallows
2 squares (1 ounce *each*)
  unsweetened chocolate,
  melted
4 cups (24 ounces) semisweet
  chocolate chips
1-1/2 cups chopped macadamia
  nuts
1 teaspoon vanilla extract
Vanilla frosting
M&M miniature baking bits

FUDGE PARTY FAVORS

COOKIE CUTTERS filled with fudge (pictured above right) make a palate-pleasing party favor for the guests at your cookie and candy exchange. Wrap them in clear or colored cellophane and tie with a ribbon for folks to take home. Don't forget to attach a copy of the recipe!

Line a 15-in. x 10-in. x 1-in. baking pan with foil. Grease the foil and 3-in. cookie cutters with 1 tablespoon butter. Place cookie cutters in pan; set aside.

In a large heavy saucepan, combine the sugar, milk and remaining butter. Cook and stir over medium heat until mixture comes to a full rolling boil. Remove from the heat; stir in marshmallows until melted. Add unsweetened chocolate and chocolate chips; stir until chips are melted. Stir in nuts and vanilla.

Spoon warm fudge into the prepared cookie cutters, filling to the top. Cool until set. Decorate with frosting and baking bits. Wrap each in plastic wrap. To remove, gently push fudge out of cookie cutters. **Yield:** about 5-1/2 pounds.

Editor's Note: Instead of using cookie cutters, fudge can be prepared in a foil-lined buttered 13-in. x 9-in. x 2-in. baking pan and cut into squares.

Gift Baskets Galore!

WHY SPEND a small fortune on specialty gift baskets seen in stores during the holiday season …especially when there's no guarantee the festive fare is going to be flavorful?

In this chapter, we present five fun gift basket ideas you can easily and inexpensively make at home. Just pair a few sure-to-please homemade treats with several purchased items, tuck them into a pretty basket and wrap.

Hurried cooks will appreciate a Savory Spaghetti Supper starring a tasty sauce that only requires reheating, while a bowl of Movie Night Munchies is perfect for the serious snack enthusiast.

And students will earn high marks when they bring in Treats for the Teacher. (All three ideas are shown at right.)

Savory Spaghetti Supper

(Pictured at right and on page 100)

TO HELP family, friends and neighbors save precious time during the hurried and hectic holiday season, present them with the fixings for a delectable Italian supper they can prepare in a snap!

Just one batch of Hearty Spaghetti Sauce (see the recipe below) can fill several 1-quart jars, so you can put together a few gift baskets at a time. We lined a basket with a dish towel, then filled it with a couple packages of dried pasta, a loaf of bread, breadsticks and some small holiday decorations.

Other gifts from the kitchen include Creamy Peppercorn Dressing and Herb Spread for French Bread (both recipes on opposite page). Or add pasta serving bowls, a wedge of Parmesan cheese, a small cheese grater and some store-bought biscotti.

Hearty Spaghetti Sauce

I received this recipe from my sister-in-law and use it all the time. The addition of pepperoni and cinnamon makes it extra special. My family says it's the best spaghetti sauce ever!
— *Wendy Prevost, Cody, Wyoming*

1-1/2 pounds ground beef
1-1/2 pounds bulk Italian sausage
   3 cans (28 ounces *each*) stewed tomatoes
   3 cans (6 ounces *each*) tomato paste
   1 can (15 ounces) tomato sauce
1/2 pound fresh mushrooms, sliced
   2 large onions, chopped

   3 medium carrots, finely chopped
   1 medium green pepper, chopped
   1 cup water
   2 packages (3 ounces *each*) sliced pepperoni, diced
   2 tablespoons sugar
   3 garlic cloves, minced
   2 teaspoons Italian seasoning
   2 teaspoons dried oregano
   1 teaspoon salt
1/2 teaspoon pepper
   2 bay leaves
1/4 teaspoon ground cinnamon, optional

In a Dutch oven, cook beef and sausage over medium heat until no longer pink; drain. Stir in the remaining ingredients. Bring to a boil. Reduce heat; simmer, uncovered, for 2-3 hours or until sauce reaches desired consistency, stirring occasionally. Discard bay leaves. Serve immediately. Or cool and pour into jars; cover and refrigerate. **Yield:** 19 cups.

Creamy Peppercorn Dressing

The home economists in our Test Kitchen tossed together some simple ingredients to create this creamy salad dressing. It conveniently keeps in the refrigerator for 2 weeks.

1 cup mayonnaise
1 cup (8 ounces) sour cream
1/3 cup grated Parmesan cheese
1/4 cup milk
3 tablespoons lemon juice
1-1/2 to 2 teaspoons coarsely ground pepper
1/2 teaspoon garlic salt
1/2 teaspoon onion powder

In a small mixing bowl, combine all ingredients; mix well. Cover and refrigerate for up to 2 weeks. **Yield:** 2-1/2 cups.

Herb Spread for French Bread

*Instead of regular garlic bread, my family requests this spread.
The flavor is best when I use parsley and basil fresh from the garden.*
—Jennie Wilburn, Long Creek, Oregon

6 tablespoons butter *or* margarine, softened
2 tablespoons minced fresh parsley
2 green onions, finely chopped
2 teaspoons minced fresh basil *or* 3/4 teaspoon dried basil
1 garlic clove, minced
1/4 teaspoon pepper
1 loaf French bread (1 pound)

In a bowl, combine the first six ingredients. Cut bread in half lengthwise; spread herb spread on cut sides. Place on an ungreased baking sheet. Broil 4 in. from the heat for 2-3 minutes or until lightly browned. **Yield:** 10-12 servings (1/2 cup spread).

Editor's Note: Herb spread may be stored in an airtight container in the refrigerator for up to 1 week.

Movie Night Munchies

(Pictured at right and on page 101)

WHEN THE WEATHER outside is frightful, it's nice to snuggle up on the sofa, watch some classic holiday movies and nibble on an assortment of snacks. This gift is brimming with goodies for the whole family.

Instead of filling a wicker basket, we used a cute seasonal serving bowl, which is perfect for dishing out Corn Puff Caramel Corn, Spicy Barbecued Peanuts and Crunchy Snack Mix (recipes below and on opposite page).

And what would the movies be without boxes of candy to satisfy every sweet tooth?

In addition to these star-studded treats, your basket could feature several cans of soda, a few favorite holiday videos or even a movie rental gift certificate.

Corn Puff Caramel Corn

Because you don't need to pop the corn or use a candy thermometer,
this is faster and easier than more traditional caramel corn recipes.
To avoid messy cleanup, consider using a disposable aluminum roasting pan.
—*Caroline Monroe, Clinton, Wisconsin*

1 **package (8 ounces) Puffcorn curls *or* popped hulled popcorn***
1 **cup salted peanuts**
1 **cup butter (no substitutes)**
1 **cup packed brown sugar**
1/2 **cup light corn syrup**
1 **teaspoon baking soda**

Place Puffcorn curls and peanuts in a large roasting pan; set aside. In a heavy 2-qt. saucepan, bring the butter, brown sugar and corn syrup to a boil, stirring occasionally; cook for 2 minutes. Remove from the heat and add baking soda; stir well (mixture will foam up). Pour over corn curl mixture and toss well to coat.

Bake at 250° for 45 minutes, stirring every 15 minutes. Spread on waxed paper to cool. Break apart and store in airtight containers. **Yield:** 5 quarts.

*Editor's Note: Puffcorn curls and popped hulled popcorn can be found in the snack aisle of most grocery stores. Regular popcorn can also be substituted.

Spicy Barbecued Peanuts

Cayenne pepper gives these sugar-glazed nuts a spicy kick. I've found that folks who favor sweet and savory flavors can't stop eating these mouth-watering morsels.

—Linda Jonsson, Marion, Ohio

  1 **egg white**
  2 **tablespoons liquid smoke**
  3 **cups salted peanuts**
1/2 **cup sugar**
  1 **teaspoon chili powder**
  1 **teaspoon ground cumin**
1/4 **teaspoon garlic powder**
1/4 **teaspoon cayenne pepper**

In a bowl, whisk egg white until foamy. Add liquid smoke and peanuts; toss to coat. Combine the remaining ingredients. Sprinkle over nuts; toss to coat. Spread in a single layer in a well-greased 15-in. x 10-in. x 1-in. baking pan. Bake at 250° for 1 hour, stirring once. Spread on waxed paper to cool. Store in an airtight container. **Yield:** 4-1/2 cups.

Crunchy Snack Mix

I got this recipe from my aunt when I wanted to make a snack for a brunch I was hosting. The brimming bowls I set out were emptied in no time!

—Milia Ziegler, Cincinnati, Ohio

   1 **cup packed brown sugar**
 1/2 **cup butter (no substitutes)**
 1/2 **cup light corn syrup**
   1 **package (12 ounces) Crispix cereal**
1-1/2 **cups coarsely chopped walnuts**

In a saucepan over medium heat, bring the brown sugar, butter and corn syrup to a boil, stirring occasionally. Spread cereal in a large roasting pan. Pour syrup mixture over cereal and stir until well coated. Sprinkle with nuts and stir. Bake at 250° for 1 hour, stirring every 15 minutes. Spread on waxed paper to cool. Break apart and store in airtight containers. **Yield:** 15 cups.

Breads 'n' Spreads Basket

(Pictured at right)

SPREAD GOOD CHEER this holiday season by assembling a basket filled with a bounty of bagels and a homemade spread, jelly or butter.

Peanut Butter Spread and Cinnamon Apple Jelly appeal to kids of all ages. Sweet Potato Butter is perfectly seasoned for the cooler months. (Recipes below and on opposite page.)

All of these tasty toppings are scrumptious over bagels as well as English muffins, toast and crackers.

The only extras needed for this pretty package are festive napkins, an ornament, candles and a spreader!

Peanut Butter Spread

As far back as I can remember, this spread has been used for sandwiches
served after church services. It's especially tasty on toast.
—Maudie Raber, Millersburg, Ohio

2 cups peanut butter
1 jar (7 ounces) marshmallow
   creme
1 cup dark corn syrup
1 cup light corn syrup

In a mixing bowl, combine all ingredients; mix well. Place in sterilized half-pint jars. Store at room temperature. **Yield:** 5 half-pints.

Sweet Potato Butter

This smooth, creamy spread has a great combination of sweet potatoes and apples.
It's a sweet and satisfying topping for a variety of breads.
—Barbara Hoard, Mathis, Texas

6 cups diced peeled sweet
   potatoes
2 cups diced peeled tart apples
4 cups water
2/3 cup orange juice concentrate
1/2 cup packed dark brown sugar
1-1/2 teaspoons ground cinnamon
1 teaspoon ground nutmeg
1/4 to 1/2 teaspoon ground cloves

In a heavy saucepan, combine all ingredients; mix well. Bring to a boil. Reduce heat; simmer, uncovered, for 2 to 2-1/4 hours or until mixture is thickened and about 1 cup of liquid remains, stirring occasionally.

In a blender, process mixture in batches until smooth. Transfer to jars or containers. Chill for at least 2 hours before serving. Store in the refrigerator. **Yield:** about 4 cups.

Cinnamon Apple Jelly

When I host a Christmas sit-down dinner, I adhere labels on small jars of this jam to use as place cards. At the end of the evening, the guests can take the sweet spread home to enjoy.
—Virginia Montmarquet
Riverside, California

7 cups unsweetened bottled apple juice
1 package (1-3/4 ounces) powdered fruit pectin
2 teaspoons butter (no substitutes)
1 cup red-hot candies
9 cups sugar

Place the apple juice in a large kettle. Stir in pectin and butter. Bring to a full rolling boil over high heat, stirring constantly. Stir in candies until dissolved. Stir in sugar; return to a full rolling boil. Boil for 1 minute, stirring constantly. Remove from the heat; skim off foam. Pour hot mixture into hot sterilized jars, leaving 1/4-in. headspace. Adjust caps. Process for 5 minutes in a boiling-water bath. **Yield:** about 13 half-pints.

Tempting Sundae Toppings

(Pictured at right)

THE LUCKY RECIPIENT of this sundae topping tray simply needs to add ice cream for some flavorful fun!

Cashew Nut Crunch—either crushed or chocolate-dipped—and Sensational Chocolate Sauce are great to serve over a variety of cool concoctions. If folks don't care for chocolate, consider giving a jar of Butterscotch sauce. (See the recipes below and on opposite page.)

Keep the theme going with maraschino cherries, salted peanuts and an assortment of sprinkles. Then round out this treat-filled tray for two with parfait glasses, an ice cream scoop and some holiday napkins.

Sensational Chocolate Sauce

My sister-in-law, Trudy, prepared this recipe one night as a topping for impromptu banana splits. The smooth yummy sauce is now my family's favorite.
—Alene Gordon, Elk, Washington

1/2 cup light corn syrup
1/3 cup boiling water
　2 squares (1 ounce *each*)
　　semisweet chocolate
　1 tablespoon butter
　　(no substitutes)
1/4 cup sugar

In a heavy saucepan, bring the corn syrup, water, chocolate and butter to a boil; boil for 4 minutes, stirring constantly. Add the sugar; boil 2-3 minutes longer or until sugar is dissolved. Cool to room temperature. Store in the refrigerator. This sauce can be reheated in the microwave. **Yield:** 3/4 cup.

Butterscotch Sauce

This is a nice alternative to traditional chocolate sauce. It doesn't last long around my house…my husband and our three boys love it.
—Arlene Bontrager, Haven, Kansas

1/4 cup light corn syrup
　1 cup packed light brown sugar
1/3 cup butter (no substitutes)
1/8 teaspoon salt
1/2 cup whipping cream

In a heavy saucepan, combine the corn syrup, brown sugar, butter and salt. Cook and stir over medium-low heat. Stir in the cream. Bring to a boil; boil for 2 minutes, stirring constantly. Cool to room temperature. Store in the refrigerator. **Yield:** about 1-1/2 cups.

Cashew Nut Crunch

This is a holiday favorite for gift giving. I coarsely chop some of the candy to sprinkle over ice cream. The remainder I break into pieces and dip in melted chocolate to serve alongside.
—Rose Randall, Derry, Pennsylvania

1 tablespoon plus 1 pound butter (no substitutes), *divided*
2 cups sugar
1/4 cup water
2 tablespoons light corn syrup
2 cups cashews, coarsely chopped
1/2 cup milk chocolate *or* vanilla *or* white chips, melted
1/4 teaspoon shortening

Grease two baking sheets using 1 tablespoon butter; set aside. In a heavy saucepan, combine the sugar, water, corn syrup and remaining butter. Cook and stir until the sugar is dissolved. Bring to a boil over medium heat; cook until a candy thermometer reads 300° (hard-crack stage), stirring constantly. Remove from the heat; stir in the cashews. Quickly pour onto prepared pans. Spread with a buttered metal spatula. Cool on wire racks.

Coarsely chop half of the candy and store in an airtight container. Use as an ice cream topping. Break remaining candy into pieces. Melt chocolate chips and shortening in a heavy saucepan or microwave at 70% power; stir until smooth. Dip one end of each candy piece into melted chips. Place on a waxed paper-lined baking sheet to dry. Store in an airtight container. **Yield:** about 2 pounds.

Treats for the Teacher

(Pictured on page 101)

YOUR STAR PUPIL will go to the head of the class when they give their teacher this basket brimming with grade A goodies.

Even the youngest of students can combine the ingredients for Hot Chocolate Mix—don't forget to include the recipe! Or have your kids press the mixture for Peppermint Cereal Squares into the pan (recipes are below).

A bevy of beverages like packaged coffee and tea plus novelty stocking stuffers will make this basket the apple of the teacher's eye.

Hot Chocolate Mix

I bring this mix along when we travel to enjoy as a bedtime snack in our hotel room.
It has a mild chocolate flavor that's not too rich or sweet.
—Leslie Meierding, Missoula, Montana

1 **package (25.6 ounces) nonfat dry milk powder**
1 **package (15 ounces) hot cocoa mix**
4 **cups confectioners' sugar**
1 **jar (6 ounces) powdered nondairy creamer**

In a large bowl, combine the first four ingredients; mix well. Store in an airtight container. **Yield:** 17 cups.

To prepare hot chocolate: Place 1/4 cup mix in a mug; stir in 3/4 cup boiling water until blended. **Yield:** 1 serving.

Peppermint Cereal Squares

Our 15 grandchildren expect me to make several batches of these minty treats each Christmas.
Their quick-and-easy preparation is appreciated during a hectic time of year.
—Carole Coe, South Sutton, New Hampshire

3 **tablespoons butter *or* margarine**
40 **large marshmallows**
6 **cups crisp rice cereal**
1/4 **cup crushed peppermint candy**

In a heavy saucepan over low heat, cook and stir butter and marshmallows until marshmallows are melted and mixture is smooth. Remove from the heat. Stir in cereal and candy; mix well. Transfer to a greased 13-in. x 9-in. x 2-in. pan; press mixture into pan. Cool; cut into squares. **Yield:** 1 dozen.

Wrap It Up!

AFTER you've filled your gift basket, you can wrap it like a pro with easy-to-find items and simple steps (see photo at right and "Wrapping a Gift Basket" below).

For wrapping material, we suggest nylon netting, fabric or ordinary cellophane. Choose colors and patterns that reflect the season or the contents of the basket.

Instead of struggling to secure the wrapped gift with ribbon, use an inexpensive chenille stem (pipe cleaner). It's simple to wrap around the gift and give a twist with just one hand.

For the finishing touch, tie on ribbon, a bow or a decorative gift tag (like the teacher tag shown at right).

WRAPPING A GIFT BASKET

1. Measure and cut a circle of nylon netting or fabric large enough to cover the outside of your assembled gift basket, adding about 4 inches of material to gather at the top. If one piece of cellophane isn't wide enough to cover the entire basket, cut two pieces.

Center the gift basket on the circle of netting or on the wrong side of the fabric. If using cellophane, center the container on two crossed lengths of the cellophane.

2. Bring the wrapping material up to the top of the gift basket, tucking in any extra pieces, and gather it in one hand. Wrap a chenille stem (pipe cleaner) around the gathers at the top.

3. Attach curling ribbon, a jute string bow or a decorative gift tag to cover the chenille stem.

GIVING *Thanks*

*You'll be thanked many times over when your
Thanksgiving table is topped with a mouth-watering
meal featuring succulent goose. Relatives and friends
will fall for a bounty of side dishes and desserts
that are guaranteed to steal the show. Instead of simply
reheating extra turkey, stuffing, potatoes and cranberry
sauce, add life to leftovers with savory second-time-
around recipes. You'll agree food is twice as nice when
dressed up in a deliciously different disguise!*

GIVING Thanks

A Thanksgiving Gala With Goose

FOR FOLKS looking to add a little twist to their traditional Thanksgiving table, this special supper showcasing succulent Goose with Corn Bread Stuffing is just the thing!

(If you think your family will cry "Foul!" when they don't find turkey on the table, we've also provided a recipe for Herb 'n' Spice Turkey Breast.)

For side dishes, you can't go wrong with Orange Whipped Sweet Potatoes, Cranberry Fruit Mold, Thyme Green Beans with Almonds and Butterfluff Rolls.

Pumpkin Cheesecake Dessert blends the wonderful flavors of pumpkin pie and cheesecake into an unforgettable finale.

FLAVORFUL FALL FARE
(Clockwise from top right)

Goose with Corn Bread Stuffing (p. 117)

Orange Whipped Sweet Potatoes (p. 119)

Thyme Green Beans with Almonds (p. 116)

Cranberry Fruit Mold (p. 119)

Pumpkin Cheesecake Dessert (p. 118)

Thyme Green Beans with Almonds

(Pictured on page 114)

Thyme is a nice addition to this classic vegetable side dish.
It's a snap to make for family, yet special enough to serve guests.
—*Kenna Baber, Rochester, Minnesota*

2 pounds fresh green beans
2 tablespoons butter *or* margarine
1 tablespoon minced fresh thyme *or* 1 teaspoon dried thyme
1/2 teaspoon salt
1/2 teaspoon pepper

1/3 cup slivered almonds, toasted

Place beans in a steamer basket. Place in a saucepan over 1 in. of water; bring to a boil. Cover and steam for 10-12 minutes or until crisp-tender. In a large skillet, melt butter; add the beans, thyme, salt and pepper. Cook and stir for 5 minutes or until heated through. Sprinkle with almonds. **Yield:** 8 servings.

THANKSGIVING DINNER AGENDA

A Few Weeks Before:
- Order a 10- to 12-pound domestic goose from your butcher.
- Buy a fresh or frozen 4-1/4- to 6-pound bone-in turkey breast; freeze.
- Prepare two grocery lists—one for non-perishable items to purchase now and one for perishable items to purchase a few days before Thanksgiving.

A Few Days Before:
- Buy goose and any remaining groceries.
- Thaw frozen turkey breast in a pan in the refrigerator. (Allow about 24 hours for a 6-pound turkey breast.)

The Day Before:
- Set the table.
- Clean and trim the fresh beans for Thyme Green Beans with Almonds.
- Make the Pumpkin Cheesecake Dessert; refrigerate.
- Prepare the Cranberry Fruit Mold; cover and refrigerate.
- For the Corn Bread Stuffing, bake corn bread as directed. Cool; store in an airtight container at room temperature. Prepare vegetables; refrigerate in airtight containers.

Thanksgiving Day:
- In the morning, peel and cube sweet potatoes for Orange Whipped Sweet Potatoes; cover with cold water and let stand at room temperature.
- Bake the Butterfluff Rolls. Cool and store in an airtight container at room temperature.
- Make the Corn Bread Stuffing; stuff goose and bake.
- Bake Herb 'n' Spice Turkey Breast.
- Make Orange Whipped Sweet Potatoes.
- Let the cooked turkey breast stand for 20 minutes before carving. Let the cooked goose stand for 10 to 15 minutes; remove the stuffing and carve.
- Make the Thyme Green Beans with Almonds.
- Set out the Cranberry Fruit Mold.
- Serve Pumpkin Cheesecake Dessert.

Goose with Corn Bread Stuffing

(Pictured at right and on page 115)

I've been making this special entree ever since my husband and I were first married many years ago. The dressing pairs well with the moist meat.

—Patsy Faye Steenbock
Riverton, Wyoming

1 package (8-1/2 ounces) corn
  bread/muffin mix
1 domestic goose (10 to 12
  pounds)
Salt
1-2/3 cups chopped onions
   2 cups sliced fresh mushrooms
   2 cups sliced celery
   6 tablespoons butter *or*
     margarine
1-1/2 cups grated peeled apples
   1 cup chopped pecans
   3/4 cup shredded carrots
   2 tablespoons minced fresh
     parsley
   3/4 teaspoon *each* dried thyme,
     marjoram and rubbed sage
   1/4 teaspoon pepper
   1 cup chicken broth
   3 medium carrots, cut into
     chunks
   1 medium onion, cut into 6
     wedges
   3 garlic cloves, minced
   1/2 cup white wine *or* additional
     chicken broth

Prepare corn bread according to package directions; cool on a wire rack. Rub inside of goose cavity with salt.

Prick skin well; set aside. Cut corn bread into cubes; place on a baking sheet. Bake at 350° for 15-20 minutes or until lightly browned. Place in a large bowl. In a skillet, saute chopped onions, mushrooms and celery in butter; add to corn bread cubes. Gently stir in apples, pecans, shredded carrots, parsley, herbs and pepper. Add broth; toss gently. Stuff the goose body and neck cavities; truss opening.

Place carrot chunks, onion wedges and garlic in a shallow roasting pan. Place goose breast side up over vegetables. Pour wine or additional broth over goose. Bake, uncovered, at 350° for 3-1/2 to 4 hours or until a meat thermometer reads 180° (cover with foil during the last hour to prevent overbrowning). Cover and let stand for 10-15 minutes before carving. **Yield:** 10-12 servings.

VERSATILE STUFFING

THE CORN BREAD STUFFING recipe (above) yields about 8 cups of stuffing and is also ideal for a 10- to 12-pound turkey. Just before baking, loosely stuff the turkey and bake at 325° for 3 to 3-1/2 hours or until a meat thermometer reads 180° in the thigh and 160° in the stuffing.

The stuffing can also be baked in a greased 2-1/2-quart baking dish. Cover and bake at 325° for 1 hour. Uncover and bake 10 to 15 minutes longer or until heated through.

Pumpkin Cheesecake Dessert

(Pictured on page 114)

*My family requests this dessert each Thanksgiving. For a change of pace,
I sometimes use cinnamon graham crackers instead of plain ones.*
—*Melissa Davies, Clermont, Florida*

3/4 cup finely chopped walnuts
3/4 cup graham cracker crumbs
   (about 12 squares)
1/4 cup sugar
1/4 teaspoon ground cinnamon
1/4 teaspoon ground ginger
1/8 teaspoon ground cloves
1/4 cup butter *or* margarine,
   melted
FILLING:
  2 packages (8 ounces *each*)
   cream cheese, softened
3/4 cup sugar
  2 eggs
  1 cup cooked *or* canned
   pumpkin

1/2 teaspoon ground cinnamon, *divided*
  2 tablespoons chopped walnuts

In a bowl, combine the first six ingredients; stir in butter. Press onto the bottom of an ungreased 10-in. tart pan with a removable bottom.

In a mixing bowl, beat cream cheese and sugar until smooth. Add eggs, beating just until blended. Add pumpkin and 1/4 teaspoon cinnamon; beat on low speed just until combined. Pour into crust; sprinkle with walnuts and remaining cinnamon.

Bake at 350° for 35-40 minutes or until center is almost set. Cool on a wire rack for 1-1/2 hours. Refrigerate until serving. **Yield:** 9-12 servings.

Herb 'n' Spice Turkey Breast

This nicely seasoned turkey breast from our Test Kitchen is a great accompaniment to goose at Thanksgiving. Or prepare it throughout the year for a delicious dinner on its own.

  3 tablespoons vegetable oil
  1 tablespoon brown sugar
  1 teaspoon salt
1/2 teaspoon rubbed sage
1/2 teaspoon dried thyme
1/2 teaspoon dried rosemary,
   crushed
1/4 teaspoon pepper
1/8 to 1/4 teaspoon ground
   allspice
  1 bone-in turkey breast
   (4-1/4 to 6 pounds)

In a small bowl, combine the oil, brown sugar, salt, sage, thyme, rosemary, pepper and allspice. Carefully loosen the skin from the turkey. Rub herb mixture under the skin; rub remaining herb mixture over the skin.

Place turkey breast side up on a rack in a roasting pan. Bake, uncovered, at 325° for 1-1/2 to 2-1/4 hours or until a meat thermometer reads 170° (cover loosely with foil if turkey browns too quickly). Cover and let stand for 20 minutes before carving. **Yield:** 10-14 servings.

Cranberry Fruit Mold

(Pictured at right and on page 114)

This special gelatin salad takes the place of ordinary cranberry sauce on my Thanksgiving table. Grapes and mandarin oranges make it deliciously different.
—Kristy Duncan
Smithfield, North Carolina

1 package (3 ounces) cranberry gelatin
1 package (3 ounces) raspberry gelatin
1 cup boiling water
1-1/2 cups ginger ale, chilled
2 cups halved seedless red *or* green grapes
1 can (11 ounces) mandarin oranges, drained

In a bowl, dissolve gelatins in boiling water. Gently stir in ginger ale. Refrigerate until slightly thickened, about 1-1/2 hours. Stir in grapes and oranges. Transfer to a 5-cup mold coated with nonstick cooking spray. Cover and refrigerate until firm. Invert onto a serving plate. **Yield:** 10-12 servings.

Orange Whipped Sweet Potatoes

(Pictured on page 115)

Orange juice adds a tantalizing twist to mashed sweet potatoes. The color and flavor are incredible!
—Shirley Bedzis, San Diego, California

3 pounds sweet potatoes, peeled and cubed
2-2/3 cups orange juice, *divided*
1/4 cup packed brown sugar
2 tablespoons butter *or* margarine
1/4 teaspoon salt
1/4 teaspoon ground nutmeg
1/4 teaspoon ground ginger

Place sweet potatoes and 2-1/3 cups orange juice in a large saucepan or Dutch oven. Cover and bring to a boil. Boil for 35-45 minutes or just until potatoes are tender. Drain and place in a large mixing bowl. Mash potatoes with the brown sugar, butter, salt, nutmeg, ginger and remaining orange juice. **Yield:** 6-8 servings.

Butterfluff Rolls

(Pictured at right)

*In my house, a meal isn't complete unless
a basket of rolls is passed around.
Just one rising time makes these
fluffy rolls easy to prepare.*
—Harriet Stichter, Milford, Indiana

    1 package (1/4 ounce) active
      dry yeast
1/4 cup warm water (110°
      to 115°)
    1 cup warm buttermilk (110°
      to 115°)*
1/4 cup sugar
1/4 cup shortening
    2 eggs
1-1/2 teaspoons salt
1/2 teaspoon baking soda
    4 to 4-1/2 cups all-purpose flour
GLAZE:
    1 egg
    1 tablespoon water

In a mixing bowl, dissolve yeast in
warm water. Add buttermilk, sugar,
shortening, eggs, salt, baking soda and
2 cups flour; beat until blended. Stir in enough remaining
flour to form a soft dough. Turn onto a floured surface; knead
until smooth and elastic, about 6-8 minutes. Divide into 18
pieces. Roll each into a 9-in. rope; coil the ends of each rope
toward center in opposite directions to form an S shape.
Place 3 in. apart on greased baking sheets. Cover and let rise
in a warm place until doubled, about 40 minutes.

In a small bowl, beat egg and water; brush over rolls. Bake
at 350° for 15-20 minutes or until golden brown. Remove
from pans to wire racks to cool. **Yield:** 1-1/2 dozen.

*Editor's Note: Warmed buttermilk will appear curdled.

Simply Elegant Thanksgiving Table

(Pictured above)

WHEN you're hosting a Thanksgiving meal at your house, the last thing you want to do is spend time worrying about how to decorate your table.

You don't need an elaborate centerpiece to make your table attractive. Simply top your table with a crisp white or ivory linen tablecloth, then run an eye-catching autumn garland down the center.

In the table setting shown above, we chose a silk garland that can be used from year to year. You can find a great selection of garlands at craft and variety stores.

For a natural look, try tucking in pinecones, gourds or Indian corn. Or replace the silk garland with boughs of dried bittersweet or fresh holly.

Thin white or ivory pillar candles placed on both sides of the garland are a simple yet striking addition. Feel free to use pillar, votive or tea light candles...or a combination of all three. If you use colored candles, make sure they pair well with your garland, linens and dishes.

Instead of traditional place mats, we added a little elegance by setting napkins matching our tablecloth on a diagonal, draping them off the side of the table and topping with plates.

For the fast finishing touch, fold a napkin into a rectangle, roll it up lengthwise and tie with a ribbon. Tuck a sprig of the garland under the ribbon and place the napkin on the plate.

GIVING *Thanks*

Thanksgiving *Side Dishes*

ALTHOUGH they don't get as much attention as main courses, side dishes and salads play an important role in rounding out a meal, especially at Thanksgiving.

In addition to your own tried-and-true mashed potatoes, dressing and gravy, why not serve up some new creative complements?

Fruited Wild Rice Pilaf, Six-Layer Gelatin Salad and Cheese Sauce Over Cauliflower (shown at right) are guaranteed to become newfound family favorites.

From vegetables and fruits to pasta and rice, these satisfying side dishes just might steal the show at your dinner table!

BOUNTIFUL HARVEST
(Clockwise from top right)

Six-Layer Gelatin Salad (p. 125)

Cheese Sauce Over
Cauliflower (p. 126)

Fruited Wild Rice Pilaf (p. 124)

Fruited Wild Rice Pilaf

(Pictured on page 122)

Crunchy apples and pecans give traditional wild rice a tasty twist.
This dish pairs well with a variety of meaty entrees.
—Becky Burch, Marceline, Missouri

1/2 cup chopped onion
1/2 cup chopped celery
2 tablespoons butter *or* margarine
1-1/4 cups hot water
3/4 cup uncooked wild rice
1-1/2 teaspoons chicken bouillon granules
1 small red apple, chopped

2 tablespoons chopped pecans, toasted
1/4 teaspoon grated lemon peel, optional

In a large saucepan, saute onion and celery in butter until tender. Stir in the water, rice and bouillon; bring to a boil. Reduce heat; cover and simmer for 50-55 minutes or until liquid is absorbed and rice is tender. Remove from the heat; fold in apple, pecans and lemon peel if desired. **Yield:** 4 servings.

Autumn Vegetables Au Gratin

I often assemble this vegetable casserole early in the morning and refrigerate.
Just before baking, I top it with the buttered bread crumbs.
—Sharon Gerow, Foothill Ranch, California

3 cups diced rutabagas
3 cups diced peeled potatoes
2 cups sliced carrots
6 tablespoons butter *or* margarine, *divided*
2 tablespoons all-purpose flour
1/2 teaspoon salt
1/2 teaspoon pepper
1/4 teaspoon ground nutmeg
1 cup milk
3/4 cup shredded cheddar cheese, *divided*
1 cup soft bread crumbs

Place rutabagas in a large saucepan or Dutch oven; cover with water. Bring to a boil. Reduce heat; cover and simmer for 25 minutes. Add potatoes. Bring to a boil. Reduce heat; cover and simmer for 5 minutes. Add carrots. Bring to a boil. Reduce heat; cover and simmer 15 minutes longer or until vegetables are crisp-tender. Drain, reserving 1 cup liquid.

In a large saucepan, melt 3 tablespoons butter. Stir in flour, salt, pepper and nutmeg until smooth. Add milk and reserved cooking liquid. Bring to a boil; cook and stir for 2 minutes or until thickened. Reduce heat. Stir in 1/4 cup cheese until melted. Add vegetables; toss to coat.

Transfer to a greased 2-qt. baking dish. Melt the remaining butter in a small skillet. Add bread crumbs; cook and stir for 3-4 minutes or until lightly browned. Sprinkle over vegetables; top with the remaining cheese. Bake, uncovered, at 350° for 25-30 minutes or until bubbly around the edges. **Yield:** 8-10 servings.

Six-Layer Gelatin Salad

(Pictured at right and on page 123)

This impressive salad does take some time to make, but the preparation itself is actually easy. It's an attractive addition to a buffet table.
— *Marcia Orlando*
Boyertown, Pennsylvania

2 packages (3 ounces *each*)
   lime gelatin
4-1/2 cups boiling water, *divided*
4-1/2 cups cold water, *divided*
1 cup whipping cream
3 tablespoons confectioners'
   sugar
2 packages (3 ounces *each*)
   orange gelatin
1 can (11 ounces) mandarin
   oranges, drained
1 package (3 ounces) lemon
   gelatin
1 can (8 ounces) crushed
   pineapple, drained
1 package (3 ounces)
   strawberry gelatin
2 medium firm bananas, thinly
   sliced

In a bowl, dissolve one package of lime gelatin in 3/4 cup boiling water; stir in 3/4 cup cold water. Refrigerate until slightly thickened. In a small mixing bowl, beat cream until slightly thickened. Add sugar; beat until soft peaks form. Fold a third of the whipped cream into the lime gelatin. Spoon into a 4-qt. bowl. Refrigerate until firm. Refrigerate remaining whipped cream.

In a bowl, dissolve one package of orange gelatin in 3/4 cup boiling water; stir in 3/4 cup cold water. Refrigerate until slightly thickened. Fold in mandarin oranges. Spoon over creamy lime layer. Refrigerate until firm.

In a bowl, dissolve lemon gelatin in 3/4 cup boiling water; stir in 3/4 cup cold water. Refrigerate until slightly thickened. Fold in a third of the whipped cream. Spoon over orange layer. Refrigerate until firm.

In a bowl, dissolve remaining package of lime gelatin in 3/4 cup boiling water; stir in 3/4 cup cold water. Refrigerate until slightly thickened. Fold in pineapple. Spoon over creamy lemon layer. Refrigerate until firm.

In a bowl, dissolve remaining package of orange gelatin in 3/4 cup boiling water; stir in 3/4 cup cold water. Refrigerate until slightly thickened. Fold in remaining whipped cream. Spoon over lime layer. Refrigerate until firm.

In a bowl, dissolve strawberry gelatin in remaining boiling water; stir in remaining cold water. Refrigerate until slightly thickened. Fold in bananas. Spoon over creamy orange layer. Refrigerate overnight. **Yield:** 16-20 servings.

Cheese Sauce Over Cauliflower

(Pictured on page 122)

The cheese sauce makes cauliflower hard to resist...even for picky eaters! I like to serve this vegetable dish at holidays and also for lunch along with pork sausage links, croissants and a green salad.
—Ruby Zein, Monona, Wisconsin

1 large head cauliflower
1-1/2 teaspoons salt
3 tablespoons butter *or* margarine
3 tablespoons all-purpose flour
1/2 teaspoon dried thyme
1-1/2 cups milk
1-1/2 cups (6 ounces) shredded cheddar cheese
Paprika
Minced fresh parsley

Place 1 in. of water in a large saucepan; add cauliflower and salt. Cover and cook for 5-10 minutes or until cauliflower is crisp-tender. In a small saucepan, melt butter; stir in flour and thyme until blended. Gradually add milk. Bring to a boil; cook and stir for 2 minutes or until thickened. Reduce heat; stir in cheese until melted.

Drain and pat cauliflower dry; place on a serving platter. Top with cheese sauce; sprinkle with paprika and parsley. Cut into wedges. **Yield:** 6-8 servings.

Brussels Sprouts Salad

My husband and I like brussels sprouts, so I'm always looking for new ways to use them. I most often serve this colorful salad with roast pork or duck.
—Nancy Korondan, Yorkville, Illinois

1-1/2 pounds fresh brussels sprouts, trimmed and halved
2 green onions, chopped
1/2 cup olive *or* vegetable oil
2 tablespoons lemon juice
1 to 1-1/2 teaspoons Dijon mustard
1/2 teaspoon salt
1/2 teaspoon dried thyme
1/4 teaspoon pepper
1 large bunch red leaf lettuce *or* radicchio, torn
2 tablespoons slivered almonds, toasted

Place 1 in. of water in a saucepan; add brussels sprouts. Bring to a boil. Reduce heat; cover and simmer for 8-10 minutes or until tender. Drain; rinse with cold water and pat dry. Place sprouts and onions in a bowl; set aside.

In a small bowl, whisk the oil, lemon juice, mustard, salt, thyme and pepper. Toss lettuce with 2 tablespoons of dressing; place in a large shallow serving bowl. Pour remaining dressing over brussels sprouts and toss to coat; mound on lettuce. Sprinkle with almonds. **Yield:** 6-8 servings.

Zucchini Twice-Baked Potatoes

(Pictured at right)

Flecks of zucchini add pretty color to these potatoes. My mother prepared them each Christmas when I was young. Now my brothers, sister and I rely on the recipe.
—Mary Maxeiner, Lakewood, Colorado

- 3 large baking potatoes (about 3/4 pound *each*)
- 3 cups shredded zucchini (about 2 medium)
- 1 medium onion, chopped
- 2 tablespoons butter *or* margarine, *divided*
- 1/2 cup sour cream
- 3/4 to 1 teaspoon salt
- 1/8 to 1/4 teaspoon pepper
- 1/2 cup shredded cheddar cheese

Scrub and pierce potatoes. Bake at 400° for 50-75 minutes or until tender. Cool until easy to handle. Reduce heat to 350°. In a skillet, saute zucchini and onion in 1 tablespoon butter until tender. Drain and set aside.

Scoop out the potato pulp, leaving a thin shell; place pulp in a bowl and mash. Add the sour cream, salt, pepper and remaining butter; mash. Stir in zucchini mixture. Spoon into potato shells. Sprinkle with cheese. Place on a baking sheet. Bake for 20-25 minutes or until heated through and cheese is melted. **Yield:** 6 servings.

Pomegranate Gelatin

As a former home economics teacher, I like to surprise family and friends with recipes
that are a little more special. This salad combines sweet and tart tastes.
—*Deidre Hobbs, Redding, California*

2 packages (3 ounces *each*)
  raspberry gelatin
2 cups boiling water
1 cup cold water
1-1/2 cups pomegranate seeds
  (about 2 pomegranates)*
1 can (8 ounces) crushed
  pineapple, drained
1/2 cup sour cream
1/2 cup mayonnaise

In a bowl, dissolve gelatin in boiling water. Stir in cold water, pomegranate seeds and pineapple. Pour into an 11-in. x 7-in. x 2-in. dish. Refrigerate until firm. Combine sour cream and mayonnaise; spread over gelatin. Refrigerate until serving. **Yield:** 10 servings.

  *Editor's Note: Refer to "Seeding a Pomegranate" on page 12.

Bow Tie Cabbage Salad

Pasta and cheese cubes make this creamy coleslaw stand out from any others.
It can conveniently be made in advance, allowing you to focus on the rest of the meal.
—*Joan Zimmerman, Earlville, Illinois*

1/2 cup evaporated milk
1/3 cup sour cream
1/3 cup cider vinegar
1/4 cup sugar
1 tablespoon prepared mustard
1-1/2 teaspoons salt
1/2 teaspoon pepper
1-1/2 cups uncooked bow tie pasta
5 cups shredded cabbage
3/4 cup chopped green onions
1/2 cup finely chopped green
  pepper
8 ounces cheddar cheese, cut
  into small cubes

In a jar with a tight-fitting lid, combine the first seven ingredients; shake well. Cover and refrigerate for 1-1/2 to 2 hours. Cook pasta according to package directions; drain and rinse in cold water. Place in a large bowl; add the cabbage, onions, green pepper, cheese and dressing. Toss to coat. Cover and refrigerate for 1-2 hours. **Yield:** 12 servings.

CABBAGE CAPERS

WHEN BUYING CABBAGE, look for those with crisp-looking leaves that are firmly packed. The head should feel heavy for its size.

  Store cabbage tightly wrapped in a plastic bag in the refrigerator for up to 2 weeks. Remove the core, rinse and blot dry just before using.

  A 1-pound cabbage will yield 4 cups shredded.

Floret Cheese Strudel

(Pictured at right)

This is a unique way to serve broccoli and cauliflower, wrapped in puff pastry. It looks so pretty on the table. Without fail, I'm asked for the recipe whenever I serve it.
—*Bonnie Zaparinuk*
Whitehorse, Yukon Territory

3-1/2 cups broccoli florets
2-1/2 cups cauliflowerets
1 small onion, chopped
1 garlic clove, minced
6 tablespoons butter *or* margarine, *divided*
2 tablespoons all-purpose flour
1 cup milk
2 tablespoons grated Parmesan cheese
1 package (17-1/4 ounces) frozen puff pastry, thawed
1 cup (4 ounces) shredded mozzarella cheese
1/2 cup shredded cheddar cheese

Place 1 in. of water in a large saucepan; add broccoli and cauliflower. Bring to a boil. Reduce heat; cover and simmer for 5-10 minutes or until crisp-tender. Drain and set aside.

In a large saucepan, saute onion and garlic in 2 tablespoons butter until tender. Stir in flour until blended. Gradually add milk. Bring to a boil; cook and stir for 2 minutes or until thickened. Remove from the heat. Stir in Parmesan cheese, broccoli and cauliflower; set aside.

Melt remaining butter. Place one sheet of puff pastry on a piece of waxed pape; brush with butter. Spoon half of the vegetable mixture along one long side of pastry. Sprinkle with mozzarella and cheddar cheeses. Roll up jelly-roll style, starting from a long side; pinch seams and ends to seal. Brush top with melted butter. Carefully place seam side down on an ungreased baking sheet. Repeat with remaining dough and vegetable mixture.

Bake at 400° for 20-25 minutes or until golden brown. Let stand for 5 minutes. Slice with a serrated knife. **Yield:** 2 strudels (4-6 servings each).

Fitting Fall Finales

PUMPKIN PIE topped with whipped cream is likely a sweet standby on every family's Thanksgiving table.

But don't limit your dessert tray to the traditional when there's a bounty of other awesome autumn choices.

Sweet and creamy Gingersnap Dip is a tasty complement to nicely spiced cookies.

Slices of Cranberry Bundt Cake are bursting with tart and tangy berries, while Frozen Pumpkin Dessert features a fun ice cream filling. (All recipes are shown at right.)

Family and friends are guaranteed to fall for these tempting desserts. And who knows? You may even start a delicious new family tradition!

SWEET TREATS
(Clockwise from top right)

Gingersnap Dip (p. 133)

Frozen Pumpkin Dessert (p. 134)

Cranberry Bundt Cake (p. 132)

Cranberry Bundt Cake

(Pictured on page 130)

Cranberry sauce gives this moist cake its pretty swirled look.
Serve slices for dessert after dinner or as coffee cake for brunch.
—Lucile Cline, Wichita, Kansas

3/4 cup butter *or* margarine, softened
1-1/2 cups sugar
3 eggs
1-1/2 teaspoons almond extract
3 cups all-purpose flour
1-1/2 teaspoons baking powder
1-1/2 teaspoons baking soda
1/2 teaspoon salt
1-1/2 cups (12 ounces) sour cream
1 can (16 ounces) whole-berry cranberry sauce
1/2 cup finely chopped pecans
ICING:
3/4 cup confectioners' sugar
4-1/2 teaspoons water
1/2 teaspoon almond extract

In a large mixing bowl, cream butter and sugar. Add eggs, one at a time, beating well after each addition. Stir in extract. Combine the flour, baking powder, baking soda and salt; add to the creamed mixture alternately with sour cream, beating well after each addition. Spoon a third of the batter into a greased and floured 10-in. fluted tube pan. Top with a third of the cranberry sauce. Repeat layers twice. Sprinkle with pecans.

Bake at 350° for 65-70 minutes or until a toothpick inserted near the center comes out clean. Cool for 10 minutes before removing from pan to a wire rack. Combine icing ingredients until smooth; drizzle over warm cake. **Yield:** 12-16 servings.

Apple Cranberry Crumble

When I first took this fruity dessert to my family's Thanksgiving dinner, it quickly became a tradition. We enjoy it for breakfast, lunch, dinner and snack time!
— Teri Roberts, Hilliard, Ohio

3 cups chopped peeled apples
2 cups fresh *or* frozen cranberries
3/4 cup sugar
1 cup old-fashioned *or* quick-cooking oats
3/4 cup packed brown sugar
1/3 cup all-purpose flour
1/2 cup butter *or* margarine, melted
1/2 cup chopped pecans, optional

In a greased 8-in. square baking dish, combine apples and cranberries; sprinkle with sugar. In another bowl, combine the oats, brown sugar, flour and butter; sprinkle over cranberry mixture. Top with pecans if desired. Bake, uncovered, at 350° for 55-60 minutes or until browned and bubbly. Serve warm. **Yield:** 6-8 servings.

Gingersnap Dip

(Pictured at right and on page 131)

I serve this dip in a clean plastic pumpkin at all of our fall church gatherings. It's a nice way to dress up packaged gingersnaps.
—*Tessie Hughes, Marion, Virginia*

1 package (8 ounces) cream cheese, softened
1 cup confectioners' sugar
2 teaspoons pumpkin pie spice
1 carton (8 ounces) frozen whipped topping, thawed
1 package (16 ounces) gingersnaps

In a small mixing bowl, combine the cream cheese, confectioners' sugar and pumpkin pie spice. Beat in whipped topping until blended. Refrigerate until serving. **Yield:** 3 cups.

HOMEMADE PUMPKIN PIE SPICE

IF YOU RARELY use pumpkin pie spice in your cooking, you may want to make your own instead of buying it. Combine 4 teaspoons ground cinnamon, 2 teaspoons ground ginger, 1 teaspoon ground cloves and 1/2 teaspoon ground nutmeg. Store in an airtight container. Substitute for store-bought pumpkin pie spice in any recipe. **Yield:** 7-1/2 teaspoons.

Frozen Pumpkin Dessert

(Pictured on page 130)

This ice cream dessert can be prepared and frozen weeks in advance.
I've found it has more mass appeal than traditional pumpkin pie.
—*Susan Bennett, Edmond, Oklahoma*

1 can (15 ounces) solid-pack
  pumpkin
3/4 cup sugar
1 teaspoon vanilla extract
1/2 teaspoon salt
1/4 teaspoon ground ginger
1/4 teaspoon ground nutmeg
1/8 to 1/4 teaspoon ground cloves

2 quarts vanilla ice cream, softened
1 cup finely chopped walnuts

In a large mixing bowl, combine the pumpkin, sugar, vanilla, salt, ginger, nutmeg and cloves. Fold in ice cream. Transfer to a greased 13-in. x 9-in. x 2-in. dish. Sprinkle with walnuts. Cover and freeze overnight. Remove from the freezer 10 minutes before serving. Cut into squares. **Yield:** 16-20 servings.

Apple Pound Cake

An apple cider glaze makes each slice of this rich pound cake nice and sweet.
It's a favorite fall treat at our house.
—*Mary Martin, Madison, North Carolina*

2 cups sugar
1-1/2 cups vegetable oil
3 eggs
2 teaspoons vanilla extract
3 cups all-purpose flour
1 teaspoon baking soda
1 teaspoon salt
1/2 teaspoon ground cinnamon
1/2 teaspoon ground nutmeg
2 cups chopped peeled tart
  apples
1 cup chopped almonds
1/2 cup raisins

APPLE CIDER GLAZE:
1/2 cup apple cider *or* juice
1/2 cup packed brown sugar
2 tablespoons butter *or* margarine

In a mixing bowl, combine sugar, oil, eggs and vanilla; mix well. Combine the flour, baking soda, salt, cinnamon and nutmeg; add to egg mixture and mix well. Stir in apples, almonds and raisins. Pour into a greased and floured 10-in. fluted tube pan.

Bake at 350° for 1-1/4 to 1-1/2 hours or until a toothpick comes out clean. Cool for 15 minutes before removing from pan to a wire rack to cool completely.

In a saucepan, combine glaze ingredients; cook over low heat until sugar is dissolved. Prick top of cake with a fork; drizzle with glaze. **Yield:** 16 servings.

Pumpkin Baked Alaska

(Pictured at right)

For years, I was a flop at making pumpkin pies. So I pulled out this recipe, which I got at a cooking class. It's been a success ever since.
—Linda Sanner, Portage, Wisconsin

1 quart vanilla ice cream, softened
2 teaspoons pumpkin pie spice
2 eggs
1-1/4 cups sugar, *divided*
3 tablespoons plus 5 teaspoons water, *divided*
1/2 teaspoon vanilla extract
2/3 cup cake flour
1/2 teaspoon baking powder
1/8 teaspoon salt
5 egg whites
1/2 teaspoon cream of tartar
1 teaspoon rum extract
2 tablespoon sliced almonds, toasted

In a bowl, combine the ice cream and pumpkin pie spice. Transfer to a 1-1/2-qt. bowl lined with plastic wrap; freeze until set.

Line a greased 9-in. round baking pan with waxed paper; grease the paper and set aside. Place a clean kitchen towel over a wire rack; dust towel with confectioners' sugar; set aside.

In a mixing bowl, beat eggs, 1/2 cup sugar, 3 tablespoons water and vanilla until thick and lemon-colored. Combine the flour, baking powder and salt; fold into egg mixture. Pour into prepared pan. Bake at 375° for 12-14 minutes or until cake springs back when lightly touched. Immediately run a knife around the edge of the pan; invert onto prepared kitchen towel. Gently peel off waxed paper; cool completely.

Place cake on an ungreased freezer-to-oven-safe platter or foil-lined baking sheet. Unmold ice cream onto cake; remove plastic wrap. Return to freezer.

In a heavy saucepan or double boiler, combine the egg whites, cream of tartar and remaining sugar and water; beat on low speed with a portable mixer for 1 minute. Continue beating over low heat until mixture reaches 160°, about 10 minutes. Remove from the heat. Add extract; beat until stiff peaks form, about 4 minutes. Spread meringue over frozen ice cream and cake, sealing meringue to the platter; sprinkle with almonds. Freeze until ready to serve, up to 24 hours.

Just before serving, broil on lowest oven rack position for 3-5 minutes or until meringue is light browned. Serve immediately. **Yield:** 12 servings.

Pecan Carrot Pie

After moving from New York to Georgia, I had many opportunities to make pecan pie.
This recipe stuns the Southerners when I tell them carrots are the secret ingredient!
— Susan Elise Jansen, Smyrna, Georgia

2 cups sliced carrots
1 cup water
1 cup half-and-half cream
1/4 cup butter *or* margarine, softened
1/2 cup packed brown sugar
2 eggs
1/2 teaspoon ground nutmeg
1/2 teaspoon ground cinnamon
1/4 teaspoon salt
1/8 teaspoon ground ginger
1 unbaked pastry shell (9 inches)

PECAN TOPPING:
2 tablespoons butter *or* margarine
1 tablespoon brown sugar
1 cup chopped pecans

In a saucepan, simmer carrots in water for 20 minutes or until tender; drain. Place carrots and cream in a blender; cover and process until smooth. In a mixing bowl, cream butter and brown sugar. Add eggs, nutmeg, cinnamon, salt, ginger and carrots; mix well. Pour into pastry shell. Bake at 450° for 15 minutes.

For topping, melt butter in a small saucepan. Stir in brown sugar until dissolved. Add pecans; stir until coated, about 2 minutes. Spoon over carrot filling. Reduce heat to 325°; bake 35-40 minutes longer or until a knife inserted near the center comes out clean. Cool completely. Store in the refrigerator. **Yield:** 8-10 servings.

Baked Stuffed Pears

This simple dessert is a tasty ending to our Thanksgiving meal of roast turkey or pork.
Pears are a yummy change from the typical apples.
— Marie Labanowski, New Hampton, New York

4 medium ripe pears (about 2 pounds)
2 tablespoons lemon juice
1/3 cup coarsely chopped walnuts
1/4 cup golden raisins
2 tablespoons maple syrup
2 teaspoons brown sugar
1 teaspoon grated lemon peel
1/8 teaspoon ground cinnamon
1 tablespoon butter *or* margarine
2/3 cup apple juice

Core pears and peel 1 in. down from the top on each. Brush peeled portion with some of the lemon juice. Place in a greased 1-qt. baking dish.

In a bowl, combine walnuts, raisins, syrup, brown sugar, lemon peel, cinnamon and remaining lemon juice. Spoon into pears. Dot with butter. Pour apple juice around pears. Bake, uncovered, at 350° for 30-40 minutes or until pears are tender, basting several times. **Yield:** 4 servings.

Bread Pudding Pumpkin

(Pictured at right)

When doing my fall decorating, I'm certain to set aside a few pumpkins for this unique dessert. It adds a festive touch to our Thanksgiving table.
—Darlene Markel, Mt. Hood, Oregon

2 medium pie pumpkins (about 3 pounds *each*)
4 eggs, lightly beaten
1 can (14 ounces) sweetened condensed milk
1/2 cup packed brown sugar
1 teaspoon salt
1 teaspoon ground cinnamon
1 teaspoon vanilla extract
3/4 teaspoon ground nutmeg
6 cups cubed crustless day-old bread
1 can (8 ounces) crushed pineapple, drained
1 cup chopped walnuts
1 cup raisins

Wash pumpkins; cut off tops and discard. Scoop out seeds and loose fibers (save seeds for another use if desired). In a large bowl, whisk the eggs, milk, brown sugar, salt, cinnamon, vanilla and nutmeg. Stir in bread cubes, pineapple, walnuts and raisins. Spoon into pumpkin shells.

Place on a greased 15-in. x 10-in. x 1-in. baking pan. Loosely cover tops with foil. Bake at 350° for 1-1/4 hours. Uncover; bake 15-30 minutes longer or until pumpkin is soft and a knife inserted near the center of bread pudding comes out clean. To serve, scoop bread pudding and cooked pumpkin into dessert dishes. **Yield:** 6-8 servings.

TOASTING PUMPKIN SEEDS

DON'T TOSS OUT the pumpkin seeds from a freshly cut pumpkin. Instead, toast them for a tasty snack.

Wash and dry the pumpkin seeds. In a skillet, saute 1 cup seeds in 2 tablespoons vegetable oil for 5 minutes or until lightly browned. Using a slotted spoon, transfer seeds to an ungreased 15-in. x 10-in. x 1-in. baking pan. Sprinkle with salt or garlic salt; stir to coat. Spread in a single layer.

Bake at 325° for 15-20 minutes or until crisp. Remove to paper towels to cool completely. Store in an airtight container for up to 3 weeks.

Give a Lift to Leftovers!

FOR MOST FAMILIES, the joy of Thanksgiving extends to the days following and the anticipation of wonderful leftovers.

Instead of simply serving those extra goodies the same old way, why not try one of this chapter's delectable second-time-around recipes? Each is sure to give a mouth-watering boost to leftover turkey, stuffing, potatoes, cranberry sauce and more.

Family and friends will clamor for second helpings of Fruited Turkey Salad, Hot 'n' Spicy Cranberry Dip and Turkey Divan Pizza (shown at right).

Even folks who typically turn up their noses at leftovers will be pleasantly surprised when you dress up the food in a deliciously different disguise!

TWICE AS NICE

(Clockwise from top left)

Fruited Turkey Salad (p. 140)

Hot 'n' Spicy Cranberry Dip (p. 143)

Turkey Divan Pizza (p. 141)

Fruited Turkey Salad

(Pictured on page 138)

A subtle tarragon flavor adds a different twist to this well-dressed turkey salad.
With cranberry sauce and a dinner roll, it's a hearty lunch or dinner.
— Donna Nole, Skokie, Illinois

6 cups cubed cooked turkey
2 cups chopped celery
1 cup green grapes
3/4 cup sour cream
3/4 cup mayonnaise
1-1/2 teaspoons dried tarragon
1 teaspoon salt
1/8 teaspoon pepper
1/2 cup chopped walnuts, toasted
Leaf lettuce

In a bowl, combine the turkey, celery and grapes. In a small bowl, combine the sour cream, mayonnaise, tarragon, salt and pepper. Add to turkey mixture and toss to coat. Cover and refrigerate for at least 5 hours. Just before serving, stir in walnuts. Serve in a lettuce-lined bowl. **Yield:** 8 servings.

SAFELY STORING THANKSGIVING LEFTOVERS

FOLLOW these guidelines to ensure that the leftovers you keep will be safe to eat.

"When in doubt, throw it out" is a good rule of thumb, whether you're questioning the safety of food you're about to store or of food you're taking out of the refrigerator or freezer to eat.

- Stock up on plastic storage bags and containers so you're prepared to store leftovers soon after the meal. Having storage supplies at the ready also makes it easy for others to help out in the kitchen.
- Immediately after cooking, remove stuffing from the turkey, chicken, duck or goose. Within 2 hours, carve all meat off the bones. Place the meat and stuffing in separate containers and refrigerate. For faster cooling, don't stack the containers.
- Leftover turkey, stuffing and pumpkin pie can be refrigerated for 3 to 4 days.
- Meat combined with gravy and gravy by itself should be used within 1 to 2 days.
- Cranberry sauce and relish can be stored in the refrigerator for 5 to 7 days.
- Cooked vegetables should be eaten within 3 to 5 days.
- Freeze any leftovers you won't eat within 3 days. Frozen cooked meat and gravy should be used within 2 to 3 months.
- When reheating leftovers, bring gravy to a full rolling boil and all others foods to a temperature of 165°.

Glazed Cranberry Carrots

(Pictured at right)

Although this is a wonderful way to use leftover carrots and cranberry sauce, I often find myself making it specifically for Thanksgiving dinner.
—Mary Ann Gilbert, Cincinnati, Ohio

2 pounds fresh baby carrots
1/2 cup jellied cranberry sauce
1/4 cup butter *or* margarine
1/4 cup packed brown sugar
1 tablespoon lemon juice
1/2 teaspoon salt

Place 1 in. of water in a large saucepan; add carrots. Bring to a boil. Reduce heat; cover and simmer for 10-12 minutes or until tender. Drain and set aside.

In the same pan, combine the cranberry sauce, butter, brown sugar, lemon juice and salt. Cook and stir until cranberry sauce is melted and mixture is smooth. Add carrots; stir to coat. Heat through. **Yield:** 6 servings.

Turkey Divan Pizza

(Pictured on page 138)

Kids who are typically picky eaters will gobble up slice after slice of this savory pizza. I often have frozen cubed cooked turkey on hand to make this meal in a moment's notice.
—Charlotte Smith, Pittsburgh, Pennsylvania

1 prebaked Italian bread shell crust (16 ounces)
2 teaspoons olive *or* vegetable oil
1/2 to 1 teaspoon garlic salt
2 cups fresh broccoli florets
1-1/2 cups cubed cooked turkey
1 can (10-3/4 ounces) condensed broccoli cheese soup, undiluted
1/3 cup milk
1/2 cup shredded cheddar cheese
2 tablespoons dry bread crumbs
1 tablespoon butter *or* margarine, melted

Place pizza crust on a baking sheet. Brush with oil; sprinkle with garlic salt. Top with broccoli and turkey. Combine soup and milk; spread over broccoli and turkey. Sprinkle with cheddar cheese. Toss bread crumbs and butter; sprinkle over the top. Bake at 400° for 13-15 minutes or until cheese is melted and broccoli is crisp-tender. **Yield:** 6-8 servings.

Thanksgiving Turkey Sandwich

I created this recipe after sampling a similar sandwich at a nearby restaurant.
At first, my husband turned up his nose. But after one bite, he was converted!
—*Jeanne Imbrigiotta, Pennington, New Jersey*

2 tablespoons cream cheese,
  softened
2 slices multigrain bread
1 tablespoon hot pepper jelly
3 slices thinly sliced deli *or*
  cooked turkey

Spread cream cheese on both slices of bread; spread jelly over cream cheese. Place turkey on one slice; cover with remaining slice. **Yield:** 1 sandwich.

Cranberry Turkey Salad

This recipe is most treasured because it's from my husband's grandmother. A savory turkey salad
is cleverly topped with cranberry-raspberry gelatin for an eye-catching dish.
—*Kim Kirven, Wadsworth, Ohio*

1 package (3 ounces) lemon
  gelatin
2 cups boiling water, *divided*
2 cups cubed cooked turkey
  or chicken
4 celery ribs, chopped
8 ounces process cheese
  (Velveeta), cubed
1 cup chopped almonds
3 hard-cooked eggs, chopped,
  optional
1 cup mayonnaise *or* salad
  dressing
1 cup whipping cream, whipped
1/2 teaspoon salt

1/2 teaspoon onion salt
1 package (3 ounces) raspberry gelatin
1 can (16 ounces) whole-berry cranberry sauce

In a mixing bowl, dissolve lemon gelatin in 1 cup of boiling water; refrigerate for 1 hour or until slightly thickened. Beat for 1 minute on high speed. Stir in turkey, celery, cheese, almonds, eggs if desired, mayonnaise, cream, salt and onion salt. Spread evenly into a 13-in. x 9-in. x 2-in. dish. Cover and refrigerate until firm, about 2 hours.

Dissolve the raspberry gelatin in remaining boiling water; stir in cranberry sauce until melted and blended. Spoon over turkey mixture. Refrigerate for 2 hours or until set. Cut into squares. **Yield:** 12-15 servings.

Hot 'n' Spicy Cranberry Dip

(Pictured at right and on page 139)

When I want to make this as an appetizer on Christmas or New Year's, I double the recipe, using one 16-ounce can of cranberry sauce.
—Marian Platt, Sequim, Washington

3/4 cup jellied cranberry sauce
1 to 2 tablespoons prepared horseradish
1 tablespoon honey
1-1/2 teaspoons lemon juice
1-1/2 teaspoons Worcestershire sauce
1/8 to 1/4 teaspoon cayenne pepper
1 garlic clove, minced
Miniature hot dogs *or* smoked sausage links, warmed
Sliced apples *or* pears

In a small saucepan, combine the first seven ingredients; bring to a boil, stirring constantly. Reduce heat. Cover and simmer for 5 minutes, stirring occasionally. Serve warm with sausage and/or fruit. **Yield:** 3/4 cup.

STAR FRUIT FACTS

CARAMBOLA is nicknamed star fruit because when it's cut crosswise, the slices are shaped like stars (see garnish on Hot 'n' Spicy Cranberry Dip above right). The more golden-colored the fruit is, the sweeter it will be. There's no need to peel the shiny skin, but you may want to remove the brown fibers from the ridges before slicing. Refrigerate completely yellow fruit in a plastic bag for 1 week.

Hearty Alfredo Potatoes

With turkey and broccoli, this special scalloped potato dish is a meal in itself.
Using a jar of Alfredo sauce makes the preparation time minimal.
—Lissa Hutson, Phelan, California

1 jar (16 ounces) Alfredo sauce
1 cup milk
1 teaspoon garlic powder
3 pounds potatoes, peeled and
    thinly sliced
5 tablespoons grated Parmesan
    cheese, *divided*
Salt and pepper to taste
2 to 3 cups diced cooked turkey
1 package (10 ounces) frozen
    chopped broccoli, thawed
2 cups (8 ounces) shredded
    Swiss cheese, *divided*

In a bowl, combine Alfredo sauce, milk and garlic powder; pour a fourth of the mixture into a greased 13-in. x 9-in. x 2-in. baking dish. Layer with a fourth of the potatoes; sprinkle with 1 tablespoon Parmesan cheese, salt and pepper.

In a bowl, combine the turkey, broccoli and 1-1/2 cups Swiss cheese; spoon a third over potatoes. Repeat layers twice. Top with remaining potatoes. Cover with remaining Swiss and Parmesan cheeses. Spread with remaining Alfredo sauce mixture.

Cover and bake at 400° for 45 minutes. Reduce heat to 350°. Bake, uncovered, 30 minutes longer or until potatoes are tender. Let stand for 15 minutes before serving. **Yield:** 6-8 servings.

PREPPING POTATOES

TO SAVE TIME, you can peel the potatoes for Hearty Alfredo Potatoes up to 2 hours in advance. Rinse and place in a bowl of cold water. Drain and thinly slice just before preparing the recipe.

Turkey Shepherd's Pie

We live way out in the country, and the nearest grocery store is 25 miles away.
So I've become quite skilled at turning leftovers into second-time-around successes like this.
—Linda Howe, Jackman, Maine

2 cups cubed cooked turkey
3/4 cup turkey gravy
1 cup shredded carrots
2 cups prepared stuffing
1 can (15-1/4 ounces) whole
    kernel corn, drained
2 cups warm mashed potatoes

In a greased 2-qt. baking dish, layer the turkey, gravy, carrots, stuffing and corn. Top with potatoes. Bake, uncovered, at 325° for 45-50 minutes or until edges of potatoes are browned. **Yield:** 4-5 servings.

All-American Turkey Potpie

(Pictured at right)

Ever since my sister-in-law shared this recipe with me, I haven't made any other kind of potpie. The crust is very easy to work with.
— Laureen Naylor
Factoryville, Pennsylvania

2 cups all-purpose flour
1/2 teaspoon salt
1/2 cup finely shredded cheddar cheese
2/3 cup shortening
2 tablespoons cold butter *or* margarine
3 to 4 tablespoons cold water

FILLING:
1 cup diced peeled potatoes
1/2 cup thinly sliced carrots
1/3 cup chopped celery
1/4 cup chopped onion
1 garlic clove, minced
1 tablespoon butter *or* margarine
1 cup chicken *or* turkey broth
2 tablespoons all-purpose flour
1/2 cup milk
1-1/2 cups cubed cooked turkey
1/2 cup frozen peas, thawed
1/2 cup frozen corn, thawed
1/2 teaspoon salt
1/4 teaspoon dried tarragon
1/4 teaspoon pepper

In a food processor, combine flour and salt; cover and pulse to blend. Add cheese; pulse until fine crumbs form. Add shortening and butter; pulse until coarse crumbs form. Gradually add water until dough forms a ball. Divide dough in half with one ball slightly larger than the other; wrap in plastic wrap. Refrigerate for 30 minutes.

For filling, in a large saucepan, saute potatoes, carrots, celery, onion and garlic in butter for 5-6 minutes. Add broth; cover and cook for 10 minutes or until vegetables are tender. In a small bowl, combine flour and milk until smooth. Gradually add to vegetable mixture. Bring to a boil; cook and stir for 2 minutes or until thickened. Add the remaining ingredients; simmer 5 minutes longer.

Roll out larger pastry ball to fit a 9-in. pie plate; transfer to pie plate. Trim pastry even with edge. Pour hot turkey filling into crust. Roll out remaining pastry to fit top of pie; place over filling. Trim, seal and flute edges. Cut slits in top or make decorative cutouts in pastry. Bake at 350° for 35-45 minutes or until crust is light golden brown. Serve immediately. **Yield:** 6-8 servings.

Country Potato Dressing

My family can't get enough dressing around the holidays. With this recipe,
I use up leftover mashed potatoes to create a tasty new dish.
—Lauren Buckner, Greenville, South Carolina

1 large onion, chopped
3/4 cup chopped celery
1/4 cup butter *or* margarine
1/4 cup turkey *or* chicken broth
8 slices day-old white bread,
  crusts removed and cubed
3 cups mashed potatoes
1 egg, beaten
1-1/2 teaspoons poultry seasoning
1 teaspoon salt
1/4 teaspoon pepper
1/4 teaspoon ground nutmeg

In a small skillet, saute onion and celery in butter until tender. Remove from the heat; stir in broth. In a large bowl, combine bread cubes, potatoes, egg and seasonings. Stir in onion mixture. Transfer to a greased 2-qt. baking dish. Cover and bake at 325° for 50-60 minutes or until a meat thermometer reads 160°. **Yield:** 6-8 servings.

Broccoli Souffle

This recipe is from my mom's fabulous collection. Without fail, I serve it every holiday
and the dish gets emptied every time. It's a clever way to get kids to eat broccoli.
—Marilyn Rockwell, Lynden, Washington

6 eggs
2 teaspoons dry bread crumbs
1/2 cup butter *or* margarine
1/2 cup all-purpose flour
1/2 teaspoon salt
1/4 teaspoon pepper
2 cups milk
4 cups cooked chopped
  broccoli, patted dry
2 tablespoons chopped onion
1 cup mayonnaise*
1/2 cup shredded cheddar cheese,
  optional

Separate the eggs. Let yolks and whites stand at room temperature for up to 30 minutes. Grease a 2-1/2-qt. souffle dish and dust with bread crumbs; set aside.

In a saucepan, melt butter. Stir in the flour, salt and pepper until smooth. Gradually add milk. Bring to a boil; cook and stir for 2 minutes or until thickened. Stir in broccoli and onion. Remove from the heat; stir in egg yolks until combined. Cool slightly. Stir in mayonnaise.

In a mixing bowl, beat egg whites until stiff peaks form. Stir a fourth of the egg whites into the broccoli mixture. Fold in remaining whites. Transfer to prepared souffle dish. Sprinkle with cheese if desired.

Bake at 325° for 38-42 minutes or until top is golden brown, a toothpick inserted near the side comes out clean and a meat thermometer reads 160°. Serve immediately. **Yield:** 8-10 servings.

*Editor's Note: Reduced-fat or fat-free mayonnaise may not be substituted for regular mayonnaise in this recipe.

Lemony Turkey Rice Soup

(Pictured at right)

While growing up in Texas, I spent a lot of time helping my grandma cook. Lemon and cilantro add a deliciously different twist to turkey soup.
—Margarita Cuellar
East Chicago, Indiana

6 cups chicken broth, *divided*
1 can (10-3/4 ounces) condensed cream of chicken soup, undiluted
2 cups cooked rice
2 cups diced cooked turkey
1/4 teaspoon pepper
2 tablespoons cornstarch
1/4 to 1/3 cup lemon juice
1/4 to 1/2 cup minced fresh cilantro *or* parsley

In a large saucepan, combine 5-1/2 cups of broth, soup, rice, turkey and pepper. Bring to a boil; boil for 3 minutes. In a small bowl, combine cornstarch and remaining broth until smooth. Gradually stir into hot soup. Cook and stir for 1-2 minutes or until thickened and heated through. Remove from the heat; stir in lemon juice and cilantro. **Yield:** 8 servings (about 2 quarts).

Swiss Creamed Peas

A creamy cheese sauce turns ordinary peas into a succulent side dish. I make this quite often for family gatherings, and it's always well received.
—Lin Carr, West Seneca, New York

1 cup chopped green onions
4-1/2 teaspoons butter *or* margarine
1 tablespoon all-purpose flour
1/2 teaspoon salt
1 cup whipping cream
3/4 cup shredded Swiss cheese
3 cups cooked peas

In a large saucepan, saute onions in butter until tender. Stir in flour and salt until blended; gradually add the cream. Bring to a boil; cook and stir for 2 minutes or until thickened. Reduce heat; stir in cheese until melted. Add peas; cook and stir until heated through. **Yield:** 4 servings.

EASTER *Gatherings*

Be a good egg this year and offer to host a
rise-and-shine brunch on Easter morning.
Brunch items such as eggs, salads, breads and desserts
are frequently fast to fix or can be started ahead of
time. For a more traditional dinner, nothing takes you
back in time like a hearty ham feast. What
a wonderful way to herald the arrival of spring!

Rise-and-Shine Easter Brunch

IF YOU'RE reluctant to invite family and friends to a fancy sit-down Easter dinner, why not offer to host a more casual brunch?

Impressive-looking fare does not have to take a lot of time to prepare, especially if you entertain early in the day.

That's because brunch items like eggs, salads, breads, desserts and more are frequently fast to fix or can be started ahead of time.

In the brunch buffet shown at right, Glazed Bacon cooks in a little more than 30 minutes, while Strawberry Cream Tarts and Asparagus Lasagna can partially be prepared in advance. Plus you can bake Easter Egg Sugar Cookies days before.

Such culinary convenience is "eggs-cellent" for any cook!

Easter Egg Sugar Cookies

(Pictured at right and on page 150)

Although they take some time to decorate, I enjoy giving these cookies to family and friends.
You can also make them for Christmas using different cookie cutters.
—Alison Benke, Chetwynd, British Columbia

1 **cup butter (no substitutes),**
    softened
1-1/4 **cups sugar**
    3 **eggs**
    1 **teaspoon vanilla extract**
    1/2 **teaspoon almond extract**
3-1/2 **cups all-purpose flour**
    1 **teaspoon baking powder**
    1/2 **teaspoon salt**
ICING:
    2 **cups confectioners' sugar**
    1 **tablespoon meringue powder***
    1/4 **cup warm water**
    1/2 **teaspoon almond extract**
Liquid food coloring
Pastel organdy ribbon (1/4 inch
    wide), cut into 12-inch lengths,
    optional

In a mixing bowl, cream butter and sugar. Add eggs, one at a time, beating well after each addition. Add extracts. Combine the flour, baking powder and salt; gradually add to creamed mixture. Cover and refrigerate for 1 hour or until easy to handle.

On a lightly floured surface, roll out dough to 1/4-in. thickness. Cut with a 2-1/2-in. egg-shaped cookie cutter. Place 1 in. apart on lightly greased baking sheets. If desired, make a hole for a ribbon by pressing a plastic straw 1/2 in. from the top of each cookie. Bake at 375° for 8-10 minutes or until lightly browned. Remove to wire racks to cool.

For icing, sift confectioners' sugar and meringue powder into a mixing bowl. Add water and extract; beat on low speed until blended. Beat on high for 5 minutes. Fill a pastry or plastic bag with 1 cup of icing; cut a small hole in the corner of the bag. Outline each cookie with icing. Tint remaining icing with food coloring if desired. Add water, a few drops at a time, until mixture is thin enough to flow smoothly. Fill in the center space of each cookie, allowing the icing to spread to the outline. Let dry overnight.

Decorate with remaining icing. Store in airtight containers. If desired, thread ribbon through holes, tie ends in a bow and hang on an Easter tree. **Yield:** about 4-1/2 dozen.

*Editor's Note: Meringue powder can be ordered by mail from Wilton Industries, Inc. Call 1-800/794-5866 or visit their Web site at *www.wilton.com*.

Easter Egg Cookie Tree

(Pictured at right)

GO OUT ON A LIMB and make an Easter tree "blooming" with colorful egg-shaped cookies!

To create the tree shown at right, we started with a small painted metal pail. Other options include a clay pot, watering can or large decorated vase. The possibilities are endless…just be sure it's watertight.

Fill the container half full with sand or aquarium gravel. Cut floral foam to fit; press into place on top of the sand or gravel and add water.

Cut and arrange several live branches (we used lilac and forsythia) in a tree shape as desired. Insert the ends of the branches into the container, making sure they reach the water.

Arrange Easter grass or shredded paper around the base of the tree to cover the floral foam. Hang cookies from the branches.

Glazed Bacon

(Pictured on page 151)

Everyone agrees this bacon tastes just like candy. My mom would make it for special-occasion breakfasts. Now I serve it when our grown kids come home to visit.
—Janet Nolan, Navesink, New Jersey

1 pound sliced bacon
1 cup packed brown sugar
1/4 cup orange juice
2 tablespoons Dijon mustard

Place bacon on a rack in an ungreased 15-in. x 10-in. x 1-in. baking pan. Bake at 350° for 10 minutes; drain. Combine the brown sugar, orange juice and mustard; pour half over bacon. Bake for 10 minutes. Turn bacon and drizzle with remaining glaze. Bake 15 minutes longer or until golden brown. Place bacon on waxed paper until set. Serve warm. **Yield:** 8 servings.

Asparagus Lasagna

(Pictured on page 150)

I received this recipe from my mother, who lives in an area known for its fine asparagus.
You can assemble the casserole the night before and refrigerate.
Just remove it from the refrigerator 30 minutes before baking.
— Bev Angebrandt, Calgary, Alberta

  3 pounds fresh asparagus, cut
    into 1-inch pieces
1/3 cup butter *or* margarine
1/2 cup all-purpose flour
1-1/2 teaspoons salt
1/4 teaspoon pepper
  5 cups milk
  1 package (8 ounces) cream
    cheese, cubed
  1 tablespoon lemon juice
  1 teaspoon grated lemon peel
1/4 teaspoon ground nutmeg
 12 lasagna noodles, cooked and
    drained
  2 cups (8 ounces) shredded
    mozzarella cheese
1/3 cup shredded Parmesan
    cheese

In a large saucepan, cook asparagus in a small amount of water until crisp-tender, about 7 minutes; drain and set aside. In another large saucepan, melt butter. Stir in flour, salt and pepper until smooth. Gradually stir in milk. Bring to a boil; cook and stir for 2 minutes or until thickened. Stir in cream cheese, lemon juice, peel and nutmeg until cheese is melted.

Spread about 3/4 cup sauce in a greased 13-in. x 9-in. x 2-in. baking dish. Layer with three noodles, a fourth of the sauce and a third of the asparagus and mozzarella. Repeat layers twice. Top with remaining noodles and sauce (dish will be full). Sprinkle with Parmesan. Bake, uncovered, at 375° for 45-50 minutes or until bubbly and golden brown. Let stand for 15 minutes before cutting. **Yield:** 12 servings.

Asparagus Tips

THE PEAK MONTHS for buying asparagus are April and May. When buying, look for firm, straight, uniform-size spears. The tips should be closed with crisp stalks.

It's best to use asparagus within a few days of purchase. For a little longer storage, place bundled stalks upright in a bowl filled with 1 inch of water; refrigerate. Or wrap the cut ends in moist paper towels. Cover the towel with plastic wrap; refrigerate.

To clean, soak asparagus in cold water. Cut or snap off the tough white portion.

Strawberry Cream Tarts

(Pictured at right and on page 151)

Dainty tarts filled with custard and fruit are fantastic for brunch. The recipe comes from our Test Kitchen. For a prettier presentation, remove the foil tins before serving. To do so, invert each shell when cool and carefully remove the foil.

> 2 packages (6 count *each*) individual graham cracker tart shells
> 2 egg whites, beaten
> 1 cup sugar
> 1/2 cup plus 2 tablespoons all-purpose flour
> 3 cups milk
> 2 eggs, beaten
> 6 tablespoons butter *or* margarine, cubed
> 2 tablespoons lemon juice
> 12 medium strawberries, sliced
> 12 blueberries
> 6 tablespoons strawberry jelly, melted

Brush insides of tart shells with egg whites. Place on two baking sheets. Bake at 350° for 5 minutes. Cool completely on wire racks.

In a heavy saucepan, combine the sugar and flour; gradually stir in milk until smooth. Bring to a boil over medium heat, stirring constantly; cook and stir for 1 minute. Remove from the heat. Stir a small amount of hot milk mixture into eggs; return all to the pan, stirring constantly. Bring to a gentle boil; cook and stir for 1 minute. Remove from the heat. Stir in butter and lemon juice. Refrigerate until chilled.

Just before serving, spoon custard into shells; top with strawberries and blueberries. Spoon jelly over fruit. **Yield:** 12 servings.

Baked Fruit Medley

Years ago, I would frequently serve my staff at work breakfast to thank them for their hard work. This comforting fruit casserole was always on the menu.
—Patricia Swanson, Cabot, Arkansas

> 1 can (29 ounces) pear halves
> 1 can (11 ounces) mandarin oranges, drained
> 1 teaspoon grated lime peel
> 1/3 cup packed brown sugar
> 1/4 cup flaked coconut

Drain pears, reserving 1/2 cup juice; set juice aside. Place pears, oranges and lime peel in an ungreased 11-in. x 7-in. x 2-in. baking dish. Combine brown sugar and pear juice; stir until sugar is dissolved. Pour over fruit. Sprinkle with coconut. Bake, uncovered, at 350° for 25-30 minutes or until heated through. Serve warm or chilled. **Yield:** 3-4 servings.

Feather-Light Doughnuts

A sweet cranberry-orange glaze is the perfect topping for these fluffy doughnuts.
Friends and family request a batch of these treats instead of a birthday present!
—Shirley Johnson, Warrens, Wisconsin

2 packages (1/4 ounce *each*)
    active dry yeast
1/2 cup warm water
    (110° to 115°)
1-1/2 cups warm milk
    (110° to 115°)
1/2 cup butter *or* margarine,
    softened
1/2 cup sugar
2 eggs, lightly beaten
2 teaspoons salt
6 to 6-1/2 cups all-purpose flour
Oil for deep-fat frying
GLAZE:
3 cups confectioners' sugar
3/4 cup cranberry juice
1 tablespoon orange extract

In a large mixing bowl, dissolve yeast in warm water. Add milk, butter, sugar, eggs, salt and 2 cups flour; beat until smooth. Stir in enough remaining flour to form a soft dough. Turn onto a floured surface; knead until smooth and elastic, about 6-8 minutes. Place in a greased bowl, turning once to grease top. Cover and let rise in a warm place until doubled, about 1 hour.

Punch dough down. Turn onto a floured surface; roll out to 1/2-in. thickness. Cut with a floured 2-1/2-in. doughnut cutter. Place on greased baking sheets. Cover and let rise until doubled, about 1 hour.

In an electric skillet or deep-fat fryer, heat oil to 375°. Fry doughnuts, a few at a time, for 2 minutes on each side or until golden brown. Drain on paper towels. In a shallow bowl, combine glaze ingredients until smooth; dip warm doughnuts. Cool on wire racks. **Yield:** 3 dozen.

Multigrain Waffles

These hearty waffles are great for breakfast and brunch.
A blend of spices makes them more special than ordinary waffles.
—Irene Greenhaw, Hobbs, New Mexico

1-1/2 cups all-purpose flour
1/2 cup whole wheat flour
1/4 cup oat bran
1 tablespoon sugar, optional
2 teaspoons baking powder
1 teaspoon baking soda
1 teaspoon ground cinnamon
1/2 teaspoon salt
1/4 teaspoon ground cloves
1/8 teaspoon ground nutmeg
3 eggs, *separated*

1-1/2 cups milk
6 tablespoons butter *or* margarine, melted
Maple *or* fruit syrup, yogurt and berries

In a mixing bowl, combine the first 10 ingredients. In another bowl, beat egg yolks, milk and butter; stir into dry ingredients just until moistened. In a small mixing bowl, beat egg whites until stiff peaks form; fold into the batter. Bake in a preheated waffle iron according to the manufacturer's directions until golden brown. Serve with syrup, yogurt and berries. **Yield:** 8 waffles.

Stuffed French Toast

(Pictured at right)

This recipe takes a little longer to prepare than regular French toast, but I think it's worth it, especially on holiday mornings. The sweet apricot syrup complements the cream cheese filling.
—*Karen Leutz, Sylvania, Ohio*

8 slices French bread (1 inch thick)
2 packages (3 ounces *each*) cream cheese, softened
1/3 cup crushed pineapple, undrained
1/2 cup chopped pecans
4 eggs
1 cup whipping cream
1/2 teaspoon vanilla extract
1-1/2 teaspoons ground ginger

APRICOT SYRUP:
1 jar (12 ounces) apricot preserves
1/3 cup orange juice

Cut a pocket through the crust of each slice of bread. In a mixing bowl, beat the cream cheese and pineapple; stir in pecans. Stuff into pockets. In a shallow bowl, beat the eggs, cream, vanilla and ginger; dip both sides of bread. Cook on a greased hot griddle until golden brown on both sides.

Combine syrup ingredients in a saucepan; heat until warmed, stirring constantly. Serve with the French toast. **Yield:** 4 servings (1-1/3 cups syrup).

Minty Lime Gelatin

Crushed butter mints in this gelatin salad's topping lend a refreshing flavor to every bite. I make it for spring luncheons.
—*Eunice Stoen, Decorah, Iowa*

1 can (20 ounces) crushed pineapple, undrained
1 package (3 ounces) lime gelatin
1 package (10-1/2 ounces) miniature marshmallows
1 package (8 ounces) butter mints, finely crushed
1 cup whipping cream, whipped

Place pineapple with juice in a large bowl. Sprinkle with gelatin; stir until dissolved. Add marshmallows. Pour into a 13-in. x 9-in. x 2-in. dish. Chill for 6 hours or until set. In a bowl, fold butter mints into whipped cream. Spread over gelatin. Cut into squares. **Yield:** 10-12 servings.

Ham 'n' Cheese Brunch Strips

These handheld sandwich strips from the home economists in our Test Kitchen pair well with scrambled eggs. If desired, substitute slices of cooked chicken for the ham.

2 tablespoons Dijon mustard
8 slices white bread, crusts removed
8 slices Swiss cheese
4 thin slices deli ham
2 tablespoons butter *or* margarine, softened

Spread mustard over four slices of bread. Top each with a slice of cheese, ham and another cheese slice. Top with remaining bread. Butter the outside of the sandwiches. Cook on a griddle or in a large skillet over medium heat until golden brown on both sides. Remove to a cutting board; cut each sandwich lengthwise into thirds. **Yield:** 4 servings.

Easter Nest Coffee Cake

The first time I made this clever coffee cake for family and friends, it was a huge hit. Our kids usually eat an "egg" and then a slice of the "nest"!
—Dian Burge, Friedheim, Missouri

3-3/4 to 4-1/4 cups all-purpose flour
1/4 cup sugar
1 package (1/4 ounce) active dry yeast
1 teaspoon salt
1/2 cup milk
1/4 cup water
1/4 cup butter *or* margarine
1 egg
GLAZE:
1 cup confectioners' sugar
1/4 teaspoon vanilla extract
2 to 3 tablespoons milk
Assorted colored sugar
1/2 teaspoon water
3 drops green food coloring
1 cup flaked coconut

In a large mixing bowl, combine 2 cups of flour, sugar, yeast and salt. In a saucepan, heat the milk, water and butter to 120°-130°. Add to dry ingredients; beat until blended. Add egg and 1/2 cup flour; beat until smooth. Stir in enough remaining flour to form a soft dough. Turn onto a lightly floured surface; knead until smooth and elastic, about 4-6 minutes. Place in a greased bowl, turning once to grease top. Cover and let rise in a warm place until doubled, about 1 hour.

Punch dough down. Turn onto a lightly floured surface; divide into thirds. Cover and let rest for 10 minutes. Shape one portion of dough into six egg-shaped rolls. Arrange rolls with sides touching in the center of a large greased baking sheet. Roll each remaining portion of dough into 24-in. ropes; twist together. Wrap around the rolls; pinch ends together to seal.

Cover and let rise in a warm place until doubled, about 45 minutes. Bake at 375° for 15-20 minutes or until golden brown. Remove from pan to a wire rack to cool.

For glaze, combine the confectioners' sugar, vanilla and enough milk to achieve drizzling consistency. Drizzle over coffee cake. Immediately sprinkle eggs with colored sugar. For grass, combine water and food coloring in a jar with a tight-fitting lid. Add coconut; shake until tinted. Sprinkle around edge of coffee cake nest. **Yield:** 1 loaf.

Spinach Crescents

(Pictured at right)

These spinach-stuffed rolls are a great way to get my son to eat his vegetables! I experimented with the recipe after tasting similar bundles years ago.
—Susan James, Manhattan, Kansas

1/2 cup sliced almonds
1 package (10 ounces) frozen chopped spinach, thawed and squeezed dry
1/2 cup grated Parmesan cheese
1/4 cup chopped onion
2 teaspoons olive *or* vegetable oil
1/4 teaspoon salt
1/8 teaspoon pepper
1 package (8 ounces) refrigerated crescent rolls

In a food processor or blender, finely chop the almonds. Add spinach, Parmesan cheese, onion, oil, salt and pepper; cover and process until well blended. Unroll and separate the crescent dough into eight pieces. Spread spinach mixture evenly over dough to within 1/8 in. of edges. Roll up and place on a greased baking sheet. Bake at 375° for 15-18 minutes or until golden brown. Serve warm. **Yield:** 8 servings.

Pink Rhubarb Punch

The grapefruit flavor really shines in this pretty punch. I serve it at family gatherings throughout the year.
—Dianne Sears, Prince George, British Columbia

8 cups chopped fresh *or* frozen rhubarb, thawed (about 2 pounds)
6 cups water
3-1/2 cups grapefruit juice
2-1/2 cups sugar
1/4 cup lemon juice
1 liter ginger ale, chilled

In a large saucepan, bring rhubarb and water to a boil. Reduce heat; simmer, uncovered, for 10-12 minutes or until rhubarb is very tender. Strain and discard pulp. Return rhubarb juice to the saucepan; add the grapefruit juice, sugar and lemon juice. Bring to a boil; cook and stir until sugar is dissolved. Cool slightly. Cover and refrigerate until chilled. Just before serving, transfer to a punch bowl and stir in ginger ale. **Yield:** 3-1/2 quarts.

Spiced Rhubarb Pork Chops

My husband and I own a small restaurant in the middle of Amish country. Our menu often features recipes using rhubarb from our garden. This savory pork dish is a favorite.
—*Connie Hamilton, Hazleton, Iowa*

1-1/2 cups chopped fresh rhubarb
    (1/2-inch pieces)
1/2 cup chicken broth
2 tablespoons sugar
1 tablespoon honey
1/2 teaspoon ground cinnamon
1/2 teaspoon ground ginger
1/4 teaspoon ground nutmeg
Red food coloring, optional
4 bone-in pork loin chops
    (3/4 inch thick)
1 tablespoon vegetable oil
Salt and pepper to taste

In a saucepan, combine the rhubarb, broth, sugar and honey; cook over medium heat until rhubarb is tender. Stir in the cinnamon, ginger, nutmeg and food coloring if desired.

In a large skillet, brown pork chops in oil. Sprinkle with salt and pepper. Pour rhubarb mixture over the chops. Cover and simmer for 35-40 minutes or until meat juices run clear, turning once. **Yield:** 4 servings.

RHUBARB BASICS

LOOK FOR rhubarb stalks that are crisp and brightly colored. Tightly wrap in a plastic bag and store in the refrigerator for up to 3 days. Wash the stalks and remove the poisonous leaves before using. One pound of rhubarb yields about 3 cups chopped.

Savory Cheddar Egg Bake

This do-head dish features three kinds of bread, giving it a deliciously different taste.
—*Shirley Roby, Johnstown, Ohio*

4 slices *each* wheat, rye and
    Italian bread, cut into
    1-inch cubes
2 cups cubed fully cooked ham
2 cups (8 ounces) shredded
    cheddar cheese, *divided*
1 teaspoon minced fresh
    parsley
1/2 teaspoon dried minced onion
1/2 teaspoon dried basil
1/8 teaspoon pepper

6 eggs
2-1/2 cups milk

Layer half of the bread cubes in a greased 13-in. x 9-in. x 2-in. baking dish. Sprinkle with ham and 1 cup cheese. Top with remaining bread cubes. Combine the parsley, onion, basil and pepper; sprinkle over bread. In a bowl, beat the eggs and milk; pour over the top. Sprinkle with remaining cheese. Cover and refrigerate overnight.

Remove from the refrigerator 30 minutes before baking. Bake, uncovered, at 350° for 40-50 minutes or until a knife inserted near the center comes out clean. **Yield:** 8 servings.

Peanut Butter Eggs

(Pictured at right)

These easy-to-make confections are a must for me at Easter. Have youngsters help shape the eggs, then reward them with some of the chocolaty candies.
— Ethel Charles
Elizabethtown, Pennsylvania

- **1 package (8 ounces) cream cheese, softened**
- **1/2 cup butter *or* margarine, softened**
- **1 jar (17.3 ounces) creamy peanut butter**
- **1 teaspoon vanilla extract**
- **1 package (2 pounds) confectioners' sugar**
- **2 cups flaked coconut, optional**
- **6 cups (36 ounces) semisweet chocolate chips**
- **1/3 cup shortening**

In a mixing bowl, beat cream cheese, butter, peanut butter and vanilla until smooth. Beat in sugar. Stir in coconut if desired. Form rounded tablespoonfuls into egg shapes. Place on waxed paper-lined baking sheets. Chill for 30 minutes.

In a microwave-safe bowl or heavy saucepan, melt chocolate chips and shortening; stir until smooth. Dip eggs until coated; place on waxed paper to harden. For more decorative eggs, place about 1/4 cup melted chocolate in a small plastic bag. Cut a hole in the corner of the bag; pipe chocolate over tops of eggs. Store in the refrigerator. **Yield:** about 5-1/2 dozen.

Family Traditions

EVERY EASTER, Grandma would bake and decorate big Italian cookies in the shape of eggs, bunnies and baskets. She and Grandpa would tuck them into baskets for all of us kids to find at their house on Easter morning. We couldn't wait to nibble on those delectable cookies! Now that I'm older, I look forward to baking and decorating the cookies as much as I do eating them.
—*Niki Malmberg-Trapp, Cudahy, Wisconsin*

Chocolate Cinnamon Crescents

I dress up ordinary crescent rolls with cinnamon and chocolate to create mouth-watering breakfast rolls. A little glaze and sprinkling of nuts tops them nicely.
—Denise Hayward, Ames, Iowa

1/4 cup sugar
3 tablespoons baking cocoa
1-1/2 teaspoons ground cinnamon
2 tablespoons butter *or* margarine, softened, *divided*
2 tubes (8 ounces *each*) refrigerated crescent rolls
1/2 cup chopped pistachios, pecans *or* almonds

GLAZE:
1/2 cup confectioners' sugar
3 to 4 teaspoons milk
Finely chopped pistachios, pecans *or* almonds

In a small bowl, combine the sugar, cocoa and cinnamon. Add 1 tablespoon butter; mix well. Separate crescent dough into 16 triangles. Melt remaining butter; brush over dough. Sprinkle cocoa mixture and nuts over each triangle; roll up. Place on ungreased baking sheets. Bake at 375° for 11-13 minutes or until golden brown. Remove to wire racks.

For glaze, in a bowl, combine confectioners' sugar and milk; drizzle over rolls. Sprinkle with nuts. **Yield:** 16 rolls.

Salmon with Herb-Mustard Sauce

This recipe has evolved over the years. It turns out moist and delicious every time and is especially wonderful served with the seasoned sauce.
—Marion Lowery, Medford, Oregon

2 cups mayonnaise
1 tablespoon Dijon mustard
1 tablespoon snipped fresh dill *or* 1 teaspoon dill weed
1 tablespoon minced fresh marjoram *or* 1 teaspoon dried marjoram
1 teaspoon minced fresh thyme *or* 1/2 teaspoon dried thyme
1 whole salmon (5 to 7 pounds), head and tail removed
2 teaspoons coarsely ground pepper
1/2 teaspoon salt

1 tablespoon balsamic vinegar
2 medium lemons, sliced
1/2 cup butter *or* margarine, melted

In a small bowl, combine the mayonnaise, mustard, dill, marjoram and thyme; cover and refrigerate until serving.

Place fish in the center of a large greased sheet of aluminum foil. Sprinkle inside of salmon with pepper and salt and drizzle with vinegar. Place overlapping lemon slices inside salmon to completely cover. Use wooden toothpicks to secure cavity along opening. Drizzle butter over the top.

Fold foil over fish and seal. Place on a large baking sheet. Bake at 325° for 80-95 minutes or until fish flakes easily with a fork. Serve with the herb-mustard sauce. **Yield:** 10 servings.

Grapefruit Alaska

(Pictured at right)

You'll easily impress guests with this dessert. It takes some time to prepare, but the rave reviews I receive make it all worth it.
—Peg Atzen, Hackensack, Minnesota

4 large grapefruit
2 teaspoons rum extract
1/2 cup whipping cream, whipped
3 egg whites
1 teaspoon cornstarch
1/4 teaspoon cream of tartar
1/4 cup sugar
8 maraschino cherries

Halve and section grapefruit; remove membranes. Return grapefruit sections to grapefruit halves. Drizzle 1/4 teaspoon rum extract over each. Top each with 1 rounded tablespoon of whipped cream; place on an ungreased foil-lined baking sheet.

In a mixing bowl, beat the egg whites, cornstarch and cream of tartar on medium speed until soft peaks form. Gradually beat in sugar, 1 tablespoon at a time, on high until stiff glossy peaks form and sugar is dissolved. Mound 1/2 cup on each grapefruit half; spread meringue to edges to seal. Bake at 350° for 15 minutes or until meringue is browned. Top each with a cherry. Serve immediately. **Yield:** 8 servings.

Creamy Fruit Salad

When my mother passed away, she left me a legacy of love—her treasured recipe collection, including this old-time favorite. She would serve this flavorful fruit salad in her best crystal bowl.
—Audrey Groe, Lake Mills, Iowa

1 can (20 ounces) pineapple chunks
1 can (11 ounces) mandarin oranges
1 package (3 ounces) cook-and-serve vanilla pudding mix
1 cup sliced fresh strawberries
1/2 cup maraschino cherries
1 to 2 medium ripe bananas, sliced

Drain pineapple and oranges, reserving juices in a 2-cup measuring cup; set fruit aside. Add enough water to juices to measure 1-1/2 cups. In a saucepan, whisk the juices and pudding mix. Cook and stir over medium heat until mixture comes to a full boil. Cool to room temperature, stirring occasionally.

Fold in the strawberries, cherries and reserved pineapple and oranges. Cover and refrigerate. Just before serving, fold in bananas. **Yield:** 6-8 servings.

Easter Feast Features Ham

THE WONDERFUL AROMA of a ham baking in the oven can take you back in taste and time to special occasions spent in Grandma's kitchen.

And nothing signals Easter and the arrival of spring in such a mouth-watering way!

Family and friends will be called to the kitchen by the sweet and tangy aroma of Plum-Glazed Gingered Ham. No one will be able to resist nibbling!

A medley of meal mates includes creamy Mustard Potatoes Au Gratin and eye-catching Spring Vegetable Bundles.

For dessert, lighter-than-air Lemon Clouds with Custard won't weigh anyone down after dinner.

MEMORABLE MEAL
(Clockwise from bottom left)

Lemon Clouds with Custard (p. 171)

Plum-Glazed Gingered Ham (p. 168)

Spring Vegetable Bundles (p. 167)

Mustard Potatoes Au Gratin (p. 166)

EASTER DINNER TIMELINE

A Few Weeks Before:
- Order a 5- to 7-pound bone-in fully cooked ham from your butcher.
- Prepare two grocery lists—one for non-perishable items to purchase now and one for perishable items to purchase a few days before Easter.
- Look for a vase and ribbon for the Carrot and Daisy Bouquet (see page 170).

Two Days Before:
- Buy ham and remaining grocery items.

The Day Before:
- Set the table.
- Buy carrots and flowers for the Carrot and Daisy Bouquet. Place flowers in water and refrigerate carrots until ready to assemble.
- Prepare and refrigerate glaze for Plum-Glazed Gingered Ham.
- Assemble and refrigerate Mustard Potatoes Au Gratin.

- Make the custard for Lemon Clouds; refrigerate.
- Bake Poppy Seed Easter Cake; let cool. Assemble and decorate as directed; chill.

Easter Day:
- In the morning, make the Carrot and Daisy Bouquet. Assemble the Spring Vegetable Bundles; refrigerate.
- Make the "clouds" for Lemon Clouds with Custard; chill for 2 hours.
- Bake the Plum-Glazed Gingered Ham.
- Remove the Mustard Potatoes Au Gratin from the refrigerator 30 minutes before baking; bake as directed.
- Cook the Spring Vegetable Bundles as directed.
- When the ham is done, prepare the gravy.
- For dessert, assemble Lemon Clouds with Custard and serve alongside Poppy Seed Easter Cake.

Mustard Potatoes Au Gratin

(Pictured on page 165)

These rich and creamy potatoes taste great with a variety of meats.
— Tangee Thaler, Silver Lake, Ohio

1/3 cup finely chopped green onions
3 tablespoons butter *or* margarine, *divided*
2 cups whipping cream

1/2 cup Dijon mustard
1 cup (4 ounces) shredded Swiss *or* Gruyere cheese, *divided*
8 medium potatoes, peeled and thinly sliced

In a small saucepan, cook onions in 1 tablespoon butter for 2 minutes or until tender. Stir in the cream, mustard and remaining butter. Bring to a boil. Reduce heat; simmer, uncovered, for 5 minutes.

Reduce heat to low; stir in half of the cheese until melted. Remove from the heat. In a greased shallow 2-1/2-qt. baking dish, layer a third of the potatoes; top with a third of the sauce. Repeat layers twice; sprinkle with remaining cheese.

Bake, uncovered, at 400° for 30 minutes. Cover and bake 25-30 minutes longer or until potatoes are tender. Let stand for 5 minutes before serving. **Yield:** 12 servings.

Spring Vegetable Bundles

(Pictured at right and on page 165)

You can assemble these bundles from our Test Kitchen before guests arrive, then cook them in mere minutes. To keep them warm while serving, place the serving platter on a heating tray.

  4 to 6 green onions
  1 cup water
  1 pound thin asparagus,* trimmed
  1 medium sweet red pepper, julienned
  1 medium sweet yellow pepper, julienned
  2 medium carrots, julienned
  12 thyme sprigs
1-1/3 cups white wine *or* 1 cup chicken broth
  3 tablespoons butter (no substitutes)

Trim both ends of onions; cut the green tops into 7-in. lengths. In a saucepan, bring water to a boil. Add onion tops; boil for 1 minute or until softened. Drain and immediately place onion tops in ice water. Drain and pat dry. Chop white portion of onions and set aside.

Divide asparagus, peppers and carrots into 12 bundles. Top each with a thyme sprig. Tie each bundle with a blanched onion top.

In a large skillet, place wine or broth, chopped onions and vegetable bundles. Bring to a boil. Cook, uncovered, for 5-7 minutes or until vegetables are tender and liquid is reduced by two-thirds. Carefully remove bundles with a slotted spoon to a serving plate. Add butter to skillet; cook and stir until melted. Spoon over bundles. **Yield:** 12 bundles.

*Editor's Note: Use asparagus spears that are 1/4 inch in diameter. Larger asparagus should be cut lengthwise in half.

Plum-Glazed Gingered Ham

(Pictured on page 164)

Our Test Kitchen home economists created a slightly sweet ham glaze that gets a little kick from ginger and mustard.

2 jars (12 ounces *each*) plum preserves
2 tablespoons lime juice
1 tablespoon grated lime peel
1 tablespoon Dijon mustard
1-1/2 teaspoons ground ginger
 or 2 tablespoons grated fresh gingerroot
3/4 teaspoon pepper

1 bone-in fully cooked ham (5 to 7 pounds)
3 tablespoons all-purpose flour
1-1/4 cups water, *divided*

For glaze, combine the first six ingredients in a saucepan; bring to a boil, stirring constantly. Remove from the heat; set aside. Place ham on a rack in a shallow roasting pan. Score surface of the ham, making diamond shapes 1/2 in. deep. Spoon half of the glaze over ham. Cover and bake at 325° for 1-1/2 hours.

Remove drippings from pan and set aside. Return ham to pan. Bake, uncovered, 30 minutes longer or until a meat thermometer reads 140°, basting twice with remaining glaze.

Skim fat from ham drippings. In a saucepan, combine flour and 1/4 cup water until smooth. Stir in 3/4 cup drippings and remaining water (discard any remaining drippings). Bring to a boil; cook and stir for 2 minutes or until thickened. **Yield:** 8-10 servings (2 cups gravy).

Poppy Seed Easter Cake

(Pictured at right)

A few years ago, this cake became our traditional Easter dinner dessert. It's so much fun to decorate...and so delicious to eat!
—Gena Aschleman
West Columbia, South Carolina

1-1/4 cups butter (no substitutes), softened
1-1/2 cups sugar
    4 eggs
    2 cups (16 ounces) sour cream
1/4 cup milk
    2 tablespoons lemon juice
    1 to 2 tablespoons grated lemon peel
    1 teaspoon vanilla extract
    3 cups all-purpose flour
    2 teaspoons baking powder
    2 teaspoons baking soda
1/4 teaspoon salt
1/4 cup poppy seeds
FROSTING:
    2 packages (8 ounces *each*) cream cheese, softened
    1 cup butter, softened
    8 cups confectioners' sugar
    2 to 3 tablespoons milk, *divided*
Green food coloring
1/2 cup jelly beans

In a large mixing bowl, cream butter and sugar. Add eggs, one at a time, beating well after each addition. Combine the sour cream, milk, lemon juice, peel and vanilla; add to creamed mixture. Combine the flour, baking powder, baking soda and salt; add to the creamed mixture and beat just until combined. Stir in poppy seeds (batter will be thick).

Transfer to three greased and floured 9-in. round baking pans. Bake at 350° for 25-30 minutes or until a toothpick inserted near the center comes out clean. Cool for 10 minutes before removing from pans to wire racks.

For frosting, in a mixing bowl, beat cream cheese and butter until light and fluffy. Gradually beat in sugar. Beat in 2 tablespoons milk. Place 1 cup of frosting in a small bowl and tint pale green; set aside.

To assemble, place one cake layer on a serving plate; frost top with white frosting. Repeat. Top with remaining cake layer. Frost top and sides of cake with remaining frosting.

Cut a small hole in the corner of a pastry or plastic bag; insert round tip No. 3. Fill bag with green frosting. Write "Happy Easter" on top of cake. With multi-opening or grass tip No. 233, pipe green frosting on top of cake to resemble a bird's nest. Pipe green frosting around top edge of cake. Place jelly beans in nest. Store in the refrigerator. **Yield:** 14-16 servings.

Editor's Note: A coupler and round tip No. 2 may be used in place of multi-opening tip No. 233.

Carrot and Daisy Bouquet

(Pictured at right and on page 165)

Folks will root for the hostess when they catch sight of this whimsical spring centerpiece. Be sure to order extra flowers to tuck into the Pocket Napkin Fold.

Fresh carrots with greens
Clear glass vase
White gerbera daisies *or* other
flowers of choice
Additional greens, optional
Coordinating wired ribbon

Cut off the greens from the carrots, leaving a bit of greens on the carrot tops. Immediately place the removed greens in water. Place the carrots, narrow ends down, inside the vase, filling it completely. The carrots should be tight and stand upright.

Fill the vase with water. Insert the daisies between carrots so the carrot tops are covered. Fill in with carrot greens and other greens if desired.

Tie a loose knot in the center of a length of ribbon. Place a strip of double-stick tape around the vase where the ribbon will be. Wrap the ribbon around the vase with the knot in front. Tie a loose knot in the ribbon on the other side of the vase; trim ribbon ends close to the knot.

THE DECORATIVE DESIGN of the Pocket Napkin Fold (pictured at left) creates a pretty place in which you can tuck in flowers, eating utensils or small party favors. Start with a cloth napkin folded into a square. (If using a patterned napkin, make sure the design is the same on both sides.)

1. Fold down the open point of the top layer so it aligns with the closed point. Fold down the open point of the next layer until it's a short distance from the previous point. Repeat with the last layer, placing the open point a short distance from the previous point.

2. Carefully turn over the napkin. Fold the side corners toward the center so they overlap. Carefully turn over the napkin. Set it on a plate; tuck the stem of a single flower in the pocket.

Lemon Clouds with Custard

(Pictured on page 164)

Cool custard on a cloud of fluffy egg whites is the perfect ending to a heavy meal.
—Jessica Wallace, Fort Worth, Texas

11 tablespoons sugar, *divided*
3 tablespoons cornstarch
2 teaspoons grated lemon peel
1-1/3 cups plus 1 tablespoon cold water, *divided*
1/3 cup lemon juice
3 egg whites
1/8 teaspoon cream of tartar
CUSTARD SAUCE:
3 tablespoons sugar
1 tablespoon cornstarch
1-3/4 cups cold milk
3 egg yolks, lightly beaten
1/2 teaspoon vanilla extract

In a heavy saucepan, combine 5 tablespoons sugar, cornstarch and lemon peel. Gradually stir in 1-1/3 cups water until blended. Bring to a boil; cook and stir for 1-2 minutes or until thickened. Remove from the heat; stir in lemon juice. Set aside.

In another heavy saucepan, combine the egg whites, cream of tartar and remaining sugar and water. With a portable mixer, beat on low speed over low heat for 1 minute. Continue beating until mixture reaches 160°. Pour into a large mixing bowl. Beat on high speed until stiff peaks form. Fold into lemon syrup. Cover and refrigerate for at least 2 hours.

For sauce, in a small saucepan, combine sugar and cornstarch. Gradually stir in milk until smooth. Bring to a boil; cook and stir for 2 minutes or until thickened. Remove from the heat. Stir a small amount of hot milk mixture into egg yolks; return all to pan, stirring constantly. Bring to a gentle boil; cook and stir for 2 minutes. Remove from the heat; stir in vanilla. Cover and refrigerate until chilled. Spoon lemon meringue into dessert cups; top with custard sauce. **Yield:** 5-6 servings.

Editor's Note: A stand mixer is recommended for beating the egg whites after they reach 160°.

SPECIAL *Celebrations*

Don't confine your entertaining to Christmas, Thanksgiving and Easter. Chase away winter blues with a satisfying selection of soups and breads, then show your heartfelt sentiments with a Valentine's Day dinner for two. A host of tried-and-true recipes and decorating ideas will prevent you from getting rattled when hosting a baby shower, family reunion picnic or party for Memorial Day or Father's Day. Plus, you'll find special birthday treats that take the cake!

Soups & Breads Warm Up Winter

AFTER you've packed away the colorful holiday decorations, a few months of winter still lay ahead.

To keep the blues at bay, host a casual dinner party for relatives and friends, featuring a slew of down-home comfort foods.

You'll chase away Old Man Winter in a flash when you ladle out hearty helpings of simmering soups like Zippy Potato Soup, Spiced Chili served in Bread Bowls and Kielbasa Bean Soup. Don't forget to pass a basket of oven-fresh Cheddar Buttermilk Biscuits. (All recipes are shown at right.)

Just place a bright bouquet of flowers on the table and you have a satisfying spread that will add a little sunshine to even the most blustery winter day.

Kielbasa Bean Soup

(Pictured on page 174)

*I usually make a double batch of this meaty vegetable soup and freeze some
in serving-size containers. It makes a nice meal for busy days or unexpected guests.*
—Emily Chaney, Penobscot, Maine

4-1/2 cups water
2 cans (14-1/2 ounces *each*) diced tomatoes, undrained
1 can (16 ounces) kidney beans, rinsed and drained
1 can (15-1/2 ounces) great northern beans, rinsed and drained
1 can (15 ounces) garbanzo beans *or* chickpeas, rinsed and drained
2 medium green peppers, chopped
2 medium onions, chopped
2 celery ribs, chopped

1 medium zucchini, sliced
2 teaspoons chicken bouillon granules
2 garlic cloves, minced
2-1/2 teaspoons chili powder
2 teaspoons dried basil
1-1/2 teaspoons salt
1/2 teaspoon pepper
2 bay leaves
3/4 pound fully cooked kielbasa *or* Polish sausage, halved lengthwise and sliced

In a soup kettle or Dutch oven, combine all ingredients except the sausage. Bring to a boil. Reduce heat; cover and simmer for 1 hour. Add sausage and heat through. Discard bay leaves. **Yield:** 12 servings (about 3 quarts).

Cheddar Buttermilk Biscuits

(Pictured on page 174)

*Every bite of these flaky biscuits gets a little kick from cayenne pepper and
sharp cheddar cheese. They're a nice accompaniment to soup and stew.*
—Kimberly Nuttall, San Marcos, California

2 cups all-purpose flour
2 tablespoons sugar
4 teaspoons baking powder
1/2 teaspoon salt
1/4 to 1/2 teaspoon cayenne pepper
1/2 cup cold butter *or* margarine
1/2 cup shredded sharp cheddar cheese
3/4 cup buttermilk

In a bowl, combine the flour, sugar, baking powder, salt and cayenne. Cut in butter until mixture resembles coarse crumbs. Add the cheese and toss. Stir in buttermilk just until moistened.

Turn onto a lightly floured surface; knead 8-10 times. Pat or roll to 1 in. thickness; cut with a floured 2-1/2-in. biscuit cutter. Place 1 in. apart on an ungreased baking sheet. Bake at 425° for 15-18 minutes or until golden brown. Serve warm. **Yield:** 6-8 biscuits.

Zippy Potato Soup

(Pictured at right and on page 175)

*This savory soup has a lot of substance,
especially for the men in the family.
We enjoy brimming bowls all winter long.*
—*Clara Lee Parsons*
Terre Haute, Indiana

3/4 pound sliced bacon, diced
1 medium onion, chopped
8 to 10 potatoes, peeled and cut
　　into chunks
1 medium carrot, grated
5 cups water
1 can (12 ounces) evaporated
　　milk
2 tablespoons butter *or*
　　margarine
4-1/2 teaspoons minced fresh
　　parsley
2 teaspoons Worcestershire
　　sauce

1/2 teaspoon ground mustard
1/2 teaspoon ground nutmeg
1/4 teaspoon salt
1/8 to 1/4 teaspoon cayenne pepper

In a large skillet, cook bacon and onion; drain and set aside. In a soup kettle or Dutch oven, cook the potatoes and carrot in water for 20 minutes or until tender (do not drain). Stir in the remaining ingredients and the bacon mixture. Cook for 10 minutes or until heated through. **Yield:** 14 servings (3-1/2 quarts).

ADD WARMTH TO A WINTER TABLE

CHASE AWAY the winter blues with these colorful ideas for warming up your dinner table.

- Instead of white linens, use brightly colored cloth or paper napkins and tablecloths.
- Add an assortment of fresh flowers in vases of various shapes and sizes. Or top the table with some potted plants.
- Buy a bunch of helium balloons in an array of colors, shapes and sizes. Set them on the table and throughout the house.
- Place tea light candles on tables, counter-

tops and mantels. Nothing creates a warm and inviting atmosphere quite like candles.
- Blanket the table in warmth by using an eye-catching quilt as a tablecloth.
- Clear bowls brimming with red and green apples or lemons and limes add beautiful color and a wonderful fragrance.
- Another "scent-sational" idea is to simmer some apple cider on the stove. The aroma appeals to all, adds a little coziness and serves as a super sipper.

Bread Bowls

(Pictured on page 175)

Instead of offering bread with your favorite kettle creation, our Test Kitchen home economists suggest serving it inside of these bread bowls!

2 packages (1/4 ounce *each*)
   active dry yeast
1 cup warm water
   (110° to 115°)
1 cup warm milk (110° to 115°)
1/2 cup shortening
1/2 cup sugar
2 eggs
2 teaspoons salt
6 to 6-1/2 cups all-purpose flour
Cornmeal

In a mixing bowl, dissolve yeast in warm water. Add the milk, shortening, sugar, eggs, salt and 2 cups flour. Beat until smooth. Stir in enough remaining flour to form a soft dough. Turn onto a floured surface; knead until smooth and elastic, about 6-8 minutes. Place in a greased bowl, turning once to grease top. Cover and let rise in a warm place until doubled, about 1 hour.

Punch dough down. Turn onto a lightly floured surface. Divide into eight pieces; shape each into a ball. Grease two baking sheets and sprinkle with cornmeal. Place four balls 3 in. apart on each prepared pan. Cover and let rise until doubled, about 30 minutes. Bake at 350° for 20-25 minutes or until golden brown. Remove from pans to wire racks to cool.

For bread bowls, cut a thin slice off the top of bread. Hollow out bottom half, leaving a 1/4-in. shell (discard removed bread or save for another use). Fill with chili, chowder or stew. **Yield:** 8 bread bowls.

Spiced Chili

(Pictured on page 175)

My father was a cook in the Army and taught me the basics in the kitchen.
My childhood baby-sitter inspired my love of cooking, too…in fact, she gave me this recipe.
—Julie Brendt, Antelope, California

1-1/2 pounds ground beef
1/2 cup chopped onion
4 garlic cloves, minced
2 cans (16 ounces *each*) kidney
   beans, rinsed and drained
2 cans (15 ounces *each*) tomato
   sauce
2 cans (14-1/2 ounces *each*)
   stewed tomatoes, cut up
1 cup water
2 bay leaves
1/4 cup chili powder
1 tablespoon salt
1 tablespoon brown sugar
1 tablespoon dried basil
1 tablespoon Italian seasoning
1 tablespoon dried thyme
1 tablespoon pepper
1 teaspoon dried oregano
1 teaspoon dried marjoram
Shredded cheddar cheese and additional chopped
   onions, optional

In a large skillet, cook beef, onion and garlic over medium heat until meat is no longer pink; drain. Transfer to a 5-qt. slow cooker. Stir in the beans, tomato sauce, tomatoes, water and seasonings. Cover and cook on low for 4-5 hours. Discard bay leaves. If desired, serve in bread bowls and garnish with cheese and onions. **Yield:** 12 servings (about 3 quarts).

Tomato Basil Bread

(Pictured at right)

This round breads' chewy crust pairs well with a steaming mug of soup. The pretty color and robust flavor are great conversation starters.
—Darlene Hoefs, Schofield, Wisconsin

1 package (1/4 ounce) active
 dry yeast
3/4 cup warm water
 (110° to 115°)
1/4 cup minced fresh basil
1/4 cup grated Parmesan cheese
2 tablespoons tomato paste
1 tablespoon sugar
1 tablespoon olive *or*
 vegetable oil
1 teaspoon salt
1/8 to 1/4 teaspoon crushed red
 pepper flakes
2-1/4 to 2-1/2 cups bread flour

In a mixing bowl, dissolve yeast in water. Stir in basil, Parmesan cheese, tomato paste, sugar, oil, salt, pepper flakes and 2 cups of flour. Stir in enough remaining flour to form a stiff dough. Turn onto a floured surface; knead until smooth and elastic, about 3-5 minutes. Place in a greased bowl, turning once to grease top. Cover and let rise in a warm place until doubled, about 1 hour.

Punch dough down; knead for 1 minute. Shape into a round loaf. Place on a greased baking sheet. Cover and let rise until doubled, about 1 hour. With a sharp knife, cut a large "X" in top of loaf. Bake at 375° for 35-40 minutes or until golden brown. Remove from pan to a wire rack to cool. **Yield:** 1 loaf.

Double Sausage Stromboli

*When the winter winds blow, my family loves this stuffed bread that
I created. Serve it as an appetizer or entree.*
—*Connie Atchley, Westport, Indiana*

1 pound bulk pork sausage
28 pepperoni slices, chopped
3/4 cup shredded mozzarella *or* cheddar cheese
1 package (16 ounces) hot roll mix
1 cup warm water (120° to 130°)
2 tablespooons butter *or* margarine, softened
1 egg, beaten
1 tablespoon dried oregano
1-1/2 teaspoons vegetable oil

In a large skillet, cook sausage over medium heat until no longer pink; add pepperoni. Drain well and pat dry with paper towels; stir in cheese and set aside.

In a bowl, combine contents of hot roll mix, water, butter and egg until dough pulls away from side of bowl and holds together. Turn onto a lightly floured surface; knead until smooth and elastic, about 5 minutes. Cover and let rest for 5 minutes. Pat dough into a greased 15-in. x 10-in. x 1-in. baking pan. Spread sausage mixture lengthwise down the center third of dough; sprinkle with oregano. Fold sides over filling; press edges lightly to seal. Cover and let rise until doubled, about 30 minutes. Brush with oil. Bake at 375° for 20-25 minutes or until golden brown. **Yield:** 6-8 servings.

Shrimp Chowder

*Pretty pink shrimp and green parsley dot this golden chowder.
It's a rich and satisfying first course or main meal.*
—*Anne Bennett, Hockessin, Delaware*

2 large onions, cut into thin wedges
1/4 cup butter *or* margarine
3 cups cubed peeled potatoes
1 cup water
2 teaspoons salt
1/2 teaspoon seasoned pepper
2 pounds uncooked small shrimp, peeled and deveined
6 cups milk
2 cups (8 ounces) shredded sharp cheddar cheese
1/4 cup minced fresh parsley

In a soup kettle or Dutch oven, saute onions in butter until tender. Add potatoes, water, salt and pepper; bring to a boil. Reduce heat; cover and simmer for 15-20 minutes or until potatoes are tender (do not drain). Add shrimp; cook until shrimp turn pink, about 5 minutes.

In a large saucepan over low heat, heat milk. Stir in cheese until melted (do not boil). Add to potato mixture; heat through (do not boil). Stir in parsley. **Yield:** 12 servings (about 3 quarts).

Apple Cider Chicken 'n' Dumplings

(Pictured at right)

I came up with this recipe one fall when I had an abundance of apple cider. Adding some to a down-home classic was a delectable decision.
—Margaret Sumner-Wichmann
Questa, New Mexico

8 chicken thighs (about 3 pounds), skin removed
2 tablespoons butter *or* margarine
1 medium red onion, chopped
1 celery rib, chopped
2 tablespoons minced fresh parsley
Salt and pepper to taste
3 tablespoons all-purpose flour
3 cups chicken broth
1 cup apple cider *or* apple juice
DUMPLINGS:
2 cups all-purpose flour
1 tablespoon baking powder
1/2 teaspoon salt
1 tablespoon cold butter *or* margarine
1 egg, lightly beaten
2/3 cup milk

In a Dutch oven, brown chicken in butter; remove and set aside. In the same pan, combine the onion, celery, parsley, salt and pepper; cook and stir until vegetables are tender. Sprinkle with flour and mix well. Add broth and cider. Bring to a boil; cook and stir for 2 minutes or until thickened. Add chicken. Cover and bake at 350° for 45-50 minutes.

Increase heat to 425°. For dumplings, combine the flour, baking powder and salt in a bowl; cut in butter until crumbly. Combine the egg and milk; stir into dry ingredients just until moistened. Drop batter into 12 mounds onto hot broth. Bake, uncovered, at 425° for 10 minutes. Cover and bake 10 minutes longer or until a toothpick inserted into a dumpling comes out clean. **Yield:** 4 servings.

Valentine's Day Dinner For Two

MAKING DINNER FROM scratch on Valentine's Day is one of the finest ways to display your love for that special someone.

And everything will be coming up rosy when you serve this magical meal for just the two of you.

The first course of Shrimp with Basil-Mango Sauce will bring romance to the table. Notice how two shrimp come together to form a heart?

Then, after dining on rich Veal Scallopini and nicely seasoned Apricot-Ginger Asparagus, dish out dreamy Orange Cheesecake Mousse garnished with easy-to-prepare chocolate hearts. (All recipes shown at right.)

ENCHANTED EATING
(Clockwise from top left)

Veal Scallopini (p. 184)

Apricot-Ginger Asparagus (p. 184)

Orange Cheesecake Mousse (p. 185)

Shrimp with Basil-Mango
Sauce (p. 186)

Veal Scallopini

(Pictured on page 182)

My husband and I prepare this veal dish for birthdays and other special occasions.
We love to cook and often entertain friends and family.
—Karen Bridges, Downers Grove, Illinois

2 tablespoons all-purpose flour
1/8 teaspoon salt
1/8 teaspoon pepper
1 egg
1/2 to 3/4 pound veal cutlets *or*
   boneless skinless chicken
   breasts, flattened to 1-inch
   thickness
2 tablespoons olive *or*
   vegetable oil
4 ounces fresh mushrooms,
   halved
1 cup chicken broth
2 tablespoons marsala wine *or*
   apple juice
Hot cooked spaghetti

In a small bowl, combine the flour, salt, and pepper. In another bowl, lightly beat the egg. Dip veal in egg, then coat with flour mixture.

   In a large skillet, brown veal in oil on both sides. Stir in the mushrooms, broth and wine or apple juice. Bring to a boil. Reduce heat; simmer, uncovered, for 5-10 minutes or until mushrooms are tender. Serve over spaghetti. **Yield:** 2 servings.

Apricot-Ginger Asparagus

(Pictured on page 183)

Our Test Kitchen home economists blend apricot preserves and a few simple seasonings to dress up
tender asparagus spears. This succulent side dish goes great with any entree.

1/2 pound fresh asparagus,
   trimmed
1/4 cup apricot preserves
1 tablespoon red wine vinegar
   or cider vinegar
1/8 teaspoon ground cinnamon
Pinch ground ginger *or* 1/8
   teaspoon minced fresh gingerroot

In a large skillet, bring 1 in. of water to a boil; place asparagus in a steamer basket over water. Cover and steam for 5 minutes or until crisp-tender; drain and keep warm.

   In a small skillet over medium heat, bring the preserves, vinegar, cinnamon and ginger to a boil. Reduce heat; simmer, uncovered, for 2-4 minutes or until glaze begins to thicken. Pour over asparagus. **Yield:** 2 servings.

Orange Cheesecake Mousse

(Pictured at right and on page 183)

This creamy dessert from our Test Kitchen will make your mouth water. It's especially pleasant after a rich meal.

1/2 cup orange marmalade
1/4 cup orange juice
1/2 teaspoon cornstarch
1 tablespoon cold water
1/2 teaspoon orange extract
1 carton (8 ounces) frozen whipped topping, thawed
Yellow and red liquid food coloring, optional
1 package (8 ounces) cream cheese, softened
1 cup (8 ounces) sour cream
1/2 cup cold milk
1 package (3.4 ounces) instant vanilla pudding mix
Chocolate hearts, optional

In a large saucepan, combine the orange marmalade and juice; cook and stir over medium heat until melted and blended.

In a small bowl, combine cornstarch and water until smooth. Gradually stir into marmalade mixture. Bring to a boil; cook and stir for 4 minutes or until thickened. Remove from the heat; stir in extract. Cool completely. Fold in whipped topping. Tint orange with yellow and red food coloring if desired.

In a large mixing bowl, beat cream cheese until smooth. Add the sour cream; mix well. In a small mixing bowl, beat the milk and pudding mix on low speed for 2 minutes. Stir into cream cheese mixture. Cut a large hole in the corner of a pastry or plastic bag; fill half full with cream cheese mixture. Press bag slightly to flatten. Cut a small hole in another bag; insert star tip No. 21. Place filled bag in empty bag; fill empty bag with orange mixture. Pipe in a swirled design in parfait glasses; chill. Garnish with chocolate hearts if desired. **Yield:** 4 servings.

CHOCOLATE HEARTS ADORN DESSERTS

IF YOUR HEART'S DESIRE is to be creative in the kitchen, try your hand at this simple garnish.

In a microwave or heavy saucepan, melt 1/2 cup semisweet chocolate chips and 1/4 teaspoon shortening; stir until smooth. Cut a small hole in the corner of a pastry or plastic bag; fill with melted chocolate. Pipe two overlapping 1-in. hearts onto waxed paper. Repeat to make three more sets of hearts. Let dry for 2-3 minutes.

Store at room temperature in an airtight container. Use as a garnish for Orange Chocolate Mousse or another dessert.

Shrimp with Basil-Mango Sauce

(Pictured on page 182)

Instead of serving cold shrimp with cocktail sauce, prepare this simple basil sauce
and top it with tender cooked shrimp. It's a fun and fancy appetizer.
—Ken Hulme, Prescott, Arizona

1 medium ripe mango *or* 2
  medium peaches, peeled and
  sliced
2 to 4 tablespoons minced fresh
  basil
1 tablespoon lemon juice
12 cooked medium shrimp,
  peeled and deveined
1 tablespoon butter *or*
  margarine
Basil sprigs, optional

In a blender or food processor, combine the mango, basil and lemon juice; cover and process until blended. Pour onto two serving plates; set aside.

Skewer two shrimp each onto six 4- to 6-in. metal or soaked wooden skewers, forming a heart shape. Cook in a large skillet in butter over medium-high heat for 4-5 minutes or until shrimp turn pink, turning once. Place over mango sauce. Garnish with basil sprigs if desired. **Yield:** 2 servings.

Chocolate Truffles

It's hard to eat just one of these chocolaty silky candies.
I like to keep some on hand for a quick sweet treat.
—DeAnn Alleva, Hudson, Wisconsin

14 squares (1 ounce *each*)
  semisweet chocolate, *divided*
1 cup whipping cream
1/3 cup butter (no substitutes),
  softened
1 teaspoon rum extract *or*
  vanilla extract
1/2 cup finely chopped pecans *or*
  walnuts, toasted

Coarsely chop 12 squares of chocolate; set aside. In a saucepan, heat cream over low heat until bubbles form around sides of the pan. Remove from the heat; add chopped chocolate, stirring until melted and smooth. Cool to room temperature. Stir in butter and extract. Cover tightly and refrigerate for at least 6 hours or until firm.

Grate remaining chocolate; place in a shallow dish. Add nuts; set aside. Shape tablespoonfuls of chilled chocolate mixture into balls. Place on waxed paper-lined baking sheets. (If truffles are soft, refrigerate until easy to handle.) Roll truffles in chocolate-nut mixture. Store in an airtight container in the refrigerator. **Yield:** 3 dozen.

Cupid's Breadsticks

(Pictured at right)

Our Test Kitchen home economists encourage you to play with your food and shape refrigerated breadsticks into hearts and arrows! A sprinkling of seasonings provides the finishing touch.

1 tube (11 ounces) refrigerated breadsticks*
2 tablespoons butter *or* margarine, melted
1/2 teaspoon dried minced onion
1/2 teaspoon dried tarragon
1/2 teaspoon dried oregano
1/2 teaspoon dried thyme
1/2 teaspoon dried parsley flakes
1/8 teaspoon onion powder

Separate breadstick dough into six pieces. For each heart, unroll four pieces and twist if desired; seal perforations and pinch ends together. Shape into hearts on an ungreased baking sheet.

For arrows, unroll remaining two pieces and separate into four breadsticks. With scissors, cut one end of each breadstick into a point. About 2 in. from the point, cut out a triangle from both sides of breadsticks (discard removed pieces). At the other end of the breadstick, make diagonal cuts on each side, creating feathers. Place on baking sheet with hearts.

In a small bowl, combine butter and seasonings. Brush over the dough. Bake at 375° for 12-14 minutes or until golden brown. **Yield:** 4 hearts and 4 arrows.

Editor's Note: This recipe was tested with Pillsbury refrigerated breadsticks.

Chocolate Chip Meringue Cookies

*This is one of my most popular recipes. Shape them into hearts for Valentine's Day
or make them as drop cookies for other occasions.*
— Debbie Tilley, Riverview, Florida

3 egg whites
1/4 teaspoon cream of tartar
1/4 teaspoon salt
1 cup sugar
3 tablespoons baking cocoa
3 tablespoons miniature
   semisweet chocolate chips
3 tablespoons finely crushed
   almonds *or* walnuts, optional

Place egg whites in a large mixing bowl; let stand at room temperature for 30 minutes. Beat egg whites until foamy. Add cream of tartar and salt; beat until soft peaks form. Gradually add sugar, 1 tablespoon at a time, beating on high until stiff peaks form, about 6 minutes. Beat in cocoa. Fold in chocolate chips and nuts if desired.

Cut a small hole in the corner of a pastry or plastic bag; insert No. 806 round tip. Spoon meringue into bag. Pipe 1-1/2-in. hearts 2 in. apart onto lightly greased baking sheets. Bake at 300° for 20-25 minutes or until firm to the touch. Remove to wire racks to cool. Store in an airtight container. **Yield:** 2 dozen.

Editor's Note: Meringue can be dropped by rounded tablespoonfuls onto lightly greased baking sheets. Bake as directed.

MAKE MERINGUE ON DRY DAYS

HUMIDITY is the most critical factor when making a successful meringue, so choose a dry day. Meringues can absorb moisture on a humid day and become limp and sticky.

Ruby-Red Strawberry Sauce

(Pictured at right)

*My best friend, Lynn Young, and I came up with this recipe after our husbands
requested it. In addition to ice cream, it can be served over pancakes and waffles.*
— Terri Zobel, Raleigh, North Carolina

1/2 cup sugar
4-1/2 teaspoons cornstarch
1/4 cup orange juice concentrate
4 cups sliced fresh strawberries
1/2 teaspoon vanilla extract

In a large saucepan, combine the sugar and cornstarch. Stir in orange juice concentrate until smooth; add strawberries. Bring to a boil; cook and stir for 2 minutes or until thickened. Remove from the heat; stir in vanilla. Cool. Store in the refrigerator. **Yield:** 2-1/2 cups.

Engaging Heart Cookies

(Pictured at right)

My husband, Brian, is an excellent cook. The first time he made these elegant cookies was the night we got engaged. He took them to the restaurant and had the staff arrange them on a plate along with my ring!
—Beth Kelley, Indianapolis, Indiana

- 1 cup butter (no substitutes), softened
- 1/2 cup sugar
- 1/2 cup packed brown sugar
- 2 eggs
- 1 teaspoon vanilla extract
- 2-1/4 cups all-purpose flour
- 1/4 cup baking cocoa
- 1/4 teaspoon salt
- 3/4 cup ground toasted hazelnuts
- 3/4 cup semisweet chocolate chips
- 2 tablespoons shortening, *divided*
- 3/4 cup vanilla *or* white chips

In a mixing bowl, cream butter and sugars. Beat in eggs and vanilla. Combine the flour, cocoa and salt; add to creamed mixture. Stir in hazelnuts. Divide dough in half. Cover and refrigerate for 1 hour or until easy to handle.

Working with one portion of dough at a time, roll to 1/4-in. thickness on a lightly floured surface. Cut with a 2-in. heart-shaped cookie cutter. Place 1 in. apart on ungreased baking sheets. Bake at 350° for 9-10 minutes (cookies will be soft). Cool for 1 minute before removing to wire racks.

In a microwave-safe bowl, melt chocolate chips and 1 tablespoon shortening; stir until smooth. Repeat with vanilla chips and remaining shortening. Dip right side of half of the cookies in semisweet chocolate; dip the left side of remaining cookies in white chocolate. Overlap two hearts before the chocolate is set. Place on waxed paper until set. **Yield:** about 3-1/2 dozen.

Be-Mine Sandwich Cookies

These simple cookies are the first thing to disappear from dessert tables.
They're cute, colorful and extremely fast to make.
—Darcie Cross, Novi, Michigan

6 ounces white *or* chocolate
    candy coating
50 to 55 chocolate cream-filled
    sandwich cookies
Assorted candy hearts, sprinkles *or*
    decorations

In a microwave-safe bowl or heavy saucepan, melt 2 ounces of candy coating at a time, stirring until smooth. Spread over cookie tops; decorate immediately. Place on waxed paper to harden. **Yield:** 50-55 cookies.

Queen-of-Hearts Salad

Red raspberries and heart-shaped croutons make this salad from our Test Kitchen
perfect for Valentine's Day. The creamy dressing hints of Dijon and lemon.

2 slices whole wheat bread
4-1/2 teaspoons butter *or*
    margarine, melted
1/4 teaspoon garlic powder
1/4 teaspoon dill weed
1/8 teaspoon salt
3 cups torn salad greens
1 jar (4-1/2 ounces) marinated
    artichoke hearts, drained and
    quartered
1/2 cup fresh raspberries
DRESSING:
1 tablespoon sugar
2-1/2 teaspoons lemon juice
1-1/2 teaspoons tarragon vinegar *or*
    cider vinegar

1/2 teaspoon salt
1 tablespoon Dijon mustard
1/4 teaspoon minced garlic
Dash coarsely ground pepper
1/4 cup vegetable oil

For croutons, cut bread into hearts with a 1-in. heart-shaped cookie cutter. In a bowl, combine butter, garlic powder, dill and salt. Add the bread hearts; toss to coat. Place in a single layer on a baking sheet. Bake at 400° for 3 minutes on each side.

On two salad plates, arrange the greens, artichokes, raspberries and croutons. In a bowl, combine sugar, lemon juice, vinegar and salt. Add mustard, garlic and pepper. Slowly whisk in oil. Drizzle over salads. Serve immediately. **Yield:** 2 servings.

Strawberry Pavlova

(Pictured at right)

I eat lots of fruits, and this recipe showcasing strawberries is a favorite. It's an impressive dessert that never fails.
—Mary Pead, Ocala, Florida

      4 egg whites
  1/4 teaspoon cream of tartar
1-1/4 cups plus 2 tablespoons sugar, *divided*
      2 teaspoons cornstarch
      1 teaspoon lemon juice
  1/2 to 1 teaspoon almond extract
      2 cups whipping cream
      1 quart fresh strawberries, sliced

PAVLOVA FOLKLORE

BOTH Australia and New Zealand claim pavlova as a national dish. It's been said that this meringue dessert with whipped cream and fruit was named after the famous Russian ballerina Anna Pavlova.

Place egg whites in a large mixing bowl; let stand at room temperature for 30 minutes. Beat egg whites on medium speed until foamy. Add cream of tartar; beat until soft peaks form. Gradually add 1-1/4 cups sugar, 1 tablespoon at a time, beating on high until stiff peaks form. Sprinkle cornstarch over egg white mixture; fold in. Fold in lemon juice and extract.

Coat a 14-in. pizza pan with nonstick cooking spray. Spoon meringue onto pan, forming a 12-in. heart; build up edges slightly. Bake at 250° for 45-55 minutes or until crisp. Cool on pan on a wire rack.

In a mixing bowl, beat cream until soft peaks form. Gradually add the remaining sugar, beating until stiff peaks form. Spoon over meringue; arrange strawberries over top. Serve immediately. **Yield:** 12 servings.

Caramel Fondue

*My brothers can't get enough of this caramel dip. We gather around the table,
dipping pieces of pound cake and fruit until the fondue pot is clean!*
—Leora Miller, Milford, Indiana

1 cup whipping cream, *divided*
3/4 cup sugar
1/2 cup light corn syrup
1/4 cup butter (no substitutes)
1/4 teaspoon salt
1/2 teaspoon vanilla extract
Pound cake and assorted fresh
   fruit, cut into pieces

In a heavy saucepan, combine 1/2 cup cream, sugar, corn syrup, butter and salt. Bring to a boil over medium heat until a candy thermometer reads 234° (soft-ball stage), stirring constantly. Cool to 220°; stir in remaining cream. Bring to a boil. Remove from the heat; stir in vanilla.

Transfer to a fondue pot and keep warm. Serve with pound cake and fruit. **Yield:** 1-3/4 cups.

Editor's Note: We recommend that you test your candy thermometer before each use by bringing water to a boil; the thermometer should read 212°. Adjust your recipe temperature up or down based on your test.

HEART-SHAPED DIPPERS

INSTEAD of simply serving cubes of pound cake with Caramel Fondue (recipe above), make some heart-shaped dippers. Thaw a 10-3/4-ounce loaf of pound cake. Slice the cake, then cut with a 1-in. heart-shaped cookie cutter.

Valentine's Day Snack Mix

*Kids of all ages will gobble up this sweet snack mix from our Test Kitchen. Best of all,
because it requires no cooking, they can help combine the ingredients.*

1 package (12.7 ounces)
   Valentine's M&M's
1 can (9-3/4 ounces) whole
   cashews
1 package (8 ounces)
   yogurt-covered raisins
1 package (3.53 ounces) dried
   cranberries

1 cup miniature pretzels
1 cup chocolate-flavored bear-shaped graham
   crackers

In a large bowl, combine all ingredients. Store in an airtight container. **Yield:** 7 cups.

Arranging Fresh Roses

ROSES can cost a pretty penny, especially around Valentine's Day. To lengthen their life—and enhance their beauty—properly prepare them for an arrangement.

- Select a vase that is about half as tall as your flowers.
- Using floral tape, create a grid on your vase. (See "Using a Grid to Arrange Flowers" below.) Then fill with water and add a floral preservative. The water should be slightly higher than your body temperature.
- With a garden shears or sharp knife, cut off any leaves and thorns that will be below the water line. Wear gardening gloves to protect your hands.
- While holding the stems under running water, cut off at least 1 inch. The flowers should be about twice the height of your vase with several stems an inch or two longer for the center of your bouquet.
- Arrange the flowers in the water as

you cut them, starting in the center and working toward the rim. Fill in with other flowers and greens as desired.

- Keep roses away from direct heat or sunlight and drafts. Add fresh water regularly and replenish the floral preservative from time to time.

USING A GRID TO ARRANGE FLOWERS

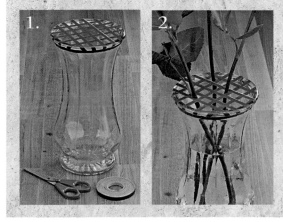

HERE'S HOW TO arrange your long-stemmed roses like a pro.

1. Place strips of waterproof floral tape parallel to one another across the top of the vase. Then place strips perpendicular to the first set to form a grid. Wrap a piece of tape to secure ends around the rim of the vase.

2. Fill the vase with water. Insert flowers, placing taller ones near the center and shorter ones near the rim to create a rounded form. Fill in with greens and baby's breath, making sure to cover the tape on the rim of the vase.

It's a Girl!

BABY SHOWERS don't always have to be a surprise. In fact, planning the party after the bundle of joy arrives gives friends and relatives an opportunity to meet the tiny guest of honor.

No matter when you host the shower, you won't get rattled thinking about the menu if you turn to these lovely lunch items.

As guests arrive, serve Celebration Punch, then top the table with Tropical Chicken Salad and Spinach Salad with Honey Dressing. The Watermelon Baby Carriage not only holds a beautiful blend of fruit but serves as a centerpiece as well.

In addition to a rich dessert, pass around pretty plates piled high with refreshing Party Mint Patties. (All shown at right.)

PRETTY IN PINK
(Clockwise from top right)

Celebration Punch (p. 197)

Party Mint Patties (p. 198)

Tropical Chicken Salad (p. 196)

Spinach Salad with
Honey Dressing (p. 198)

Watermelon Baby
Carriage (p. 199)

Tropical Chicken Salad

(Pictured on page 195)

Pineapple and almonds give this chicken salad its tropical taste.
Every forkful is loaded with chicken, making this a hearty luncheon entree.
—*Russell Moffett, Irvine, California*

1 can (20 ounces) pineapple
  tidbits
4 cups cubed cooked chicken
4 hard-cooked eggs, chopped
1 cup thinly sliced celery
1 cup slivered almonds
1/2 cup mayonnaise
1/2 cup sour cream

1 teaspoon poppy seeds
Salt and pepper to taste

Drain pineapple, reserving 1 tablespoon juice (discard remaining juice or save for another use). In a large bowl, combine the pineapple, chicken, eggs, celery and almonds. In a small bowl, combine the remaining ingredients; stir in reserved pineapple juice. Pour over chicken mixture; mix well. Refrigerate until serving. **Yield:** 8 servings.

Chocolate Cheesecake Squares

These bite-size bars are very rich, so small servings are satisfying.
They're perfect for parties because they don't require a fork and plate to eat.
—*Helen Longmire, Austin, Texas*

1 cup all-purpose flour
1/2 cup sugar
3 tablespoons baking cocoa
1 teaspoon baking powder
1/4 teaspoon salt
1/2 cup cold butter *or* margarine
1 egg yolk
1 teaspoon vanilla extract
1/2 cup finely chopped walnuts
FILLING:
1 package (8 ounces) cream
  cheese, softened
1/3 cup sugar
1/2 cup sour cream
1 tablespoon all-purpose flour
2 teaspoons grated orange peel
1/4 teaspoon salt
1 egg
1 egg white

1/2 teaspoon vanilla extract
Chocolate sprinkles, optional

Line a 9-in. square baking pan with foil; grease the foil and set aside. In a bowl, combine the first five ingredients. Cut in butter until fine crumbs form. Stir in egg yolk, vanilla and walnuts; mix well. Press onto the bottom of the prepared pan. Bake at 325° for 15 minutes.

In a small mixing bowl, beat cream cheese and sugar until smooth. Add the sour cream, flour, orange peel and salt; mix well. Add egg, egg white and vanilla; beat on low speed just until combined. Pour over warm crust. Bake for 20-25 minutes or until center is almost set. Cool on a wire rack for 1 hour.

Garnish top with chocolate sprinkles if desired. Refrigerate overnight. Using foil, lift out of pan. Discard foil; cut into 1-in. squares. **Yield:** 25 servings.

Celebration Punch

(Pictured at right and on page 195)

This pretty fruit punch has just the right amount of sweetness. The ice ring keeps it cool for hours without diluting the flavor.
—Marci Carl
Northern Cambria, Pennsylvania

ICE RING:
1-3/4 cups orange juice
1-1/2 cups water
   1 cup halved fresh strawberries
Fresh mint springs
PUNCH:
   2 packages (10 ounces *each*)
     frozen sweetened
     strawberries, thawed
   4 cans (5-1/2 ounces *each*)
     apricot nectar
3/4 cup orange juice concentrate
   3 cups cold water
   1 cup lemon juice
3/4 cup sugar
   1 liter ginger ale, chilled

For ice ring, in a bowl, combine orange juice and water. Pour 2 cups into a 4-1/2-cup ring mold. Freeze until solid. Top with fresh strawberries and mint. Slowly pour remaining juice mixture into mold to almost cover strawberries and mint. Freeze until solid.

For punch, place thawed strawberries in a blender; cover and puree until smooth. Pour into a large serving bowl or punch bowl. Add the apricot nectar, orange juice concentrate, water, lemon juice and sugar; stir until sugar is dissolved. Just before serving, stir in ginger ale and add ice ring. **Yield:** about 1 gallon.

UNMOLDING AN ICE RING

TO REMOVE an ice ring from a mold, wrap the bottom of the mold with a hot, damp dish towel. Invert onto a baking sheet; place fruit side up in a punch bowl.

Spinach Salad with Honey Dressing

(Pictured on page 195)

Guests are always impressed by this elegant salad's taste and appearance.
They never leave the table without requesting the recipe.
—Emilie Hinton, Bradley, Illinois

1 medium red apple
Lemon juice
6 cups torn fresh spinach
6 cups torn red leaf lettuce
1 small red onion, sliced and
   separated into rings
1 can (11 ounces) mandarin
   oranges, drained
1/3 cup sunflower kernels,
   toasted
6 bacon strips, cooked and
   crumbled
DRESSING:
1/2 cup vegetable oil

1/4 to 1/3 cup sugar
2 tablespoons plus 1-1/2 teaspoons cider vinegar
2 tablespoons plus 1-1/2 teaspoons honey
1/2 teaspoon celery salt
1/2 teaspoon onion salt
1/2 teaspoon paprika
1/2 teaspoon ground mustard
1/2 teaspoon lemon juice

Thinly slice apple; brush with lemon juice. In a large salad bowl, toss the spinach, lettuce, onion, oranges and apple slices. Sprinkle with sunflower kernels and bacon.

In a microwave-safe bowl, whisk the dressing ingredients. Microwave, uncovered, on high for 1 minute. Stir and drizzle over salad. Serve immediately. **Yield:** 12 servings.

Party Mint Patties

(Pictured on page 195)

These easy-to-make mint candies are perfect for any occasion throughout the year.
Simply tint the dough the appropriate color. Friends and family will gobble these up in a jiffy!
—Mrs. William Yoder, Bloomfield, Iowa

1/4 cup butter (no substitutes),
   softened
1/3 cup light corn syrup
4 cups confectioners' sugar,
   divided
1/2 to 1 teaspoon peppermint
   extract
2 drops red food coloring
2 drops yellow food coloring
Granulated sugar (about 1 cup)

In a small mixing bowl, combine butter and corn syrup. Add 2 cups confectioners' sugar and extract; beat well. Stir in 1 cup confectioners' sugar. Turn onto a work surface sprinkled with remaining confectioners' sugar; knead until sugar is absorbed and mixture is smooth.

Divide into three portions. Tint one portion pink and one yellow; leave remaining portion white. Shape into 3/4-in. balls; roll in granulated sugar. Flatten with a fork. Let stand, uncovered, at room temperature for 1 day. Store in an airtight container. **Yield:** about 7-1/2 dozen.

Watermelon Baby Carriage

(Pictured at right and on page 194)

This fruit-filled carriage was made for my daughter's baby shower and was a huge hit. Fill it with any fruit you fancy and serve purchased poppy seed dressing alongside if you desire.
—Angie Schaff
St. Anthony, North Dakota

1 medium watermelon
5 toothpicks
4 orange slices
4 lime slices
2 cups seedless red grapes, *divided*
1 medium cantaloupe, cut into balls *or* cubes
2 cups seedless green grapes
2 cups halved fresh strawberries
Poppy seed salad dressing

With a sharp knife, cut a thin slice from bottom of melon it sits flat. Lightly score a horizontal line halfway up sides and around the melon, leaving 5 in. from one end unmarked on each side for baby carriage hood.

For hood, make another line around top of watermelon, connecting both sides of the horizontal line. Using the rounded edge of a biscuit cutter as a guide, mark a scalloped edge along all straight lines. With a long sharp knife, cut into melon along the scalloped lines, making sure to cut all the way through the melon rind. Gently pull off rind. Remove fruit from melon and removed section; cut fruit into balls or cubes and set aside.

For the U-shaped handle (see diagram at right), cut out a 5-in. square from the removed section of rind. Cut out the center and one end, leav-

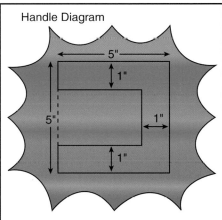

Handle Diagram

ing a 1-in.-wide handle. Break one toothpick in half. Attach handle to watermelon with toothpick halves.

For wheels, position orange slices at base of watermelon and attach with toothpicks. Top each orange slice with a lime slice and a red grape.

In a large bowl, combine the cantaloupe, green grapes, strawberries, remaining red grapes and reserved watermelon. Spoon into baby carriage. Serve with poppy seed salad dressing. **Yield:** 20-24 servings.

Lemon Squares

*I'm expected to bring these bars to bridal showers and family gatherings.
The combination of sweet and tart tastes is sure to please.*
—Mary Larson, Maplewood, Minnesota

3 cups all-purpose flour
3/4 cup confectioners' sugar
1/2 teaspoon salt
1-1/2 cups cold butter (no substitutes)
TOPPING:
6 eggs, lightly beaten
3 cups sugar
1/2 cup lemon juice
1-1/2 teaspoons baking powder
1/2 teaspoon salt
Confectioners' sugar

In a bowl, combine the flour, confectioners' sugar and salt. Cut in butter until crumbly. Pat into a greased 15-in. x 10-in. x 1-in. baking pan. Bake at 350° for 16-20 minutes or until set and top is golden brown.

For topping, combine the eggs, sugar, lemon juice, baking powder and salt in a bowl. Pour over crust (pan will be full). Bake 16-20 minutes longer or until set and top is golden brown. Cool. Dust with confectioners' sugar. Cut into squares. **Yield:** 4 dozen.

STARTING A TIME CAPSULE FOR THE BABY

LOOKING for a fun tradition to begin at a baby shower? Help the parents start a "time capsule" of the baby's first year of life.

- Select a durable container that will last for years, such as a heavy cardboard box or plastic container with tight-fitting lid.
- When you send out the invitations, inform the guests you're starting a time capsule and ask each guest to bring an item to add. Assign a specific object to each guest or provide them with a list of possibilities to spark their creativity. Here are some ideas:

  Newspapers and television guides with the year of the child's birth
  Magazines featuring current clothing styles
  Grocery store ads showing food prices
  Stamps or coins
  Music compact discs
  Television video tapes or DVDs
  Popular toys (Beanie Babies, etc.)
  Copy of the baby's family tree
  Handwritten letters to baby
  Copies of family-favorite recipes
  Recent pictures of family and friends
  Clean newborn diapers or clothes

- In lieu of party games, present the time capsule container to the mother-to-be. Go around the room and have each guest add their own item.
- After the party, encourage Mom and Dad to add pictures from the shower and other mementos from the baby's first year (lock of hair, favorite rattle, discarded pacifiers, etc.).
  Note: To avoid yellowing, place all papers in resealable plastic bags. Put photos on acid-free pages to prevent deterioration.
- On the baby's first birthday, have the parents seal the capsule, adhere a "Do Not Open Until" label (indicating a special date in the future, such as the child's 16th birthday, high school graduation day or birth of their own baby) and tuck it away in a cool dry place like a closet.

Strawberry Cheese Bundles

(Pictured at right)

When I first served these turnovers, folks thought I bought them from a bakery. Everyone was surprised to hear they start with refrigerated crescent rolls and pie filling.
—Jolene Spray, Van Wert, Ohio

1 package (3 ounces) cream cheese, softened
2 tablespoons confectioners' sugar
1/4 teaspoon almond extract
1 tube (8 ounces) refrigerated crescent rolls
1/3 cup strawberry pie filling
1/3 cup crushed pineapple, drained
2 to 3 tablespoons apricot spreadable fruit

In a small mixing bowl, beat the cream cheese, sugar and extract until smooth. Unroll crescent dough and separate into eight triangles. Place 1 heaping teaspoonful of cream cheese mixture in the center of each triangle. Top with 1 teaspoon of pie filling and 1 teaspoon of pineapple.

With one long side of pastry facing you, fold right and left corners over filling to top corner, forming a square. Seal edges. Place on an ungreased baking sheet. Bake at 375° for 15-17 minutes or until lightly browned. Brush with spreadable fruit. Serve warm or cold. **Yield:** 8 servings.

Candy Pacifiers

(Pictured at right)

These cute candy pacifiers are a clever addition to any baby shower.
—Lori Vigstol
Thief River Falls, Minnesota

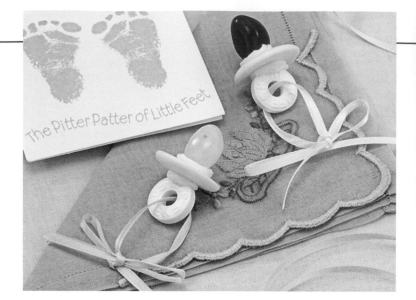

1/4 cup vanilla frosting
Liquid food coloring, optional
  24 candy coating wafers
  24 jelly beans
  24 peppermint Life Savers
   8 feet of ribbon (1/8 inch), cut
     into 4-inch lengths

Tint frosting with food coloring if desired. Place a pea-size amount of frosting on the rounded side of each candy wafer; position a jelly bean standing upright in the frosting. Let stand for 10-20 minutes or until set. Place wafers jelly bean side down on a wire rack with jelly beans between the wires.

Carefully place another pea-size amount of frosting on the flat side of each candy wafer; position a Life Saver on edge in the frosting. Let stand for at least 1 day to dry. Tie a ribbon through each Life Saver. **Yield:** 2 dozen.

PAPER CLIP STOPS KNOTS

TO PREVENT the knot from slipping when making a loop on the Candy Pacifiers, place a paper clip on ribbon about 1 inch above top of pacifier; tie a knot. Remove paper clip. Tie ends of ribbon into a bow.

Cucumber Party Sandwiches

When I serve these refreshing sandwiches at ladies' luncheons and potlucks, the platter is always emptied. They are so simple to prepare that you'll find yourself making them often.
—Veronica Smith, Donnelly, Minnesota

1 package (8 ounces) cream
  cheese, softened
2 teaspoons Italian salad
  dressing mix
1 loaf (16 ounces) snack rye
  bread
2 large cucumbers, thinly sliced

2 tablespoons minced fresh dill *or* 2 teaspoons
  dill weed

In a small mixing bowl, beat the cream cheese and salad dressing mix until smooth. Spread on one side of each slice of bread. Top with a cucumber slice and sprinkle with dill. Serve immediately. **Yield:** about 3-1/2 dozen.

Broccoli Chicken Braid

(Pictured at right)

I work outside the home, so I appreciate recipes like this that are fast and delicious.
— Diane Wampler
Morristown, Tennessee

2 cups chopped cooked chicken
1 cup chopped fresh broccoli florets
1 cup (4 ounces) shredded cheddar cheese
1/4 cup chopped green pepper
1/4 cup chopped sweet red pepper
1 garlic clove, minced
1 teaspoon dill weed
1/4 teaspoon salt
1/2 cup mayonnaise

2 tubes (8 ounces *each*) refrigerated crescent rolls
1 egg white, lightly beaten
2 tablespoons slivered almonds

In a bowl, combine the first eight ingredients. Stir in mayonnaise. Unroll both tubes of crescent roll dough into one long rectangle on an ungreased baking sheet. Roll into a 15-in. x 12-in. rectangle, sealing seams and perforations. Spoon chicken mixture down center third of dough.

On each long side, cut eight strips about 3-1/2 in. into the center. Bring one strip from each side over filling and pinch ends to seal; repeat. Brush with egg white. Sprinkle with almonds. Bake at 375° for 15-20 minutes or until filling is heated through and top is golden brown. **Yield:** 8 servings.

Sunflower Cheese Ball

Having lived in the Sunflower State all my life, I've loved using sunflower kernels in a variety of recipes. Here, those crunchy kernels coat a creamy cheese spread.
— Karen Ann Bland, Gove, Kansas

1 package (8 ounces) cream cheese, softened
1 teaspoon Dijon mustard
1/2 teaspoon garlic powder
2 cups (8 ounces) shredded cheddar cheese
1/2 cup chopped ripe olives
2 tablespoons minced fresh parsley

1/2 cup salted sunflower kernels
Assorted crackers

In a small mixing bowl, beat cream cheese and mustard until smooth. Add garlic powder. Stir in the cheese, olives and parsley. Cover and refrigerate for 15 minutes. Shape into a ball; roll in sunflower kernels. Store in the refrigerator. Serve with crackers. **Yield:** 2-1/2 cups.

Backyard Memorial Party

WHEN YOU GATHER with family and friends to remember those who lost their lives defending their country, proudly display your patriotism with this tried-and-true menu.

Family and friends will be in their glory when you tap into the merry mood and make a Flag Cake.

Add to the spirited celebration by serving Orange Fruit Dip with an assortment of red, white and blue produce.

For many people, Memorial Day marks the beginning of summer. Herald the arrival of warmer weather with pleasing picnic fare like Herb Burgers and Potato Chip Chicken Strips.

STARS AND STRIPES SUPPER
(Clockwise from top right)

Herb Burgers (p. 206)

Orange Fruit Dip (p. 210)

Potato Chip Chicken Strips (p. 208)

Flag Cake (p. 207)

Herb Burgers

(Pictured on page 205)

These tasty burgers have lots of flavor! My dear Uncle Mickey shared the recipe with me years ago.
—*Brenda Sorrow, Kannapolis, North Carolina*

1 egg, lightly beaten
1 medium onion, chopped
2 teaspoons ketchup
2 garlic cloves, minced
1 teaspoon salt
1 teaspoon Worcestershire sauce
1/2 teaspoon pepper
1/4 teaspoon dried oregano
1/4 teaspoon dried parsley flakes
1/4 teaspoon rubbed sage

1/8 to 1/4 teaspoon hot pepper sauce
2 pounds ground beef
8 hamburger buns, split
Mayonnaise, lettuce leaves, and sliced tomatoes and red onion

In a bowl, combine the first 11 ingredients. Crumble beef over mixture and mix well. Shape into eight patties. Grill, uncovered, over medium heat for 5-6 minutes on each side or until meat is no longer pink. Serve on buns with mayonnaise, lettuce, tomatoes and onion. **Yield:** 8 servings.

Deli-Style Pasta Salad

This salad is wonderful for a crowd. Men love the robust flavor, women enjoy the colorful vegetables and kids gobble up the tender pasta.
—*Lana Boyd, Laredo, Texas*

1 package (1 pound) ziti, penne, bow tie *or* tricolor spiral pasta
2 large cucumbers, peeled, seeded and chopped
2 large red onions, sliced into thin strips
2 large green peppers, chopped
2 large tomatoes, chopped
1 bottle (16 ounces) Italian salad dressing
1 container (2.62 ounces) Salad Supreme Seasoning*

Cook pasta according to package directions; drain and rinse with cold water. In a large bowl, combine the pasta, cucumbers, onions, green peppers and tomatoes. In a small bowl, whisk the salad dressing and seasoning. Drizzle over pasta mixture and toss to coat. Cover and refrigerate for at least 1 hour. Gently toss just before serving. **Yield:** 20-24 servings.

   ***Editor's Note:** This recipe was tested with McCormick's Salad Supreme Seasoning. Look for it in the spice aisle of your grocery store.

Flag Cake

(Pictured at right and on page 204)

This impressive cake makes for a pretty presentation on a Memorial Day table. It conveniently starts with a boxed cake mix, then is topped with a sweet homemade frosting.
—Glenda Jarboe, Oroville, California

- 1 package (18-1/4 ounces) white cake mix
- 1 cup shortening
- 1 package (2 pounds) confectioners' sugar
- 1/2 cup water
- 1/2 teaspoon salt
- 1/2 teaspoon vanilla extract
- **Blue and red food coloring**

Prepare and bake cake according to package directions, using two greased 9-in. round baking pans. Cool for 10 minutes before removing from pans to wire racks.

For frosting, in a mixing bowl, com-

bine the shortening, sugar, water, salt and vanilla. Beat on medium speed for 5-8 minutes or until fluffy. Place one cake on a serving plate; spread with 2/3 cup frosting. Top with remaining cake.

In a small bowl, combine 2/3 cup frosting and blue food coloring. In another bowl, combine 1-1/2 cups frosting and red food coloring. Fill a pastry or plastic bag with 1/4 cup white frosting; cut a small hole in the corner of the bag and set aside.

Frost cake top and sides with remaining white frosting. With blue frosting, frost a 3-in. section in the upper left corner of the cake. Pipe white stars over blue frosting. Fill another pastry or plastic bag with red frosting; cut a large hole in the corner of the bag. Pipe stripes across top of cake. **Yield:** 12-14 servings.

Potato Chip Chicken Strips

(Pictured on page 204)

This novel recipe is a fast and tasty change from fried chicken.
—*Sister Judith LaBrozzi, Canton, Ohio*

1 cup (8 ounces) sour cream
1/8 teaspoon garlic salt
1/8 teaspoon onion salt
1/8 teaspoon paprika
1 package (12 ounces) potato chips, crushed
2 pounds boneless skinless chicken breasts, cut into 1-inch strips
1/4 cup butter *or* margarine, melted

Salsa, barbecue sauce *or* sweet-and-sour sauce

In a shallow bowl, combine sour cream and seasonings. Place crushed potato chips in another shallow bowl. Dip chicken strips in sour cream mixture, then coat with potato chips. Place in a greased 15-in. x 10-in. x 1-in. baking pan. Drizzle with butter. Bake at 400° for 20-22 minutes or until chicken is no longer pink. Serve with salsa or sauce. **Yield:** 6 main-dish or 10 appetizer servings.

Berry Sour Cream Cake

Add this delightful dessert from our Test Kitchen to your Memorial Day menu. The moist white cake is laden with colorful raspberries and blueberries and drizzled with a sweet glaze.

1 cup butter *or* margarine, softened
1-1/4 cups sugar
2 eggs
1 cup (8 ounces) sour cream
1 teaspoon vanilla extract
2 cups all-purpose flour
1 teaspoon baking powder
1/2 teaspoon baking soda
2 cups fresh raspberries
1 cup fresh blueberries
GLAZE:
2 cups confectioners' sugar
1/4 cup butter *or* margarine, melted
1/2 teaspoon vanilla extract
2 to 3 tablespoons milk

In a mixing bowl, cream butter and sugar. Add the eggs, sour cream and vanilla; mix well. Combine the flour, baking powder and baking soda; gradually add to creamed mixture. Spread into a greased 13-in. x 9-in. x 2-in. baking dish. Sprinkle with raspberries and blueberries. Bake at 325° for 40-45 minutes or until a toothpick inserted near the center comes out clean.

For glaze, in a mixing bowl, beat confectioners' sugar, butter, vanilla and enough milk to achieve drizzling consistency. Drizzle over warm cake. Cool on a wire rack before cutting. **Yield:** 12-15 servings.

Rhubarb Terrine with Raspberry Sauce

(Pictured at right)

I'm a retired home economist who loves to make desserts and share them with family and friends. To easily cut this dessert, first dip a sharp knife in warm water, dry it, then slice.
—Lucile Cline, Wichita, Kansas

1-1/4 pounds fresh rhubarb, cut into 1-inch pieces
1-1/2 cups sugar, *divided*
   1 cup whipping cream
  1/2 teaspoon vanilla extract
  1/8 teaspoon ground ginger
    or 1/2 teaspoon grated fresh gingerroot
   3 cups vanilla ice cream, softened
   3 packages (10 ounces *each*) frozen sweetened raspberries, thawed

Line a 9-in. x 5-in. x 3-in. loaf pan with plastic wrap; set aside. In a large saucepan, bring rhubarb and 1 cup sugar to a boil. Reduce heat; simmer, uncovered, for 12-14 minutes or until thickened and rhubarb is tender, stirring several times. Remove from the heat. Cool completely, about 25 minutes, stirring several times to break apart rhubarb.

In a small mixing bowl, combine whipping cream, 2 tablespoons sugar and vanilla; beat until soft peaks form. Fold into rhubarb mixture. Transfer half to prepared pan. Cover and freeze for 1 hour. Cover and refrigerate remaining rhubarb mixture.

Stir ginger into ice cream; spread 1-1/2 cups over rhubarb layer. Cover and freeze for 30 minutes. Refrigerate remaining ice cream mixture. Spread remaining rhubarb mixture over the ice cream layer. Cover and freeze for 1 hour. Spread with remaining ice cream mixture. Freeze until firm.

For sauce, drain raspberries, reserving juice. In a blender, combine raspberries and 2 tablespoons of juice; cover and process until pureed. Press through a fine sieve; discard seeds and pulp. Stir remaining sugar into raspberry mixture. Add enough of the remaining juice to measure 1-1/2 cups.

Remove terrine from the freezer 15 minutes before cutting. Serve with raspberry sauce. **Yield:** 10-12 servings.

BERRY BEAUTIFUL CENTERPIECE

TABLE TOPPERS don't have to take a lot of thought or effort. A patriotic bowl brimming with red raspberries and blueberries (as shown in the photo above) is a simple Memorial Day centerpiece you can produce in minutes!

Orange Fruit Dip

(Pictured on page 205)

This refreshing dip is the perfect complement to fresh summer fruit.
Folks just can't seem to get enough of it…the bowl is always scraped clean!
— *Tiffany Anderson-Taylor, Gulfport, Florida*

1 cup sugar
2 tablespoons plus 1 teaspoon cornstarch
1/4 teaspoon salt
1 cup orange juice
1/2 cup water
1/4 cup lemon juice
1/2 teaspoon grated orange peel
1/2 teaspoon grated lemon peel
Assorted fresh fruit

In a small saucepan, combine the sugar, cornstarch and salt; stir in the orange juice, water, lemon juice, and orange and lemon peel until blended. Bring to a boil; cook and stir or 2 minutes or until thickened. Cover and refrigerate until chilled. Serve with fruit. **Yield:** 2 cups.

Chilled Blueberry Soup

With 100 blueberry bushes in my garden, I'm always looking for recipes calling for this
sweet-tart fruit. So I was delighted when my granddaughter shared this one with me.
— *Edith Richardson, Jasper, Alabama*

1/2 cup sugar
2 tablespoons cornstarch
2-3/4 cups water
2 cups fresh *or* frozen blueberries
1 cinnamon stick (3 inches)
1 can (6 ounces) frozen orange juice concentrate
Sour cream, optional

In a large saucepan, combine sugar and cornstarch. Gradually stir in water until smooth. Bring to a boil over medium heat; cook and stir for 2 minutes or until thickened. Add blueberries and cinnamon stick; return to a boil. Remove from the heat. Stir in orange juice concentrate until melted. Cover and refrigerate for at least 1 hour. Discard cinnamon stick. Garnish with sour cream if desired. **Yield:** 4 servings.

Patriotic Taco Salad

(Pictured at right)

One year, my daughter decided to celebrate her July birthday with a patriotic theme. This colorful and refreshing salad was the main dish on the menu. The kids gobbled it up!
—Glenda Jarboe, Oroville, California

1 pound ground beef
1 medium onion, chopped
1-1/2 cups water
1 can (6 ounces) tomato paste
1 envelope taco seasoning
6 cups tortilla *or* corn chips*
4 to 5 cups shredded lettuce
9 to 10 pitted large ripe olives, sliced lengthwise
2 cups (8 ounces) shredded cheddar cheese
2 cups cherry tomatoes, halved

In a large skillet over medium heat, cook beef and onion until meat is no longer pink; drain. Stir in the water, tomato paste and taco seasoning. Bring to a boil. Reduce heat; simmer, uncovered, for 20 minutes.

Place chips in an ungreased 13-in. x 9-in. x 2-in. dish. Spread beef mixture evenly over the top. Cover with lettuce. For each star, arrange five olive slices together in the upper left corner. To form stripes, add cheese and tomatoes in alternating rows. Serve immediately. **Yield:** 8 servings.

*Editor's Note: If you wish to prepare this salad in advance, omit the layer of chips and serve them with the salad.

Summertime Fruit Tea

Pineapple-orange juice gives ordinary iced tea a refreshing citrus flavor. It never lasts long, so I keep plenty of these ingredients on hand.
—Rosalee Dixon, Sardis, Mississippi

12 cups water, *divided*
1-1/2 cups sugar
9 individual tea bags
1 can (12 ounces) frozen lemonade concentrate, thawed
1 can (12 ounces) frozen pineapple-orange juice concentrate, thawed

In a Dutch oven, bring 4 cups water to a boil. Stir in sugar until dissolved. Remove from the heat; add tea bags. Steep for 5-8 minutes. Discard tea bags. Stir in juice concentrates and remaining water. Serve over ice. **Yield:** 3-1/2 quarts.

Strawberry Cookies

My family finds these fruity cookies to be a light treat in summer.
I sometimes use lemon cake mix in place of the strawberry.
—Nancy Shelton, Boaz, Kentucky

1 package (18-1/4 ounces)
    strawberry cake mix
1 egg, lightly beaten
1 carton (8 ounces) frozen
    whipped topping, thawed
2 cups confectioners' sugar

In a mixing bowl, combine the cake mix, egg and whipped topping until well combined. Place confectioners' sugar in a shallow dish. Drop dough by tablespoonfuls into sugar; turn to coat. Place 2 in. apart on greased baking sheets. Bake at 350° for 10-12 minutes or until lightly browned around the edges. Remove to wire racks to cool. **Yield:** about 5 dozen.

German Chocolate Cupcakes

These cupcakes disappear in a dash when I take them to the school where I teach.
Pecans, coconut and brown sugar dress up the topping nicely.
—Lettice Charmasson, San Diego, California

1 package (18-1/4 ounces)
    German chocolate cake mix*
1 cup water
3 eggs
1/2 cup vegetable oil
3 tablespoons chopped pecans
3 tablespoons flaked coconut
3 tablespoons brown sugar

In a large mixing bowl, combine the cake mix, water, eggs and oil. Beat on medium speed for 2 minutes. Fill paper-lined muffin cups three-fourths full. Combine pecans, coconut and brown sugar; sprinkle over batter. Bake at 400° for 15-20 minutes or until a toothpick comes out clean. Cool for 5 minutes before removing from pans to wire racks. **Yield:** about 2 dozen.

*Editor's Note: This recipe was tested with Betty Crocker German chocolate cake mix.

Patriotic Picnic Table

(Pictured above)

WHEN DINING OUTDOORS on Memorial Day, show your patriotic colors with this red, white and blue table trim.

First, cover your picnic or patio table with a white tablecloth, allowing it to hang over the sides of the table. You can use cloth if you choose, but disposable paper tablecloths are less expensive and require no laundering afterward. They can be found at variety and party supply stores.

Next, gather red and blue ribbon in assorted widths. Cut lengths of ribbon equal to the length of the tablecloth. Center the widest ribbon down the length of the table. Place a bit of double-stick tape on the underside of the ribbon at each edge of the table. Add additional ribbons on each side of the wide ribbon, and tape as before. Trim the ribbons even with the tablecloth.

Now cut lengths of ribbon equal to the width of the table. Place them across the width of the table between each place setting, weaving them through the lengthwise ribbons, and tape as before. Trim ribbons even with the tablecloth.

Place red and white geraniums in a patriotic container on the center of the table. Wrap tableware in a festive napkin; tie in a bow with a contrasting ribbon.

SPECIAL
Celebrations

A Special Day for Dad

TO SHOW Pop he's tops, head to the great outdoors for a tried-and-true barbecue!

The selection of stick-to-your-ribs fare in this chapter will surely satisfy Dad's big appetite.

Hot pepper sauce, salsa and taco sauce turn up the heat on Zesty Grilled Pork Medallions. It's bound to be a surefire success at your family gathering.

To round out this manly meal, pair the meaty entree with generous slices of Peppered Corn Bread and hearty helpings of Simple Cabbage Slaw.

Packed with oats and candy bar pieces, the recipe for Championship Cookies will become a prized possession in your kitchen.

FATHER'S DAY FARE
(Clockwise from top left)

Championship Cookies (p. 218)

Peppered Corn Bread (p. 219)

Zesty Grilled Pork Medallions (p. 217)

Simple Cabbage Slaw (p. 219)

Tangy Sirloin Strips

My love of cooking started when I was trying to earn my Girl Scout cooking badge.
My family savors the sweet sauce on these skewers.
—Joanne Haldeman, Bainbridge, Pennsylvania

1/4 cup vegetable oil
  2 tablespoons Worcestershire
    sauce
  1 garlic clove, minced
1/2 teaspoon onion powder
1/2 teaspoon salt
1/4 teaspoon pepper
  1 pound boneless sirloin steak
    (1 inch thick)
  4 bacon strips
Lemon-pepper seasoning
GLAZE:
1/2 cup barbecue sauce
1/2 cup steak sauce
1/2 cup honey
  1 tablespoon molasses

In a large resealable plastic bag, combine the first six ingredients. Cut steak into four wide strips; add to the marinade. Seal bag and turn to coat; refrigerate for 2-3 hours or overnight, turning once.

Drain and discard marinade. Wrap a bacon strip around each steak piece; secure with a toothpick. Sprinkle with lemon-pepper. Coat grill rack with nonstick cooking spray before starting the grill.

Grill steak, covered, over medium-low heat for 10-15 minutes, turning occasionally, until meat reaches desired doneness (for rare, a meat thermometer should read 140°; medium, 160°; well-done, 170°). Combine the glaze ingredients; brush over steak. Grill until glaze is heated. Discard toothpicks. **Yield:** 4 servings.

GREAT GRILLING TIPS

GRILLING is a wonderful way to get summer suppers sizzling. Before you head to your backyard for some fun outdoor cooking, refresh your grilling skills with these tips:

- Before grilling meats, trim excess fat to avoid flare-ups.
- Marinades can be used to add flavor to meat and vegetables or to tenderize less-tender cuts of meat. Always marinate in the refrigerator in a glass container or resealable plastic bag.

  In general, do not reuse marinades. If a marinade is also used as a basting or dipping sauce, reserve a portion before adding the uncooked foods, or bring it to a rolling boil after removing the raw meat.

- Bring foods to a cool room temperature before grilling. Cold foods may burn on the outside before the interior is cooked.
- Use tongs to turn meat instead of a meat fork to avoid piercing and losing juices. Also, salting meats after cooking helps retain juices.
- Brush on thick or sweet sauces during the last 10 to 15 minutes of cooking. Baste and turn every few minutes to prevent burning.
- Use a meat or instant-read thermometer to check the internal temperature of meat and poultry before the recommended cooking time is up.

Zesty Grilled Pork Medallions

(Pictured at right and on page 214)

Some of our friends made up this marinade but weren't able to give me exact measurements. I experimented until I came up with this recipe, which tastes as good as theirs.
—Patty Collins, Morgantown, Indiana

 2 cups salsa
 1/4 cup sugar
 4-1/2 teaspoons sweet-and-sour sauce
 1 tablespoon vegetable oil
 1 tablespoon green taco sauce
 2 teaspoons balsamic vinegar
Dash hot pepper sauce
 2 pork tenderloins (about 1 pound *each*)

In a bowl, combine the first seven ingredients; mix well. Set aside 1 cup for dipping; cover and refrigerate. Pour remaining marinade into a large resealable plastic bag; add the pork. Seal bag and turn to coat; refrigerate overnight.

Drain and discard marinade. Grill pork, covered, over indirect medium heat for 30-40 minutes or until a meat thermometer reads 160°. Warm the dipping sauce; serve with sliced pork. **Yield:** 6-8 servings.

Peanut Butter Ice Cream Pie

This recipe has been a family favorite for nearly 30 years. I often have a pie handy in the freezer to serve unexpected guests.
—Sharon Mensing, Greenfield, Iowa

1-1/2 cups chocolate wafer crumbs, *divided*
 1/4 cup sugar
 1/2 cup butter *or* margarine, melted
 1 quart vanilla ice cream, softened
 1/2 cup chunky peanut butter
 1 cup whipped topping
Peanuts, optional

Set aside 1 tablespoon of wafer crumbs for garnish. In a bowl, combine the sugar and remaining crumbs. Stir in butter. Press onto the bottom and up the sides of greased 9-in. pie plate. Refrigerate for 1 hour or until set.

In a bowl, combine ice cream and peanut butter. Fold in whipped topping. Pour into pie shell. Top with reserved crumbs and peanuts if desired. Cover and freeze for at least 2 hours. Remove from the freezer 15 minutes before cutting. **Yield:** 6-8 servings.

Championship Cookies

(Pictured on page 214)

I got this recipe from a friend who baked at a conference center.
Snickers candy bar pieces make them irresistible.
—*Patricia Miller, North Fork, California*

2/3 cup shortening
1-1/4 cups packed brown sugar
1 egg
1 teaspoon vanilla extract
1-1/2 cups all-purpose flour
1 teaspoon baking powder
1 teaspoon baking soda
1/2 teaspoon ground cinnamon
1/4 teaspoon salt
2 Snickers candy bars (2.07 ounces *each*), chopped
1/2 cup quick-cooking oats

In a mixing bowl, cream shortening and brown sugar. Beat in egg and vanilla. Combine the flour, baking powder, baking soda, cinnamon and salt; gradually add to the creamed mixture. Stir in chopped candy bars and oats.

Drop by rounded tablespoonfuls 2 in. apart onto greased or parchment-lined baking sheets. Bake at 350° for 10-12 minutes or until lightly browned. Remove to wire racks to cool. **Yield:** about 5 dozen.

Hot Wings

For parties, I like to make these wings in advance and keep them warm
in a slow cooker. The mild sauce is finger-licking good!
—*Tracie Calkin, Casper, Wyoming*

20 whole chicken wings (about 4 pounds)*
Vegetable oil for deep-fat frying
1/2 cup butter *or* margarine
1-1/2 teaspoons brown sugar
1 teaspoon lemon juice
1 garlic clove, minced
2 to 3 tablespoons Louisiana hot sauce
3 to 4 teaspoons hot pepper sauce
Celery and carrot sticks
Ranch *or* blue cheese salad dressing

Cut chicken wings into three sections; discard wing tips. In an electric skillet or deep-fat fryer, heat oil to 375°. Fry chicken wings, a few at a time, until juices run clear. Drain on paper towels.

In a large skillet, melt butter. Stir in the brown sugar, lemon juice, garlic and hot sauces; bring just to a boil. Add chicken wings; turn to coat. Cook and turn for 5-10 minutes or until well coated. Serve with celery and carrot sticks and salad dressing for dipping. **Yield:** 10 servings.

*Editor's Note: 4 pounds of uncooked chicken wing sections may be substituted for the whole chicken wings. Omit the first step of the recipe.

Peppered Corn Bread

(Pictured at right and on page 215)

Pretty flecks of jalapeno and red peppers peek out from this golden corn bread. It has a mild flavor, which appeals to all palates.
—Ila Bray, Pelham, North Carolina

1-1/2 cups cornmeal
   1 tablespoon all-purpose flour
   1 tablespoon sugar
2-1/4 teaspoons baking powder
  3/4 teaspoon salt
  1/2 teaspoon baking soda
   2 eggs, beaten
   1 can (8-3/4 ounces) cream-style corn
   1 cup buttermilk
  2/3 cup vegetable oil
   2 cups (8 ounces) shredded cheddar cheese
   1 medium sweet red pepper, chopped
   2 jalapeno peppers, seeded and diced*
   4 to 5 green onions, chopped

In a bowl, combine the cornmeal, flour, sugar, baking powder, salt and baking soda; set aside. Combine the eggs, corn, buttermilk and oil; stir into the dry ingredients just until blended. Fold in the cheese, peppers and onions. Pour into a greased 13-in. x 9-in. x 2-in. baking dish. Bake at 350° for 30-35 minutes or until a toothpick comes out clean. Cut into squares; serve warm. **Yield:** 12-16 servings.

   *Editor's Note: When cutting or seeding hot peppers, use rubber or plastic gloves to protect your hands. Avoid touching your face.

Simple Cabbage Slaw

(Pictured on page 214)

When I was growing up, my father would make this salad as part of our Sunday dinner. Now I carry on the tradition with my own family.
—Sandra Lampe, Muscatine, Iowa

   4 cups coleslaw mix
   1 medium sweet red *or* green pepper, finely chopped
   5 tablespoons sugar
   5 tablespoons cider vinegar
  1/4 cup water
  1/4 teaspoon salt
  1/8 teaspoon pepper

In a large bowl, combine all ingredients and toss to coat. Cover and refrigerate for at least 4 hours or overnight. **Yield:** 6 servings.

Skewered Potatoes

Here's a unique way to prepare red potatoes. Cooking them in the microwave ensures
they're tender inside, while grilling gives them a crisp outside.
—Sarah Steinacher, Geneva, Nebraska

2 **pounds small red potatoes,**
  quartered
1/3 **cup cold water**
1/2 **cup mayonnaise *or* salad**
  dressing
1/4 **cup dry white wine *or***
  chicken broth
2 **teaspoons dried rosemary,**
  crushed
1 **teaspoon garlic powder**

Place potatoes and water in a 2-qt. microwave-safe dish. Cover and cook on high for 10-15 minutes or until tender, stirring halfway through; drain. In a large bowl, combine the remaining ingredients. Add potatoes; stir gently to coat. Cover and refrigerate for 1 hour. Drain, reserving marinade. Thread potatoes on metal or soaked wooden skewers. Grill, covered, over hot heat for 6-8 minutes or until potatoes are golden brown. Turn and brush occasionally with reserved marinade. **Yield:** 6-8 servings.

Editor's Note: This recipe was tested in an 850-watt microwave.

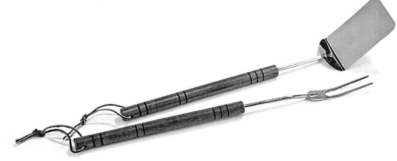

Saucy Orange Shrimp

On a trip to New Orleans, my husband picked up some fresh Gulf shrimp. The wife of the
shrimp boat captain sent this recipe along with him. It's our favorite way to prepare shrimp.
—Gloria Jarrett, Loveland, Ohio

4 **pounds uncooked large**
  shrimp in the shell
2 **cups butter (no substitutes)**
2 **medium navel oranges, peeled**
  and thinly sliced
1 **cup orange juice concentrate**
2 **tablespoons Worcestershire**
  sauce

1 **teaspoon *each* lemon-pepper seasoning, paprika,**
  dried parsley flakes, garlic powder, onion powder
  and barbecue *or* hickory seasoning
Dash cayenne pepper

Place shrimp in two 13-in. x 9-in. x 2-in. baking dishes. In a saucepan, melt butter. Add orange slices; cook and stir until oranges fall apart. Stir in the remaining ingredients; heat through. Pour over the shrimp. Bake, uncovered, at 375° for 15-20 minutes or until shrimp turn pink. **Yield:** 8-10 servings.

Peach Streusel Pie

(Pictured at right)

Dad will want to save room for dessert when this peach pie from our Test Kitchen is on the menu. Serve each warm juicy slice with a scoop of vanilla ice cream.

Pastry for single-crust pie
  (9 inches)
  1/4 cup sugar
    2 tablespoons cornstarch
    2 tablespoons lemon juice
    5 cups sliced fresh *or* frozen
      peaches, thawed
TOPPING:
  2/3 cup packed brown sugar
  1/2 cup granola cereal (without
      raisins)
  1/4 cup all-purpose flour
    1 teaspoon ground cinnamon
  1/4 cup cold butter *or* margarine
Vanilla ice cream

Line a 9-in. pie plate with pastry; flute edges. Line the pastry shell with a double thickness of heavy-duty foil. Bake at 450° for 5 minutes. Remove foil; bake 5 minutes longer. Cool on a wire rack.

In a bowl, combine the sugar, cornstarch, lemon juice and peaches. Spoon into pastry shell. In another bowl, combine the brown sugar, granola, flour and cinnamon; cut in butter until crumbly. Sprinkle over filling. Bake at 375° for 35-40 minutes or until filling is bubbly. Cool on a wire rack. Serve warm with ice cream. **Yield:** 6-8 servings.

Grilled Corn with Chive Butter

When our son was young, corn was the only vegetable he'd eat. My husband and I soon got bored with the simple salt and butter topping, so I stirred in some lemon juice and chives.
—Sue Kirsch, Eden Prairie, Minnesota

    6 medium ears sweet corn
      in husks
  1/2 cup butter (no substitutes),
      melted
    2 tablespoons snipped chives
    1 tablespoon sugar
1-1/2 teaspoons lemon juice
Salt and pepper to taste

Soak corn in cold water for 1 hour. In a small bowl, combine the butter, chives, sugar, lemon juice, salt and pepper. Carefully peel back corn husks to within 1 in. of bottom; remove silk. Brush with butter mixture. Rewrap corn in husks and secure with kitchen string. Grill corn, uncovered, over medium heat for 25-30 minutes, turning occasionally. **Yield:** 6 servings.

SPECIAL Celebrations

Family Reunion Picnic

SUMMER is the perfect time for relatives from near and far to come together for a reunion picnic in the park.

Such a grand gathering isn't complete without those treasured recipes that have been in the family for generations.

In addition, branch out and make some new memories with Grilled Picnic Chicken, Southwestern Pasta Salad, Summer Sub Sandwich, Brownies in a Cone, Root Beer Cookies and Marinated Vegetable Salad. (All shown at right.)

Every recipe in this chapter is a tried-and-true favorite of a family just like yours and is perfectly portioned for larger groups.

COOKING FOR A CROWD
(Clockwise from top center)

Marinated Vegetable Salad

(Pictured on page 222)

*This recipe is so versatile because you can use whatever vegetables your family prefers.
It's a nice change from typical mayonnaise-based salads.*
—*Rita Wagers, Emporia, Kansas*

3 cups broccoli florets
2 cups cauliflowerets
1-1/2 cups sliced baby carrots
2 celery ribs, cut into 1/2-inch
   pieces
1 medium zucchini, sliced
1 can (14 ounces) water-packed
   artichoke hearts, drained and
   quartered
1 can (6 ounces) pitted ripe
   olives, drained
1 jar (4-1/2 ounces) whole
   mushrooms, drained

DRESSING:
3/4 cup vegetable oil
1/3 cup cider vinegar
1 teaspoon garlic salt
3/4 teaspoon sugar
1/2 teaspoon salt
1/2 teaspoon lemon-pepper seasoning

In a large salad bowl, combine the first eight ingredients. In a jar with a tight-fitting lid, combine the dressing ingredients; shake well. Pour over the vegetable mixture and toss to coat. Cover and refrigerate for 8 hours or overnight, stirring occasionally. **Yield:** 14 servings.

FOOD QUANTITIES FOR A CROWD

WHEN PLANNING a buffet, use this guide to estimate how much you'll need per person.
   Keep in mind, if you offer more than one item from each category, the less you'll need per serving.

Beverages
3/4 cup of coffee or tea
24 ounces of soft drinks, juices, lemonade
   or bottled water
1 cup of milk

Breads
1 to 2 slices of bread
1 biscuit, roll or muffin

Salads
1 cup of green salads
1/2 cup of fruit, potato or pasta salads

Condiments
3 to 4 pickle slices or 1 pickle spear

3 olives
1 ounce of ketchup, mustard and
   pickle relish

Dairy
1 teaspoon (1 pat) of butter or margarine
   for bread and rolls
1 ounce of sliced cheese for sandwiches
2 tablespoons of cream for coffee

Desserts
1/2 cup of ice cream or frozen yogurt
1 portion of cake or pie

Meats
4 to 6 ounces of meat, fish or poultry
2 hot dogs
1 to 2 ounces of sliced luncheon meat

Miscellaneous
1 ounce of potato or corn chips
3 to 4 ounces of ice for beverages

Summer Sub Sandwich

(Pictured at right and on page 223)

*When I cook for a large group,
I turn to this super sandwich.
It can be assembled in minutes.*
*—Laverne Renneberg
Chelan, Saskatchewan*

1 package (3 ounces) cream cheese, softened
1 loaf (20 inches) unsliced French bread, halved lengthwise
6 slices deli ham
6 slices provolone cheese
1 jar (4-1/2 ounces) sliced mushrooms, drained
2 medium tomatoes, thinly sliced, optional

1 small onion, thinly sliced
2 banana peppers, thinly sliced
2 cups shredded lettuce

Spread cream cheese on bottom half of bread. Layer with the ham, cheese, mushrooms, tomatoes if desired, onion, peppers and lettuce. Replace top. Cut into 1 1/2 in. slices. **Yield:** 10-15 servings.

Grilled Picnic Chicken

(Pictured on page 223)

This tasty chicken marinates overnight. The next day, I just pop it on the grill for dinner in no time.
—Cindy DeRoos, Iroquois, Ontario

1-1/2 cups white vinegar
3/4 cup vegetable oil
6 tablespoons water
4-1/2 teaspoons salt
1-1/2 teaspoons poultry seasoning
3/4 teaspoon garlic powder
3/4 teaspoon pepper
3 broiler/fryer chickens (3 to 4 pounds *each*), quartered *or* cut up

In a bowl, combine the first seven ingredients. Remove 1 cup for basting; cover and refrigerate. Pour remaining marinade into a gallon-size resealable plastic bag; add chicken. Seal bag and turn to coat; refrigerate for 4 hours or overnight, turning once or twice.

Drain and discard marinade. Grill chicken, uncovered, over medium heat for 30 minutes, turning once. Baste with the reserved marinade. Grill 10-20 minutes longer or until the juices run clear, turning and basting several times. **Yield:** 12 servings.

Brownies in a Cone

(Pictured at right and on page 223)

These brownie-filled ice cream cones are a fun addition to any summer gathering. They appeal to the child in everyone.
—*Mitzi Sentiff, Greenville, North Carolina*

> 1 package fudge brownie mix (13-inch x 9-inch pan size)
> 17 ice cream cake cones* (about 2-3/4-inches tall)
> 1 cup (6 ounces) semisweet chocolate chips
> 1 tablespoon shortening
> Colored sprinkles

Prepare brownie batter according to package directions, using 3 eggs. Place the ice cream cones in muffin cups; spoon about 3 tablespoons batter into each cone. Bake at 350° for 25-30 minutes or until a toothpick comes out clean and top is dry (do not overbake). Cool completely.

In a microwave, melt chocolate chips and shortening; stir until smooth. Dip tops of brownies in melted chocolate; decorate with sprinkles. **Yield:** 17 servings.

***Editor's Note:** This recipe was tested with Keebler ice cream cups. These brownie cones are best served the day they're prepared.

Olive Potato Salad

My mother shared this recipe with me at my bridal shower more than 45 years ago.
—*Margaret Matson, Metamora, Illinois*

> 10 hard-cooked eggs
> 10 medium potatoes, cooked, peeled and cubed
> 2 celery ribs, chopped
> 2 cans (2-1/4 ounces *each*) sliced ripe olives, drained
> 1 tablespoon minced fresh parsley
> 1-1/2 teaspoons salt
> 1/4 teaspoon pepper
> DRESSING:
> 1/4 cup sugar
> 1-1/2 teaspoons all-purpose flour
> 1/4 to 1/2 teaspoon salt
> 1/4 teaspoon ground mustard
> 4 egg yolks, lightly beaten
> 6 tablespoons white vinegar
> 6 tablespoons water
> 1-1/2 teaspoons butter *or* margarine
> Paprika

Chop six hard-cooked eggs; set aside. Slice remaining hard-cooked eggs and refrigerate. In a large serving bowl, combine the chopped eggs, potatoes, celery, olives, parsley, salt and pepper; refrigerate.

For dressing, combine the sugar, flour, salt and mustard in a saucepan. Combine the egg yolks, vinegar and water; gradually whisk into saucepan. Add butter. Bring to a boil, stirring constantly. Cook and stir for 1-2 minutes or until thickened. Cool to room temperature, stirring several times. Pour over potato mixture; gently stir to coat. Cover and refrigerate for at least 2 hours. Top with sliced eggs; sprinkle with paprika. **Yield:** 12-14 servings.

Root Beer Cookies

(Pictured at right and on page 222)

Since it's too difficult to take along root beer floats on a picnic, take these cookies instead! I've found the flavor is even better the next day. The hard part is convincing my family to wait that long before sampling them.
— *Violette Bawden*
West Valley City, Utah

1 cup butter (no substitutes), softened
2 cups packed brown sugar
2 eggs
1 cup buttermilk
3/4 teaspoon root beer concentrate *or* extract
4 cups all-purpose flour
1 teaspoon baking soda
1 teaspoon salt
1-1/2 cups chopped pecans
FROSTING:
3-1/2 cups confectioners' sugar
3/4 cup butter, softened
3 tablespoons water
1-1/4 teaspoons root beer concentrate *or* extract

In a mixing bowl, cream butter and brown sugar. Add eggs, one at a time, beating well after each addition. Beat in buttermilk and root beer concentrate. Combine the flour, baking soda and salt; gradually add to creamed mixture. Stir in pecans.

Drop by tablespoonfuls 3 in. apart onto ungreased baking sheets. Bake at 375° for 10-12 minutes or until lightly browned. Remove to wire racks to cool. In a mixing bowl, combine frosting ingredients; beat until smooth. Frost cooled cookies. **Yield:** about 6 dozen.

Southwestern Pasta Salad

(Pictured on page 223)

*This satisfying salad has a nice blend of textures and flavors. I appreciate
its make-ahead convenience when I'm entertaining.*
—*Ann Brown, Bolivar, Missouri*

1 package (1 pound) small
  shell pasta
2/3 cup cider vinegar
2 celery ribs, chopped
6 green onions, thinly sliced
1/2 cup chopped green pepper
1 can (15-1/2 ounces)
  black-eyed peas, rinsed
  and drained
1 can (11 ounces) whole kernel
  corn, drained
1 can (2-1/4 ounces) sliced ripe
  olives, drained
1/2 cup sliced stuffed olives

3 tablespoons diced pimientos
1/3 cup mayonnaise
1/4 cup vegetable oil
1 to 2 teaspoons chili powder
1 teaspoon salt
1/4 teaspoon Worcestershire sauce
1/8 to 1/4 teaspoon hot pepper sauce

Cook pasta according to package directions; drain and rinse with cold water. Place in a large bowl; add the vinegar and toss to combine. Stir in the celery, onions, green pepper, peas, corn, olives and pimientos. In a small bowl, combine the remaining ingredients; stir into pasta mixture. Cover and refrigerate overnight. **Yield:** 10-12 servings.

Apple Broccoli Salad

*I came up with this recipe in an attempt to combine the flavors of Waldorf salad
and my favorite broccoli salad. It appeals to family and friends.*
—*Brenda Sue Huntington, Clemons, New York*

6 medium tart apples, chopped
3 cups broccoli florets
1 small onion, chopped
1/2 cup raisins
1-1/2 cups mayonnaise
2 tablespoons white vinegar
1-1/2 teaspoons sugar
1/2 teaspoon lemon juice
1/2 teaspoon salt
10 bacon strips, cooked and
  crumbled
1/2 cup coarsely chopped walnuts

In a large bowl, combine the apples, broccoli, onion and raisins. In a small bowl, combine the mayonnaise, vinegar, sugar, lemon juice and salt; pour over apple mixture and toss to coat. Cover and chill for at least 2 hours. Just before serving, stir in the bacon and walnuts. **Yield:** 10-12 servings.

Tropical Fruit Salad

(Pictured at right)

Flavored whipped cream makes each bite of this salad taste like candy. The bowl always empties quickly.
—Carol Gillespie
Chambersburg, Pennsylvania

2 large bananas, cut into 1/4-inch slices
4 teaspoons lemon juice
2 large cantaloupe melons, cut into cubes *or* balls
5 cups cubed fresh pineapple
3 cups halved fresh strawberries
1 cup whipping cream
1/2 cup confectioners' sugar
1 teaspoon rum extract, optional
1/2 cup flaked coconut, toasted
2 tablespoons slivered almonds, toasted

In a 4-qt. serving bowl, toss the bananas and lemon juice. Stir in the cantaloupe, pineapple and strawberries. In a small mixing bowl, beat cream until it begins to thicken. Add sugar and extract if desired; beat until soft peaks form. Spoon over fruit. Sprinkle with coconut and almonds. Serve immediately. **Yield:** 16-20 servings.

Family-Style Baked Beans

My mother has been making these baked beans for more than 30 years.
Whenever I serve them at cookouts or family gatherings, I receive many compliments.
—Cathy Weidner, Cincinnati, Ohio

3 cans (16 ounces *each*) pork and beans
1-1/2 cups ketchup
1 large onion, chopped
3 tablespoons brown sugar
3 tablespoons Worcestershire sauce
1 tablespoon white vinegar
3/4 teaspoon chili powder
1/4 to 1/2 teaspoon hot pepper sauce

In a large bowl, combine all ingredients. Transfer to an ungreased 2-1/2-qt. baking dish or bean pot. Cover and bake at 350° for 30-35 minutes or until bubbly. **Yield:** 10 servings.

Cheddar Pan Rolls

Cheddar cheese gives these rich rolls golden color and fabulous flavor.
—Esther Current, Kitchener, Ontario

4-1/2 cups all-purpose flour
2 tablespoons sugar
1 tablespoon salt
1 package (1/4 ounce) active dry yeast
2 cups milk
1 tablespoon butter *or* margarine
2 cups (8 ounces) shredded cheddar cheese
1 egg white, beaten

In a large mixing bowl, combine 2 cups flour, sugar, salt and yeast. In a saucepan, heat milk and butter to 120°-130°. Add to dry ingredients; beat until smooth. Stir in cheese and enough remaining flour to make a soft dough. Do not knead. Cover and let rise in a warm place until doubled, about 45 minutes (dough will be soft).

Punch dough down; divide into three portions. Shape each portion into 12 balls. Place in three greased 9-in. round baking pans. Cover and let rise in a warm place until nearly doubled, about 30 minutes. Brush with egg white. Bake at 350° for 20-25 minutes or until golden brown. Serve warm. **Yield:** 3 dozen.

Potluck Strawberry Trifle

This recipe is a great way to serve dessert to a crowd. Frozen pound cake, strawberries and whipped topping add to the ease of preparation for this trifle, which is made in a jelly roll pan.
—Celia Clark, New Tazewell, Tennessee

2 packages (3 ounces *each*) cook-and-serve vanilla pudding mix
2 packages (3 ounces *each*) strawberry gelatin
1 package (10-3/4 ounces) frozen pound cake, thawed
1 package (20 ounces) unsweetened frozen strawberries, thawed and halved
1 carton (8 ounces) frozen whipped topping, thawed

Prepare pudding according to package directions; cool. Prepare gelatin according to package directions; refrigerate until partially set. Meanwhile, slice the pound cake into 26 pieces. Place in an ungreased 15-in. x 10-in. x 1-in. baking pan. Top with strawberries. Spoon gelatin over strawberries. Refrigerate until set.

Carefully spread cooled pudding over gelatin (pan will be full). Carefully spread with whipped topping. Refrigerate until serving. **Yield:** 24-30 servings.

Fiesta Chili Dogs

(Pictured at right)

*These hot dogs are a hit with
my grandchildren.*
—Marion Lowery, Medford, Oregon

3 cans (15 ounces *each*) chili
   without beans
2 cans (10-3/4 ounces *each*)
   condensed cheddar cheese
   soup, undiluted
1/2 cup minced fresh cilantro
   or parsley, *divided*
1 jalapeno pepper, seeded and
   minced*
2 garlic cloves, minced
24 hot dogs
24 hot dog buns, split and
   toasted
2 cans (4 ounces *each*) sliced
   ripe olives, drained
1 medium onion, chopped
3 cups crushed corn chips

In a large saucepan, combine the chili and soup; stir in 1/4 cup cilantro, jalapeno and garlic. Add hot dogs. Bring to a boil. Reduce heat; cover and simmer for 35-40 minutes, stirring occasionally. Stir in the remaining cilantro. To assemble, place hot dogs in buns; top with chili sauce, olives, onion and chips. **Yield:** 24 servings.

   ***Editor's Note:** When cutting or seeding hot peppers, use rubber or plastic gloves to protect your hands. Avoid touching your face.

Crisp Onion Relish

*I take this relish to picnics for people to use as a condiment on
hamburgers and hot dogs. It adds a special zip!*
—Marie Patkau, Hanley, Saskatchewan

4 medium sweet onions, halved
   and thinly sliced
1/2 cup sugar
1/3 cup water
1/3 cup cider vinegar
1 cup mayonnaise
1 teaspoon celery seed

Place onions in a large bowl. In a small bowl, combine the sugar, water and vinegar; stir until sugar is dissolved. Pour over onions. Cover and refrigerate for at least 3 hours. Drain. Combine mayonnaise and celery seed; add to onions and mix well. Store in the refrigerator. **Yield:** about 6 cups.

Barbecued Pork Sandwiches

Although my cooking experience is limited, I can prepare these sandwiches successfully every time. My grandma's recipe has been in the family for years.
—Pat Lemmer, Greenville, Ohio

1 pork shoulder *or* butt roast
 (3 to 4 pounds)
2 tablespoons vegetable oil
1-1/2 cups water
2 cans (14-1/2 ounces *each*)
 beef broth
2 cans (10-3/4 ounces *each*)
 condensed tomato soup,
 undiluted
1 large onion, chopped
3/4 cup steak sauce
3 tablespoons Worcestershire
 sauce
2 tablespoons sugar
2 tablespoons cider vinegar

1/2 teaspoon salt
1/2 teaspoon pepper
1/8 teaspoon hot pepper sauce
12 to 14 sandwich buns, split

In a Dutch oven over medium heat, brown roast in oil; drain. Add water; bring to a boil. Reduce heat; cover and simmer for 2-1/2 to 3 hours or until meat is tender. Remove meat; discard cooking juices or save for another use. Cool meat; shred and refrigerate.

In a large saucepan over medium heat, combine the next 10 ingredients; bring to a boil. Reduce heat; simmer, uncovered, for 1-1/2 to 2 hours or until thickened. Add shredded pork; simmer, uncovered, for 30 minutes or until heated through. Serve on buns. **Yield:** 12-14 servings.

Smoky Barbecue Sauce

My mother has been relying on this recipe for years. We especially enjoy it on a beef brisket.
—Carla Holland, Oktaha, Oklahoma

2-1/2 cups ketchup
1/4 cup packed brown sugar
1/4 cup chopped onion
2 tablespoons Worcestershire
 sauce
2 to 3 teaspoons liquid smoke
1 teaspoon garlic powder
1 teaspoon hot pepper sauce
1/2 teaspoon pepper

In a large saucepan, combine all ingredients. Bring to a boil over medium heat, stirring often. Reduce heat; simmer, uncovered, for 10-15 minutes or until heated through. **Yield:** 2-1/2 cups.

THE HISTORY OF WORCESTERSHIRE SAUCE

IN 1835, Englishman Lord Sandys commissioned two chemists from Worcestershire, John Lea and William Perrins, to duplicate a sauce he had acquired during his travels in India. The pungent batch proved disappointing and wound up in the cellar. When the pair stumbled upon the aged concoction 2 years later, they tasted it and were pleasantly surprised by its wonderfully unique taste.

Mandarin Pasta Salad

(Pictured at right)

I developed this recipe when I was asked to bring a salad to a birthday party for my husband's grandfather. Guests raved about my creative dish!
—Kathleen Dougherty
Williamsville, Illinois

1 package (1 pound) angel hair pasta *or* thin spaghetti, broken into thirds
1 pound boneless skinless chicken breasts, cut into 1-inch cubes
2 garlic cloves, minced
2 tablespoons butter *or* margarine
1-1/2 teaspoons seasoned salt
1 can (8 ounces) sliced water chestnuts, drained
2 cans (11 ounces *each*) mandarin oranges
1 package (6 ounces) frozen snow peas, thawed and drained
2 cups sliced fresh mushrooms
2 cups shredded carrots
2 bunches green onions, sliced
DRESSING:
2/3 cup vegetable oil
1/2 cup white wine vinegar *or* cider vinegar
3 tablespoons soy sauce
1 garlic clove, minced
1 tablespoon sugar
1 tablespoon honey
1/2 teaspoon ground ginger
3 tablespoons sesame seeds, toasted

Cook pasta according to package directions. Drain and rinse with cold water; set aside. In a large skillet, saute chicken and garlic in butter until chicken juices run clear; sprinkle with seasoned salt. Remove with a slotted spoon; set aside.

In the same skillet, saute water chestnuts for 2-3 minutes. Drain oranges, reserving 1/2 cup juice. In a large serving bowl, combine oranges, pasta, chicken, water chestnuts, peas, mushrooms, carrots and onions.

In a jar with a tight-fitting lid, combine the oil, vinegar, soy sauce, garlic, sugar, honey, ginger and reserved mandarin orange juice; shake well. Pour over pasta mixture and toss. Sprinkle with sesame seeds. Refrigerate until serving. **Yield:** 20-25 servings.

Birthday Treats Take the Cake

FOR young and old alike, birthday celebrations revolve around friends and family, prettily wrapped packages and—most importantly—a scrumptious cake topped with candles!

Make someone's day extra special by taking a little time to prepare showstopping treats like Raspberry Fudge Torte, Cookies 'n' Cream Cake and Posy Cupcakes (shown at right).

This chapter also provides some do-it-yourself decorating techniques that let you easily create impressive cakes.

So turn the pages and spread the fun with innovative ideas for fancy layered cakes, creative cupcakes and more!

Cookies 'n' Cream Cake

(Pictured on page 235)

This cake is the perfect size when you're feeding a smaller crowd and don't want leftovers.
Chunks of chocolate sandwich cookies are in every biteful.
— Dorothy Smith, El Dorado, Arkansas

1/4 cup butter *or* margarine,
    softened
3/4 cup sugar
   1 egg
3/4 cup sour cream
   1 cup all-purpose flour
1/2 teaspoon baking soda
1/2 teaspoon baking powder
1/4 cup water
   8 cream-filled chocolate
    sandwich cookies, coarsely
    chopped
WHIPPED CREAM TOPPING:
3/4 cup whipping cream
   2 tablespoons sugar

Additional coarsely chopped cream-filled chocolate
   sandwich cookies, optional

In a small mixing bowl, cream butter and sugar. Add egg; beat well. Beat in sour cream. Combine the flour, baking soda and baking powder; add to creamed mixture alternately with water. Stir in chopped cookies. Pour into a greased and floured 9-in. round baking pan. Bake at 350° for 30-35 minutes or until a toothpick inserted near the center comes out clean. Cool for 10 minutes before removing from pan to a wire rack to cool completely.

   For topping, beat cream in a small mixing bowl until soft peaks form. Gradually add sugar, beating until stiff peaks form. Spread over top of cake; sprinkle with additional chopped cookies if desired. **Yield:** 6-8 servings.

Clove Bundt Cake

This old-fashioned bundt cake is so moist, it doesn't need any frosting.
But I sometimes sprinkle it with confectioners' sugar for a pretty presentation.
—Mary Zawlocki, Gig Harbor, Washington

   1 cup butter *or* margarine,
    softened
   2 cups sugar
   3 eggs, lightly beaten
   3 cups all-purpose flour
   1 tablespoon ground cinnamon
   2 to 3 teaspoons ground cloves
3/4 teaspoon baking soda
1/4 teaspoon salt
   1 cup buttermilk
Confectioners' sugar, optional

In a mixing bowl, cream butter and sugar. Add eggs; mix well (mixture will appear curdled). Combine the flour, cinnamon, cloves, baking soda and salt; add to creamed mixture alternately with buttermilk.

   Pour into a greased and floured 10-in. fluted tube pan. Bake at 350° for 50-55 minutes or until a toothpick inserted near the center comes out clean. Cool for 10 minutes before inverting onto a wire rack; cool completely. Dust with confectioners' sugar if desired. **Yield:** 12-14 servings.

Posy Cupcakes

(Pictured at right and on page 234)

Our Test Kitchen staff suggests dressing up cupcakes from a mix with canned frosting and candied flowers. Don't want to fuss with perfectly placing the flowers? Crumble them for a fun confetti look.

1 package (18-1/4 ounces) white *or* yellow cake mix
1 can (16 ounces) white *or* vanilla frosting
40 to 50 Candied Flowers (recipe below)

Prepare cake batter according to package directions. Fill greased, foil or paper-lined muffin cups two-thirds full. Bake at 350° for 18-24 minutes or until a toothpick comes out clean. Cool for 5 minutes before removing from pans to wire racks to cool completely. Frost cupcakes. Decorate with candied flowers. **Yield:** 2 dozen.

Candied Flowers

(Pictured above and on page 234)

Sugarcoated edible flowers are a quick and easy way to add a little flair to many desserts and serving trays. They need to be made in advance, which is a real time-saver on party day.

2 teaspoons meringue powder*
2 tablespoons water
40 to 50 edible blossoms of your choice, such as rose petals, violas (Johnny-jump-ups), calendula petals (pot marigold) and dianthus
1-1/4 cups superfine sugar*

In a small bowl, dissolve meringue powder in water. Lightly brush over all sides of flowers to coat completely. Sprinkle with sugar. Allow to dry on a waxed paper-lined baking sheet for 1 to 2 days. Use as a garnish for desserts. **Yield:** 40 to 50 candied flowers.

*Editor's Note: Meringue powder can be ordered by mail from Wilton Industries, Inc. Call 1-800/794-5866 or visit their Web site at *www.wilton.com*.

Superfine sugar can be found in the baking aisle alongside granulated sugar. As a substitute for superfine sugar, place granulated sugar in a blender or food processor; cover and pulse until fine.

EDIBLE FLOWER REMINDER

ONLY harvest blooms from plants that have not been treated with chemicals. When using any flowers for cooking, be certain of what you are picking.

Raspberry Fudge Torte

(Pictured on page 234)

This special-occasion cake impresses all who see and taste it. People are surprised to hear this torte starts with a simple cake mix…they're sure I bought it at a bakery.
—Julie Hein, York, Pennsylvania

1 package (18-1/4 ounces)
  devil's food cake mix
1 cup (8 ounces) sour cream
3/4 cup water
3 eggs
1/3 cup vegetable oil
1 teaspoon vanilla extract
1 cup miniature semisweet
  chocolate chips
GANACHE:
1 cup semisweet chocolate chips
1/2 cup whipping cream
1 tablespoon butter (no
  substitutes)
RASPBERRY CREAM:
1 package (10 ounces) frozen
  sweetened raspberries,
  thawed
3 tablespoons sugar
4 teaspoons cornstarch
1/2 cup whipping cream, whipped
Fresh raspberries and mint,
  optional

In a mixing bowl, combine the cake mix, sour cream, water, eggs, oil and vanilla; beat on low speed until moistened. Beat for 2 minutes on medium. Fold in miniature chips. Pour into three greased and floured 9-in. round baking pans. Bake at 350° for 25-30 minutes or until a toothpick inserted near the center comes out clean. Cool for 10 minutes before removing from pans to wire racks to cool completely.

For ganache, combine chips and cream in a small saucepan. Cook and stir over low heat until melted and smooth. Remove from the heat; stir in butter. Refrigerate for 1-2 hours or until cold, stirring occasionally. Beat for 1-2 minutes or until mixture achieves spreading consistency.

For raspberry cream, mash and strain raspberries, reserving juice; discard seeds. In a small saucepan, combine sugar and cornstarch; stir in raspberry juice. Cook and stir over low heat for 1-2 minutes until thickened and bubbly. Cover and refrigerate for 30 minutes or until cold. Fold in whipped cream.

To assemble, place one cake layer on serving plate; spread with half of the ganache. Place second cake layer over ganache; spread with raspberry cream. Top with remaining cake; spread with remaining ganache. Garnish with raspberries and mint if desired. Cover and store in the refrigerator. **Yield:** 12 servings.

Scaredy Cakes

(Pictured at right)

Our Test Kitchen home economists guarantee kids of all ages will delight in these funny-faced cupcakes. You can even enlist your little ones to help decorate them, using the candies we suggest or other candies to suit your tastes.

> 1 package (18-1/4 ounces) yellow cake mix
> 1 can (16 ounces) vanilla frosting
> **Green gel food coloring, optional**
> **Assorted candies of your choice (Chiclets, black licorice nips, red shoestring licorice, Gummi Worms, M&M's, Life Savers, gumballs, strawberry sour belts, Tart 'n' Tangy's, Tic Tacs)**

Prepare cake batter according to package directions. Fill greased or paper-lined muffin cups two-thirds full. Bake at 350° for 18-24 minutes or until a toothpick comes out clean. Cool for 5 minutes before removing from pans to wire racks to cool completely.

Tint some of the frosting green if desired. Frost cupcakes. Decorate with assorted candy to create monster faces. **Yield:** 2 dozen.

CAKE DECORATING TIPS

EVEN a novice can master decorating techniques to create impressive cakes. To make the task easier, use pastry bags or heavy-duty resealable bags, metal or plastic cake decorating tips and a coupler. A coupler lets you switch tips without changing pastry bags when using the same color frosting.

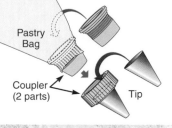

To use a coupler, place the large part of the coupler inside the pastry bag (see illustration at right). Trim the top of the bag if necessary in order to let the coupler extend about 1/4 inch outside the bag. Place the coupler ring over the tip and screw both parts of the coupler together. To change tips and continue using the same color frosting, unscrew the coupler ring, replace tip and screw on the ring.

Below are some common cake decorating techniques. Unless otherwise noted, hold the pastry bag at a 45° angle.

1. Shell Border. Using a No. 16-21 star tip, hold the bag just above the surface. Squeeze bag; slightly lift tip as frosting builds and fans out. Relax pressure as you lower tip to make tail. Stop pressure completely and pull tip away. Work from left to right, resting the head of one shell on the tail of the previous shell.

2. Writing, Outline, Facial Features, Zigzag. Using a No. 1-3 round tip, touch surface lightly, squeezing frosting out evenly as you go. Release pressure and gently touch cake surface to stop. To zigzag, continue piping up and down with steady pressure.

3. Star Fill-in. Using a No. 16-21 star tip, hold bag at a 90° angle with tip just above the surface. Squeeze bag; hold tip in place as star is formed. Stop pressure and pull tip up. Pipe rows of stars evenly and close together until entire area is filled.

4. Ruffle Garland. Using a No. 102-104 tip, angle the narrow end of the tip slightly away from the surface. Squeeze bag, moving your hand up and down slightly to ruffle the icing and positioning the bag to form the curve.

5. Sotas (Lace). Using a No. 1-3 round tip, squeeze bag and allow frosting to drop randomly in a series of overlapping loops.

Clown Cake

(Pictured at right)

You can't go wrong planning a circus theme for your child's birthday party, especially with this colorful cake from our Test Kitchen. Use some of the clown cookies on the cake and serve the remainder alongside.

1 tube (18 ounces) refrigerated sugar cookie dough
1 package (18-1/4 ounces) yellow *or* chocolate cake mix
3/4 cup butter *or* margarine, softened
6 tablespoons shortening
9 cups confectioners' sugar
3 teaspoons vanilla extract
1/8 teaspoon salt
1/2 cup milk
Red, blue, yellow and green gel *or* paste food coloring

On a lightly floured surface, roll out cookie dough to 1/4-in. thickness. Cut out with a 3-in. to 3-1/2-in. gingerbread man cookie cutter. Bake according to package directions. Cool on wire racks.

Prepare and bake cake according to the package directions, using two greased and floured 9-in. round baking pans. Cool for 10 minutes before removing from pans to wire racks to cool completely.

For frosting, in a large mixing bowl, cream butter and shortening. Beat in the confectioners' sugar, vanilla and salt. Beat in milk until smooth. Place 1/2 cup of frosting each in four small bowls; tint one red, one blue, one yellow and one green. Place 3/4 cup frosting in a small bowl and leave white. Cover the bowls with plastic wrap and set aside.

To assemble, place one cake layer on a 10-in. round serving plate. Using some of the remaining frosting, frost top of cake. Top with second layer; frost top and sides of cake.

Using 1/2 cup of the reserved white frosting, spread a thin layer on the front side of nine cookies; let stand until dry. (Set aside remaining cookies for another use or decorate and serve alongside.) Cut a small hole in the corner of four pastry or plastic bags; insert a tip and fill each bag with a tinted frosting. Decorate frosted side of cookies with zigzag, star fill-in, ruffle garland or sotas (lace) to resemble clowns. Let stand until dry.

Gently press a clown cookie into the lower left side of top of cake. Using frosting, make three balloons. Pipe strings from balloons to the clown's hand. Pipe "Happy Birthday" on cake. Pipe a shell border around top edge. Pipe two large dots on the back of each clown with remaining white frosting. Evenly space clowns around sides of cake; gently press into cake. **Yield:** 8-10 servings (about 2 dozen cookies).

Coconut Pecan Torte

An apricot filling is the sweet surprise in this moist, pretty cake.
Every forkful is filled with a wonderful combination of flavors.
—Mary Somers, Enid, Oklahoma

1/2 cup butter *or* margarine,
    softened
1/2 cup shortening
  2 cups sugar
  5 eggs, *separated*
1/2 teaspoon almond extract
1/2 teaspoon vanilla extract
  2 cups all-purpose flour
  1 teaspoon baking soda
  1 cup buttermilk
  1 cup flaked coconut
  1 cup finely chopped pecans,
    toasted

APRICOT FILLING:
  1 cup dried apricots
  1 cup boiling water
1/4 cup packed brown sugar
1/8 teaspoon ground mace

FROSTING:
1/2 cup butter *or* margarine,
    softened
  1 package (8 ounces) cream
    cheese, softened
3-3/4 cups confectioners' sugar
  1 teaspoon vanilla extract
  1 cup chopped pecans, toasted

In a mixing bowl, cream butter, shortening and sugar. Add egg yolks, one at a time, beating well after each. Beat in extracts. Combine flour and baking soda; add to the creamed mixture alternately with buttermilk. Stir in the coconut and pecans.

In a mixing bowl, beat egg whites until stiff peaks form; fold into cake batter. Pour into three greased and floured 9-in. round baking pans. Bake at 325° for 25-30 minutes or until a toothpick inserted near the center comes out clean. Cool for 10 minutes before removing from pans to wire racks to cool completely.

For filling, place apricots and boiling water in a small bowl; let stand until completely cooled. Drain, reserving 1/3 cup liquid. In a small saucepan, combine apricots, brown sugar and reserved liquid. Cook over medium heat for 20 minutes or until thickened, stirring frequently. Remove from the heat; stir in mace. Cool completely. Place in a blender or food processor; cover and process until smooth.

For frosting, in a mixing bowl, cream the butter, cream cheese and confectioners' sugar. Beat in vanilla.

To assemble, place bottom cake layer on a serving plate; spread with half of the filling. Repeat layers. Top with the third cake layer; spread frosting over top and sides of cake. Garnish with pecans. Cover and store in the refrigerator. **Yield:** 12-15 servings.

Family Traditions

I PURCHASED a plate with "Happy Birthday" painted on it. On each of my son's birthdays, they get to eat off of this special plate for breakfast, lunch, dinner and snacks. I've even toted it to restaurants! It's the first thing my kids run to get as soon as they wake up on their birthday.
—Chris Kallies, Oldsmar, Florida

Checkerboard Birthday Cake

(Pictured at right)

Although this cake from our Test Kitchen does take some time to prepare, no special pan is needed. The different batters are simply added in rings in three 9-inch round pans.

- 1 cup butter *or* margarine, softened
- 2 cups sugar
- 4 eggs
- 3 cups cake flour, *divided*
- 4 teaspoons baking powder
- 1/4 teaspoon salt
- 1 cup milk
- 1 square (1 ounce) unsweetened chocolate, melted and cooled
- 1/2 teaspoon vanilla extract
- 1/2 teaspoon almond extract
- Red liquid food coloring
- 1/2 teaspoon lemon extract
- Yellow liquid food coloring

FROSTING:
- 6 tablespoons butter *or* margarine, softened
- 6-1/2 to 7-1/2 cups confectioners' sugar, *divided*
- 5 squares (1 ounce *each*) unsweetened chocolate, melted and cooled
- 3/4 cup milk
- 1-1/2 teaspoons vanilla extract

Grease three 9-in. round baking pans; set aside. In a mixing bowl, cream butter and sugar. Add eggs, one at a time, beating well after each addition. Combine 2-1/2 cups of cake flour, baking powder and salt; add to the creamed mixture alternately with milk. Divide batter into thirds. To one portion, fold in melted chocolate and vanilla. To second portion, fold in 1/4 cup flour, almond extract and 3-4 drops red food coloring. To third portion, fold in lemon extract, 3-4 drops yellow food coloring and remaining flour.

Spoon a ring of chocolate batter around edge of one prepared pan; spoon a ring of pink batter inside chocolate ring and fill center with yellow batter. Spoon a ring of yellow batter around edge of second pan; add a chocolate middle ring and a pink center. Spoon a ring of pink batter around edge of third pan; add a yellow middle ring and a chocolate center.

Bake at 350° for 20-25 minutes or until a toothpick inserted near the center comes out clean. Cool for 10 minutes before removing from pans to wire racks to cool completely.

For frosting, in a mixing bowl, cream butter and 2 cups confectioners' sugar. Beat in melted chocolate until smooth. Add milk and vanilla. Beat in enough of the remaining confectioners' sugar until frosting achieves spreading consistency. Spread between layers and over top and sides of cake. **Yield:** 12-14 servings.

Chocolate Fudge Cake

(Pictured at right)

I first made this cake in my junior high home economics class. I've changed the recipe through the years to make the cake a little richer, and the icing is my own invention.
— Katarina Greer
Victoria, British Columbia

1/2 cup butter *or* margarine, softened
1-1/4 cups packed brown sugar
1 egg
1 teaspoon vanilla extract
3/4 cup water
1/2 cup milk
1-1/2 cups all-purpose flour
6 tablespoons baking cocoa
1-1/2 teaspoons cream of tartar
1 teaspoon baking soda
1 teaspoon baking powder
1/4 teaspoon salt
FROSTING:
1/2 cup butter *or* margarine, softened
1 cup confectioners' sugar
1/4 cup baking cocoa
1 to 2 tablespoons milk
1 can (16 ounces) vanilla frosting

Grease a 13-in. x 9-in. x 2-in. baking pan; line with parchment paper. Grease the paper; set aside. In a mixing bowl, cream butter and brown sugar. Beat in egg and vanilla. Combine water and milk. Combine the flour, cocoa, cream of tartar, baking soda, baking powder and salt; add to creamed mixture alternately with milk mixture.

Pour into prepared pan. Bake at 350° for 22-27 minutes or until a toothpick inserted near the center comes out clean. Cool for 10 minutes before inverting onto a wire rack. Remove and discard parchment paper. Cool cake completely.

For frosting, in a mixing bowl, cream butter, confectioners' sugar and cocoa until smooth. Beat in enough milk to achieve spreading consistency. Transfer cake to a serving platter or covered board. Spread with chocolate frosting; decorate with vanilla frosting. **Yield:** 16-20 servings.

Creative Cake Boards

(Pictured above)

CAKES baked in convenient 13-inch x 9-inch x 2-inch baking pans are great because they don't call for any tricky layering and they often feed a larger group. But to make the cake look a little more special for occasions like birthday parties, you may want to take it out of the pan (see "Removing a Cake from a Pan" at right) and serve it on a cake board.

While the cake cools on the wire rack, prepare your cake board, making sure it's large enough to hold your cake.

For the Chocolate Fudge Cake shown on opposite page, we covered a piece of foam core with wrapping paper, then with clear cellophane. The same can be done with a sturdy gift box. Another option is to invert an everyday jelly roll pan and top it with an inexpensive paper doily. You can also place the cake directly onto a clean marble or plastic cutting board.

If you're serving a round cake but don't have a traditional cake plate or pedestal, any large round plate will do.

Or to make your own pedestal, invert a soup bowl, custard cup, footed dessert dish, ice cream sundae dish or a similar bowl and top it with a coordinating cake plate, dinner plate or round serving plate. Although you can use florist's clay between the inverted dish and plate to add some stability, this type of cake pedestal is for presentation only, and the plate should be removed from the pedestal dish before cutting and serving the cake.

REMOVING A CAKE FROM A PAN

HERE'S a trick that will make it easy to remove a cake from a baking pan. Before adding the batter, grease the pan. Line the bottom only with parchment paper, trimming the paper as needed to fit; grease the paper. Add batter and bake as directed.

1. Let the cake cool in the pan for 10 minutes. Carefully run a knife around the edges of the pan. Invert the pan onto a wire rack and lift up.

2. Lift off the parchment paper and discard. Let the cake cool completely before transferring to a serving plate for frosting.

REFERENCE INDEX

Use this index as a guide to the many helpful hints, food facts, decorating ideas and step-by-step instructions throughout the book.

GENERAL RECIPE INDEX

This handy index lists every recipe by food category, major ingredient and/or cooking method.

ALPHABETICAL INDEX

Refer to this index for a complete alphabetical listing of all recipes in this book.

Here's *Your* Chance To Be Published!

Send us your special-occasion recipes and you could have them featured in a future edition of this classic cookbook.

YEAR AFTER YEAR, the recipe for success at every holiday party or special-occasion celebration is an attractive assortment of flavorful food.

So we're always on the lookout for mouth-watering appetizers, entrees, side dishes, breads, desserts and more…all geared toward the special gatherings you attend or host throughout the year.

Here's how you can enter your family-favorite holiday fare for possible publication in a future *Holiday & Celebrations Cookbook*:

Print or type each recipe on one sheet of 8-1/2" x 11" paper. Please include your name, address and daytime phone number on each page. Be specific with directions, measurements and the sizes of cans, packages and pans.

Please include a few words about yourself, when you serve your dish, reactions it's received from family and friends and the origin of the recipe.

Send to "Celebrations Cookbook", 5925 Country Lane, Greendale WI 53129 or E-mail to *recipes@reimanpub.com*. Write "Celebrations Cookbook" on the subject line of all E-mail entries and *include your full name, postal address and phone number on each entry.*

Contributors whose recipes are printed will receive a complimentary copy of the book…so the more recipes you send, the better your chances of "being published"!